Developmental Cognitive Neuroscience

B

Fundamentals of Cognitive Neuroscience

General Editors: *Martha J. Farah* and *Mark H. Johnson*

The "decade of the brain" has seen a growing *rapprochement* among cognitive scientists, specialists in artificial intelligence, neuropsychologists, and brain scientists in their various efforts to understand human mental activity. New theoretical frameworks in cognitive science are being constructed, while new technologies enable unprecedented observations of the live brain at work. Graduate and undergraduate syllabuses are advancing closely behind the research frontiers, but the task of synthesizing the new knowledge being produced by such diverse enterprises is a daunting one not only for students but also for instructors.

Fundamentals of Cognitive Neuroscience will address this problem. Each book will constitute a concise, readable, and up-to-date review of a particular problem area by a leading scientist. The aim will be both to provide balanced coverage and to convey the excitement and challenge of new developments. Major emphasis will be placed on contrasting theoretical approaches to the masses of new data now being collected, though each author will be encouraged to express a point of view and to discuss the relative merits of these approaches as he or she sees them.

Developmental Cognitive Neuroscience

An Introduction

Mark H. Johnson

MRC Cognitive Development Unit
and
University College London

First published 1997

2 4 6 8 10 9 7 5 3 1

Blackwell Publishers Inc.
238 Main Street
Cambridge, Massachusetts 02142
USA

Blackwell Publishers Ltd
108 Cowley Road
Oxford OX4 1JF
UK

Library of Congress Cataloging-in-Publication Data

Johnson, Mark H. (Mark Henry), 1960–
    Developmental cognitive neuroscience : an introduction / Mark H. Johnson.
        p.   cm. — (Fundamentals of cognitive neuroscience ; v. 1)
    Includes bibliographical references and index.
        ISBN 0–631–20200–5 (hbk. : alk. paper). — ISBN 0–631–20201–3 (pbk. : alk. paper)
        1. Cognitive neuroscience.   2. Developmental psychology.
    I. Title.   II. Series.
    QP360.5.J64   1997
    612.8'2—dc20   96–16493
                                                                                CIP

British Library Cataloguing in Publication Data

A CIP catalogue record for this book is available from the British Library.

Typeset in 11 on 13½pt Palatino
by Graphicraft Typesetters Ltd, Hong Kong
Printed in Great Britain by Hartnolls Ltd, Bodmin, Cornwall

This book is printed on acid-free paper

For Annette, and all future
developmental cognitive neuroscientists

Contents

Figures

Tables

Series Editors' Preface

Science often seems to proceed in an excruciatingly slow and incremental manner. Between initial grant submissions and renewals, between first-year projects and doctoral defenses, it is rare to see significant change in our theories or methods. For researchers in cognitive psychology and behavioral neuroscience, the 1970s and early 1980s were periods of this type of steady but not terribly exciting progress.

By the mid-eighties, however, something decidedly non-incremental happened: a new field, called cognitive neuroscience, was born. Those of us lucky enough to have been working in the parent disciplines of cognitive science and neuroscience at this time experienced a major change in our thinking about mind and brain. Before, they had seemed related in principle, but not in any way that was tractable in research practice. Now the relation between mind and brain seemed not only tractable, but essential for further progress in understanding mind and brain. By the end of the decade, cognitive scientists were using data from brain-damaged patients and functional neuroimaging to test theories of normal cognition, and neuroscientists were using cognitive theories and methods, including computational modeling, to interpret brain anatomy and physiology. A host of new meetings, societies, journals, and funding initiatives signaled that a new field had been established.

From the perspective of the late 1990s, cognitive neuroscience continues to flourish, and to attract new researchers from the ranks of graduate students and senior scientists alike. Unfortunately, these individuals face a problem: the dearth of general, introductory reading in cognitive neuroscience. It was with this problem in mind that we undertook to edit the *Fundamentals of Cognitive Neuroscience* series. The books in this series are primers on the essential topics of cognitive neuroscience. Each volume provides a theory-oriented overview of the current state of the art in its area, drawing upon the results of multiple research techniques. In addition to the present volume, other volumes currently in press or in preparation will cover Attention, Language, Memory, Motor Control, and Vision. Additional volumes are likely to be commissioned in the near future.

While most of the books in the series focus on a particular domain of cognition, such as attention or language, we felt the need to include a volume on the broader topic of development. Development concerns the progressive emergence of structure within the individual from birth to adulthood. This book has two fundamental themes that we believe to be central, not just for those interested in development, but to cognitive neuroscience in general. First, the issue of brain plasticity is addressed. A critical point made in the book is that plasticity is a fundamental property of brain development, and not just a specialized response to injury. This motivates a need to determine the factors, both intrinsic and extrinsic to the individual, that determine the specialization and localization of cognitive abilities. Second, the book focusses on changes in representations as a bridge between neural and cognitive development. It attempts to move beyond the traditional nature versus nurture debate by adopting a constructivist approach within which the constraints on representations that emerge within neural networks can be investigated.

Martha J. Farah
Mark H. Johnson

Philadelphia and London, 1996

Preface

In the first chapter of this book I describe some of the factors responsible for the recent emergence of a subdiscipline at the interface between developmental psychology and cognitive neuroscience. I have chosen to refer to this new field as "developmental cognitive neuroscience," though it has been known under a number of other terms such as "developmental neuro-cognition" (de Boysson-Bardies et al., 1993). Though a series of edited volumes on the topic has recently appeared, like most newly emerging disciplines there is a time lag before the first books suitable for teaching appear. This book and the Reader which I edited in 1993 (Johnson, 1993a) are initial attempts to fill the gap. While some may believe these efforts to be premature, my own view is that the lifeblood of any new discipline is in the students and postdocs recruited to the cause. And the sooner they are recruited, the better.

Is developmental cognitive neuroscience really significantly different from other fields that have a more extended history, such as developmental neuropsychology or cognitive development? Clearly, it would be unwise to rigidly demarcate developmental cognitive neuroscience from related, and mutually informative, fields. However, it is my belief that the emerging field has a number of characteristics that makes it distinctive.

First, while there is some disagreement about exact definitions, the fields of developmental neuropsychology and developmental psychopathology focus on abnormal development, while commonly comparing them to normal developmental trajectories. In contrast, cognitive neuroscience (including the developmental variant outlined in this book) focuses on normal cognitive functioning, but uses information from deviant functioning and development as "nature's experiments" which can shed light on the neural basis of normal cognition. This book is therefore not intended as an introduction to the neuropsychology of developmental disorders. For such information the reader is referred to the excellent introductions by Cicchetti and Cohen (1995) and Spreen et al. (1995).

Second, unlike many in cognitive development, this book adopts the premise that information from brain development is more than just a useful additional source of evidence for supporting particular cognitive theories. Rather, information about brain development is viewed as both changing and originating theories at the cognitive level. Third, developmental cognitive neuroscience restricts itself to issues at the neural, cognitive, and immediate environmental levels. In my view it is a hazard of some interdisciplinary fields that the focus of interest is diffused across many different levels of explanation. This is not to deny the importance of these other levels, but a mechanistic interdisciplinary science needs to restrict both the domains (in this case aspects of cognitive processing) and levels of explanation with which it is concerned. Finally, developmental cognitive neuroscience is specifically concerned with understanding the relation between neural and cognitive phenomena. For this reason, I have not discussed evidence from the related field of developmental behavior genetics. In general, developmental behavior genetics tends to be concerned with correlations between the molecular level (genetics) and gross behavioral measures such as IQ. With some notable exceptions, little effort is made to specifically relate these two levels of explanation via the intermediate neural and cognitive levels. Having pointed out the different focus of developmental cognitive neuroscience, my hope is that this book is written to be both accessible and informative to those in related and overlapping disciplines.

The above comments go some way to explaining the choice of material that I have presented in the book. However, I have no doubt that there is a substantive amount of excellent experimentation and theorizing that could have been included but was not. Since this is intended as a brief introduction to the field, I have chosen to focus on a few particular issues in some detail. Of course, the choice of material also reflects my own biases and knowledge since the book is intended as an introductory survey of the field as viewed from my own perspective. I apologize in advance for the inevitable omissions and errors.

The book is aimed at the advanced-level student and assumes some introductory knowledge of both neuroscience and cognitive development. Students without this background will probably need to refer to more introductory textbooks in the appropriate areas. I also hope that the book will attract developmentalists with an interest in learning more about the brain, and cognitive neuroscientists curious as to how developmental data can help constrain their theories about adult functioning. But most of all I hope that the book inspires readers to find out more about the field, and to consider a developmental cognitive neuroscience approach to their own topic.

Acknowledgments

The book was written thanks to the happy coincidence of two projects. First, the initiation of the Fundamentals of Cognitive Neuroscience series co-edited with Martha Farah, originally conceived with Stephan Chambers of Blackwell, and now under the benevolent guidance of Alison Mudditt (also of Blackwell). And, second, the kind invitation to contribute a review chapter on the neural basis of development to the latest (Mussen) *Handbook of Child Psychology*. I thank Deanna Kuhn and Bob Siegler for their invitation and comments on the structure of that chapter which influenced the preparation of this book. Chuck Nelson, Bob Siegler, and Paul Quinn provided detailed comments on a draft of that chapter, and thus indirectly contributed to this book. I also thank John Wiley and Sons, Inc. for permission to reproduce substantive sections of the chapter in this book (sections of chapters 3–7, and 9).

Other parts of this book are derived from works co-authored with colleagues. Some sections of chapters 1 and 3 are due to collaborative writing and discussion with Rick Gilmore. Chapter 2 was written concurrently with chapter 5 of Elman et al., *Rethinking Innateness* (1996) and has text in common. I especially thank Liz Bates for her extensive input to this text and sections of chapter 6. My collaborators have, of course, also contributed to the general viewpoints expressed in the book. Specifically, chapter 3 owes much to discussion with Mike Posner, chapter 4 reports ideas developed with Johan Bolhuis, Gabriel Horn, John Morton, and Randy O'Reilly, chapter 5 benefited from discussion with Charles Nelson, and chapter 9 contains material and ideas developed in collaboration with Shaun Vecera, Annette Karmiloff-Smith, Yuko Munakata, Jay McClelland, Jeff Shrager, Andrew Oliver, and Bob Siegler.

Annette Karmiloff-Smith, Bruce Pennington, Paul Quinn, and Sarah Hesketh provided useful feedback on a draft of this book. Thanks are also due to members of my current research team, especially Sarah Hesketh, Sarah Minister, and Leslie Tucker, who all contributed both directly and indirectly to the completion of this book.

The MRC Cognitive Development Unit remains a stimulating and supportive environment in which to work. Thanks for this are largely due to the director, John Morton, and continuing financial support from the UK Medical Research Council. A productive and enjoyable three and a half years spent at Carnegie Mellon University greatly influenced my thinking, and left me with many fond memories.

Finally, I thank Annette Karmiloff-Smith, not only for many stimulating breakfast and dinner conversations concerning issues in development, but also for ensuring that I sometimes forgot about these topics at the cinema or theater. My cat, Ella, is also intensely grateful to Annette for feeding, watering, and playing during my writing-induced absences.

The author and publishers gratefully acknowledge permission to reproduce the following figures in this volume:

Figure 1.3 is reproduced from C. H. Waddington, *The Evolution of an Evolutionist* (1975) by kind permission of Edinburgh University Press.

Figure 2.1 is from *The Development of the Brain* by W. Maxwell Cowan. Copyright 1979 by Scientific American, Inc. All rights reserved.

Figure 2.6 is reproduced from figure 12.2 by K. Brodmann in A. Brodal (ed.), *Neurological Anatomy in Relation to Clinical Medicine.* Copyright 1981. By permission of Oxford University Press.

Figure 2.7 is taken from P. Rakic, "Intrinsic and extrinsic determinants of neocortical parcellation: a radial unit model," in P. Rakic and W. Singer (eds), *Neurobiology of Neocortex.* Report of the Dahlem Workshop on Neurobiology of Neocortex, Berlin, 17–22 May, 1987. Copyright 1987. Reprinted by permission of John Wiley and Sons, Ltd.

Figure 2.8 is reproduced from D. D. M. O'Leary, "Do cortical areas emerge from a protocortex?," *Trends in the Neurosciences,* vol. 12, pp. 400–406. Copyright 1989. Reprinted by permission of Elsevier Trends Journals, Cambridge, UK.

Figure 2.9 is reprinted with permission from A. W. Roe, S. L. Pallas, J. O. Hahm and M. Sur, "A map of visual space induced in primary auditory cortex," *Science,* vol. 250, pp. 818–820. Copyright (1990) American Association for the Advancement of Science.

Figure 2.10 is reproduced from H. T. Chugani, M. E. Phelps and J. C. Mazziotta, "Positron emission tomography study of human brain functional development," *Annals of Neurology,* 1987, vol. 22, pp. 487–497. Reprinted with permission of the editors and publishers of the journal.

Figure 3.1 and 3.3 are both taken from K. D. Miller, J. B. Keller and M. P. Stryker, "Ocular dominance column development: analysis and simulation," *Science,* vol. 245, pp. 605–615. Copyright 1989. Reprinted with permission of the American Association for the Advancement of Science.

Figure 3.2 is reproduced from R. Held, "Binocular vision: behavioral and neuronal development," in J. Mehler and R. Fox (eds), *Neonate Cognition: Beyond the Blooming, Buzzing Confusion,* chapter 3. Copyright (1985) Lawrence Erlbaum Associates, Inc., Mahwah, New Jersey.

Figure 3.8 is reprinted with the permission of Cambridge University Press from J. E. Richards and B. J. Casey, "Heart rate variability during attention phases in young infants," *Psychophysiology*, vol. 28. Copyright 1991.

Figure 6.1 is reprinted with permission from G. Dehaene-Lambertz and S. Dehaene, "Speed and cerebral correlates of syllable discrimination in infants," *Nature*, vol. 370, p. 294. Copyright (1994) Macmillan Magazines Limited.

Figure 7.1 is reprinted with the kind permission of Academic Press, Inc., Florida, from R. W. Thatcher, "Cyclic cortical reorganization during early childhood," *Brain and Cognition*, vol. 20, p. 31. Copyright 1992.

Figure 7.2 is reprinted with the kind permission of Academic Press, Inc., Florida, from R. Case, "The role of the frontal lobes in the regulation of cognitive development," *Brain and Cognition*, vol. 20, p. 55. Copyright 1992.

Figure 8.1 is reproduced from I. C. McManus and M. P. Bryden, "Geschwind's theory of cerebral lateralization: developing a formal, causal model," *Psychological Bulletin*, vol. 110, pp. 237–253. Copyright (1991) by the American Psychological Association. Reprinted with permission.

chapter one

The Biology of Change

In this introductory chapter I discuss a number of background issues relating to the developmental cognitive neuroscience approach, beginning with historical approaches to the nature–nurture debate. Constructivism, in which biological forms are an emergent product of complex dynamic interactions between genes and environment, is presented as a superior approach to development than accounts which seek to identify pre-existing information in the genes or external environment. However, giving up existing ways of analyzing development into "innate" and "acquired" components raises the question of how to analyze developmental processes. One scheme for taking account of the various levels of interaction between genes and environment is put forward. In addition, a dissociation between innate representations and architectural constraints on the emergence of representations within neural networks is introduced. Following this, a number of factors that make a cognitive neuroscience approach to development important are discussed, including the increasing availability of brain-imaging and molecular approaches. Conversely, the importance of development for analyzing the relation between brain structure and cognition is assessed. In reviewing ways that development and cognitive neuroscience can be put together, a distinction is drawn between the currently popular static neuropsychology approach (based on the assumption of causal epigenesis), and the promising but relatively unexplored constructivist approach (based on the assumption of probabilistic epigenesis). Finally, the content of the rest of the book is outlined.

1.1 Viewpoints on development

Developmental cognitive neuroscience has emerged at the interface between two of the most fundamental questions that challenge mankind. The first of these questions concerns the relation
between mind and body, and specifically between the physical
substance of the brain and the mental processes it supports.
This issue is fundamental to the scientific discipline of cognitive
neuroscience. The second question concerns the origin of organized biological structures, such as the highly complex structure
of the adult human brain. This issue is fundamental to the study
of development. In this book I will suggest that light can be
shed on these two fundamental questions by tackling them both
simultaneously, and specifically by focusing on the relation
between the postnatal development of the human brain and the
cognitive processes it supports.

The second of the two questions above, that of the origin of
organized biological structures, can be posed in terms of phylogeny or ontogeny. The phylogenetic (evolutionary) version of this
question concerns the origin of species, and has been addressed
by Charles Darwin among others. The ontogenetic version of
this question concerns individual development within a lifespan.
The ontogeny question has been somewhat neglected relative to
phylogeny, since some scientists have held the view that once a
particular set of genes has been selected by evolution, ontogeny
is simply a process of executing the "instructions" coded by
those genes. On this view, the ontogeny question essentially
reduces to phylogeny. By contrast, in this book I demonstrate
that ontogenetic development is an active process through which
biological structure is "created" afresh in each individual by
means of complex and variable interactions between genes and
their environments. The information is not in the genes, but
emerges from the constructive interaction between genes and
their environment (see also Oyama, 1985). However, since both
ontogeny and phylogeny concern the origin of biological structure, some of the same mechanisms of change have been invoked in the two cases.

The debate about the extent to which the ontogenetic question (individual development) is subsidiary to the phylogenetic question (evolution) is otherwise known as the nature–nurture issue, and has been central in developmental psychology throughout its history. Broadly speaking, at one extreme the belief is that most of the information necessary to build a human brain, and the mind it supports, is latent within the genes of the individual. While most of this information is common to the species, each individual has some specific information that will make him or her differ from others. By this view, development is a process of unfolding or triggering the expression of information within the genes.

At the opposing extreme, others believe that most of the information that shapes the human mind comes from the structure of the external world. Some facets of the environment, such as gravity, patterned light etc., will be common throughout the species, while other aspects of the environment will be specific to the individual. It will become clear in this book that both of these extreme views are ill conceived since they assume that the information for the structure of an organism exists (either in the genes or in the external world) prior to its construction. In contrast to this, it appears that biological structure emerges anew within each individual's development from constrained dynamic interactions between genes and various levels of environment, and is not easily reducible to simple genetic and experiential components.

It is more commonly accepted these days that the mental abilities of adults are the result of complex interactions between genes and environment. However, the nature of this interaction remains controversial and poorly understood. We will see that by simultaneously considering brain and psychological development we can shed light on the nature of this interaction. Before going further, however, it is useful to briefly review some historical perspectives on the nature–nurture debate. This journey into history may help us avoid slipping back into ways of thinking that are deeply embedded in the Western intellectual tradition.

Throughout the seventeenth century, there was an ongoing

Figure 1.1   Drawings such as this influenced a seventeenth-century school of thought, the "spermists," who believed that there was a complete preformed person in each male sperm and that development merely consisted in increasing size.

debate in biology between the so-called "vitalists," on the one hand, and the "preformationists," on the other. The vitalists believed that ontogenetic change was driven by "vital" life forces. Belief in this somewhat mystical and ill-defined force was widespread and actively encouraged by some members of the clergy. Following the invention of the microscope, however, some of those who viewed themselves as being of a more rigorous scientific mind championed the preformationist viewpoint. This view argued that a complete human being was contained in either the male sperm ("spermists") or the female egg ("ovists.") In order to support their claim, spermists produced drawings of a tiny, but perfect, human form enclosed within the head of sperm (see figure 1.1). They argued that there was a simple and direct mapping between the seed of the organism and its end state: simultaneous growth of all the body parts. Indeed, pre-formationists of a religious conviction argued that God, on the sixth day of his work, placed about two hundred thousand million fully formed human miniatures into the ovaries of Eve or the sperm of Adam (Gottlieb, 1992)!

Of course, we now know that such drawings were the result of overactive imagination, and that no such perfectly formed miniature human forms exist in the sperm or ovaries. However, as we shall see, the general idea behind preformationism, that there is a pre-existing blueprint or plan of the final state, remained a pervasive one for many decades in biological development. In fact, Oyama (1985) suggests that the same notion of a "plan" or "blueprint" which exists prior to the developmental process has persisted to the present day, with genes replacing the little man inside the sperm. As it became clear that genes do not contain a simple "code" for body parts, in more recent years, "regulator" and "switching" genes have been invoked to orchestrate the expression of the others. In all of these versions of the nativist viewpoint is the belief that there is a fixed mapping relation between a pre-existing set of coded instructions and the final form.

On the other side of the nature–nurture dichotomy, those who believe in the structuring role of experience also view the information as existing prior to the end state, only the source of that information is different. This argument has been applied to psychological development, since it is obviously less plausible for physical growth. For example, some of the more extreme members of the behaviorist school of psychology believed that a child's psychological abilities could be entirely shaped by his or her early environment. More recently, some developmental psychologists from the "connectionist" modeling school have argued that the infant's mind is shaped largely by the statistical regularities latent in the external environment. It will become evident in this book that the connectionist modeling approach need not necessarily be associated with such an empiricist standpoint. Indeed, it can be an excellent method of exploring types of interaction between intrinsic and extrinsic structure.

The viewpoints discussed above have the common assumption that the information necessary for constructing the final state (in this case, the adult mind) is present prior to the developmental process. While vitalist beliefs were sometimes more dynamic in character than preformationists, the forces that guided development were still assumed to originate with an external creator. Preformationism in historical or modern guises involves the execution of plans or codes (from genes) or the incorporation of information from the structure of the environment. Oyama (1985) argued that these views on ontogenetic development resemble pre-Darwinian theories of evolution in which a creator was deemed to have planned all the species in existence. In both the ontogenetic and phylogenetic theories of this kind, a plan for the final form of the species or individual exists prior to its emergence.

A more recent trend in thinking about ontogenetic development is "constructivism." Constructivism differs from preformationist views in that biological structures are viewed as an emergent property of complex interactions between genes and environment. Perhaps the most famous proponent of such a view with regard to cognitive development was the Swiss epistemologist Jean Piaget. The essence of constructivism is that the relationship between the initial state and the final product can only be understood by considering the progressive construction of information. This construction is a dynamic process to which multiple factors contribute. There is no simple sense in which information either exclusively in the genes or in the environment can specify the end product. Rather, these two factors combine in a constructive manner such that each developmental step will be greater than the sum of the factors that contributed to it. The upshot of this viewpoint is not that we can never understand the mapping between genetic (or environmental) information and the final product, but rather that this mapping can only be understood once we have unraveled some of the key interactions that occur between genetic and environmental factors during ontogeny.

Until recently, the constructivist view suffered from the same problem as vitalism, in that the mechanisms of change were poorly specified and the emergence of new structures from old resembled the conjuror's trick of making a rabbit appear from a hat. Even the "mechanisms" proposed by Piaget appeared somewhat elusive on closer inspection. Another problem with the constructivist approach was that, despite its emphasis on interaction, it was unclear how to analyze development in the absence of the traditional dichotomy between innate and environmental factors. By taking a cognitive neuroscience approach to psychological development, in conjunction with a number of new theoretical approaches, we will see that it is possible to reinforce the constructivist approach to development and to provide new ways to analyze cognitive and brain development.

1.2 Analyzing development

Viewpoints on cognitive development that involve reducing behavior to information derived from genes, on the one hand, and/or information derived from the external environment, on the other, have commonly used the distinction between "innate" and "acquired" components. The term "innate" has rarely been explicitly defined, and has a somewhat checkered history in developmental science. Indeed, it has been dropped from use, and even actively banned, in many areas of developmental biology. The main reason for the term's disuse in fields of biology such as ethology and genetics is simply because it is no longer useful since it has become evident that genes interact with their environment at many levels, including the molecular. One compelling example of this point, discussed by Gottlieb (1992), concerns the formation of the beak in the chick embryo.

The production of the (toothless) beak in the chick embryo results from the coaction of two types of tissue, avian oral epidermal tissue and avian oral mesenchyme. However, if, in an experimental situation, the avian oral mesenchyme is replaced with mouse molar mesenchyme then teeth will form instead of a beak! Thus, as Gottlieb (1992) points out, the genetic component

Table 1.1 Levels of interaction between genes and their environment

Levels of interaction	Term
Molecular	Internal environment
Cellular	Internal environment (innate)
Organism–external environment	Species-typical environment (primal) Individual-specific environment (learning)

that is necessary for the chick oral epithelium to produce teeth has been retained from the reptilian ancestry of birds. More generally, the phenotype that emerges from these chick genes can vary dramatically according to the molecular and cellular context in which they are located.

Thus, there is no aspect of development that can be said to be strictly "genetic;" that is, exclusively a product of information contained within particular genes. If the term "innate" is taken to refer to structure that is specified exclusively by genetic information, it refers to nothing that exists in the natural world, except for genes themselves. In cognitive science, however, use of the term "innate" has persisted despite repeated calls for it to be dropped from use (e.g. Hinde, 1974; Oyama, 1985; Johnston, 1988; Gottlieb, 1992). Presumably its persistent usage reflects the need for a term to describe the interaction between factors intrinsic to the developing child, and features of the external environment. In considering this issue, Johnson and Morton (1991) suggest that it is useful to distinguish among the various levels of interaction between genes and their environment. Some of these are shown in table 1.1. Within this analysis, the term "innate" refers only to changes that arise as a result of interactions that occur within the organism, and does not equate with genetic factors. That is, it refers to the *level of the interaction between genes and environment, and not to the source of the information*. I will adopt this working definition of the term in this book. Interactions between the organism and aspects of the external environment that are common to all members of the species, the species-typical environment, (such as patterned light, gravity, etc.) are referred to as "primal" by Johnson and Morton (1991). Interactions between the organism and aspects of the environment unique to an individual, or subset of members of a species, are referred to as "learning."

Based on a series of experiments on the effects on brain structure of rearing rats in impoverished or comparatively enriched early environments, Greenough et al. (1987) proposed a similar distinction between two types of information storage induced by the environment. Changes induced by aspects of the environment that are common to all members of a species were classified as "experience-expectant" information storage (= "species-typical,") and are associated with selective synaptic loss. The second type of information incorporated by the brain through interaction with the environment was referred to as "experience-dependent" (= "individual-specific.") This referred to interactions with the environment that are, or can be, specific to an individual and are associated with the generation of new synaptic connections. Clearly, the boundary between these types of experience is often difficult to ascertain, and there have been many instances from ethological studies where behaviors thought to be innate turn out to be primal on closer study.

Using this framework, it is possible to analyze aspects of development into underlying components. Normally in developmental psychology this is done in terms of components of cognition or behavior. In a cognitive neuroscience approach, by contrast, we can use evidence from different components of brain structure to constrain our thinking about cognitive development. Specifically, we can inquire into the extent to which aspects of a given neural circuit are innate (defined as above as the product of interactions within the organism, and not sensitive to experience). Different aspects of brain structure and function are probably differentially sensitive to the effects of postnatal experience. The following analysis, which for simplicity I apply to the example of a simple abstract neural network, will assist in the later discussion of brain development and plasticity. A

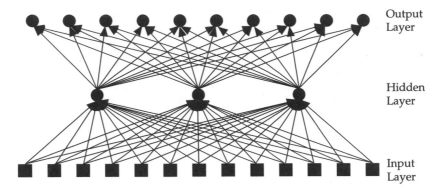

Figure 1.2   A simple three-layered connectionist neural network in which groups of nodes are joined by links. Changes in the strength of links as a result of training are determined by a learning rule.

similar, but more detailed, analysis is presented in Elman et al. (1996).

The human brain is composed of very complex neural circuits bathed in a variety of chemicals which can regulate and modulate function. Therefore, when considering ways to analyze plasticity in such circuits it is useful to start with a simpler system that shares the same general properties. Connectionist neural network models involve nodes (simplified neurons) and links that can vary in strength (simplified synapses and dendrites). Learning in such networks takes place by varying the strength or extent of connections between nodes according to learning rules, some of which approximate those thought to be used in real brains (such as "Hebbian" learning rules).

Figure 1.2 shows a simple connectionist neural network. There are several ways in which it could be sensitive to training. First, the basic architecture of the network could alter as a result of experience. This could involve a change in the number of nodes, the learning rule, or the extent to which the nodes are interconnected. There are, in fact, a few neural network models that change in this way. Another possibility is that while the basic architecture of the network is relatively fixed, the strength of the connections between the nodes varies according to a weight-adjustment learning rule. This is the way that most connectionist neural networks encode information. Since representations in artificial connectionist networks are dependent on the particular pattern of link strengths between nodes, allowing these to vary with the input means that different representations may emerge as a result of experience. In terms of the brain, we can think of these changes as residing in the details of microcircuits and synaptic efficacy. When the basic architecture of the network is fixed but the link strengths vary, we may say that the network shows an *innate architecture*. *More specifically, the representations that emerge as a result of training are constrained by the architecture of the network.* In chapter 2 we will review evidence consistent with the view that the primate cerebral cortex imposes architectural constraints on the development of representations.

Within this framework, there are, however, also two other possibilities. The first of these is that both the basic architecture of the network and the patterns and strengths of links between nodes are innate (as defined in table 1.1), and thus insensitive to external input. I will refer to this as the network possessing *innate representations*. In later chapters we will see that there is little evidence that the human neocortex possesses innate representations. The second possibility is that both the architecture and the detailed pattern and strength of links are malleable as a result of training. In the next chapter we will see that only under extremely abnormal environmental conditions, or in cases of genetic abnormality, do we see changes in the basic architecture of the primate brain.

1.3   Why take a cognitive neuroscience approach to development?

Until recently, the majority of theories of perceptual and cognitive development were generated without recourse to evidence from the brain. Indeed, some authors argued strongly for the independence of cognitive level theorizing from considerations of the neural substrate (Morton et al., 1984). Evidence from the brain was thought to be distracting, irrelevant, or hopelessly complex. However, our understanding of brain function has improved significantly over the past decade or so. Accordingly, some believe that the time is now ripe for exploring the interface between cognitive development and brain development (Elman et al., 1996; Johnson and Gilmore, in press). Further, the integration of information from biology and cognitive development sets the stage for a more comprehensive psychology and biology of change than was previously thought possible: a developmental cognitive neuroscience. By the term "cognitive neuroscience" I include not only evidence about brain development, such as that from neuroanatomy, brain imaging, and the behavioral or cognitive effects of brain lesions, but also evidence from ethology. Ethology, a science pioneered by Tinbergen, Lorenz, and others in the 1940s and 1950s, concerns the study of a whole organism within its natural environment (see Tinbergen, 1951; Lorenz, 1965; Hinde, 1974). We shall see that ethology is a powerful complement to neuroscience, and that the two fields combined can change the way we think about critical issues in perceptual and cognitive development.

In general, insights from biology have begun to play a more central role in informing thinking about perceptual and cognitive development for a number of reasons. First, a range of powerful new methods and tools is becoming available to cognitive neuroscientists. These techniques permit questions to be asked about the biological basis of cognitive and perceptual development more directly than can be posed at present. One set of tools relates to neuroimaging: the generation of "functional" maps of brain activity based on changes in cerebral metabolism, blood flow or electrical activity. Some of these imaging methods, such as positron emission tomography (PET), are of limited utility for studying transitions in cognitive development in normal infants due to their invasive nature (requiring the intravenous injection of radioactivity-labeled substances) and their relatively coarse temporal resolution (in the order of tens of seconds). In contrast, two techniques currently being developed may be readily applied to development in normal children:

high-density event-related potentials (HD-ERP), and functional magnetic resonance imaging (F-MRI). HD-ERP is a method of recording from the scalp the electrical activity of the brain.

The electrical activity of the brain can be recorded by means of sensitive electrodes that rest on the scalp surface. These recordings can either be of the spontaneous natural rhythms of the brain (electroencephalography or EEG), or the electrical activity time locked to a stimulus presentation or action (ERPs). Since the ERP from many trials is averaged, the spontaneous natural rhythms of the brain that are unrelated to the stimulus presentation average to zero. With a high density of electrodes on the scalp, algorithms can be employed which infer the position and orientation of the brain sources of electrical activity (dipoles) for the particular pattern of scalp surface electrical activity. Some of the assumptions necessary for the successful use of these algorithms are actually more likely to be true of infants than adults. For example, lower levels of skull conductance and fewer cortical convolutions may improve the accuracy and interpretability of HD-ERP results in infants relative to adult subjects (but see Nelson, 1994, for a comprehensive analysis of the difficulties in applying the ERP methodology to infants).

Functional-MRI allows the non-invasive measurement of cerebral blood flow (Raichle and Malinkrodt, 1987; Kwong et al., 1992), with the prospect of spatial resolution in the order of millimeters and temporal resolution of several seconds, using MRI machines commonly available in modern medical facilities. This technique has already being applied to children, though factors such as noise, vibration levels, and enclosure may still make it difficult to apply to infants.

Another useful tool for linking brain development to behavior is the "marker task." This method involves the use of specific behavioral tasks which have been related to one or more brain regions in adult humans and non-human primates by neurophysiological, neuropsychological, and/or brain imaging studies, and preferably by at least two of these methods. By studying the development of performance on the task at different ages and in different contexts, the researcher can gather evidence about how the observed behavioral change is accounted for by known patterns of brain development.

In this book, I will survey several lines of inquiry which illustrate the marker task approach. There are also weaknesses in the marker task approach, such as the generalizability of findings from one task to others, and the interpretability of results between subject pools that differ significantly. Another challenge stems from the design of a task that is sufficiently limited in its demands as to give interpretable results with infants or young children, and yet sufficiently demanding to call upon "interesting" cognitive capacities. Moreover, since different brain regions may be critical for the same task at different ages (Goldman-Rakic, 1971), the interpretation of results is made more complex. Nevertheless, the marker task approach is a useful methodology that promises to provide insight into the development of neurocognitive systems.

Marker tasks need to be based on the cognitive abilities of young infants. Obviously, behavioral tasks involving verbal instruction or output are not feasible. Further, young infants only have a short attention span in terms of the length of time they are prepared to cooperate with the experimenter. Consequently, studies involving extensive training are not feasible either. Fortunately, however, several methods have been developed for testing infants that utilize their natural tendencies to look at conspicuous and novel visual stimuli. One of these procedures, called "preferential looking," involves presenting paired visual stimuli, and recording the time that the infants chooses to look at each. Another procedure, called "habituation," involves showing the same stimulus repeatedly until the infant shows a clear decrease in the time it spends looking at it. When a certain criterion for the looking decrement is reached, a novel stimulus is presented and the recovery in looking time recorded. If there is significant recovery of looking time, we may infer that the infant can discriminate between the two. If there is little or no recovery, we may infer that the infant is unable to discriminate between them. Other techniques for eliciting discriminative responses from young infants that will be mentioned in this book include using rate of sucking to measure habituation, and the use of heart rate measures.

Beyond neuroimaging and the marker task, techniques exist in molecular genetics which allow the lesioning of particular genes from the genome of an animal (mainly mice and rats so far). An example of this is the deletion of the alpha-calcium calmodulin kinase II gene which results in rats being unable to perform certain learning tasks when adults (Silva et al., 1992a, b). This method opens new vistas in the analysis of genetic contributions to cognitive and perceptual change in animals, and may be particularly fruitful when applied to well-studied animal models of development such as visual imprinting in chicks and song learning in passerine birds.

Animal models are another way that the cognitive neuroscience approach can contribute to the study of development. A number of animal models of behavioral development have reached a stage where some of the principles discovered may be applicable to aspects of human development (see Blass, 1992). One example discussed later in this book is the work of Horn and collaborators on the neural basis of visual imprinting in the chick (see Horn, 1985; Johnson, 1991, for reviews). This line of research has implicated particular regions of the chick brain in visual imprinting, and has identified electrophysiological, neuroanatomical, and molecular correlates of this process. A neuronal network model of one of these brain regions has been developed, allowing the computational analysis of such phenomena as sensitive periods for learning (O'Reilly and Johnson, 1994). Further, the dissociation of neural systems underlying components of filial preference behavior in the chick has been used to argue for a similar dissociation in the development of face recognition in human infants (see chapter 4). Consequently, while homologies between species must be made with great care, well-studied animal models increasingly provide useful theoretical and empirical insights into cognitive development in humans. Importantly, theories which incorporate and reveal relationships between brain structures and cognitive functions will be useful in understanding the effects of early brain injury or genetic disorder on cognitive development. Evidence derived from infants with congenital and acquired brain damage will be discussed throughout later chapters. Beyond its clinical utility, this line of evidence can also contribute to the development of theories about functional specification, critical periods, and plasticity in the brain. Thus, there is a two-way interaction between clinical evidence and basic research in developmental cognitive neuroscience.

1.4   Why take a developmental approach to cognitive neuroscience?

Ontogentic development is the constructive process by which genes interact with their environment at various levels to yield complex organic structures such as the brain and the cognitive processes it supports. The study of development is necessarily multidisciplinary since new levels of structure that emerge as a result of this process (such as particular neural systems) often require different levels and methods of analysis from those that preceded them. The flip side of this is that development can be used as a tool for unraveling the interaction between seemingly disparate levels of organization, such as that from the molecular biology of gene expression to the development of cognitive abilities such as object recognition. Further, the human adult brain and the mind it sustains is composed of a complex series of hierarchical and parallel systems which has proven very difficult to analyze in an exclusively "top-down" manner. Brain damage induced by surgical lesions, or by accident or stroke, are unlikely to cleanly dissociate different levels of hierarchical organization. The developmental approach may allow different levels of hierarchical control to be observed independently. Specifically, it presents the opportunity to observe how various neurocognitive systems emerge and become integrated during development. This approach is reminiscent of the "synthetic psychology" advocated by Braitenberg (1984) in which he evolved increasingly complex "vehicles" (organisms) capable of seemingly sophisticated behaviors.

1.5   Putting development and cognitive neuroscience together

This book provides an introduction to the interface of development and cognitive neuroscience. Views of the integration of these two disciplines differ as a function of the general approaches to biological development discussed earlier. Those inclined to see development as the unfolding of pre-existing information in the genes tend to adopt a "static" view of developmental psychology in which infants have reduced versions of the adult mind which increase by steps as particular brain pathways or structures mature. In contrast, taking a constructivist view of development involves attempting to unravel the dynamic relations between intrinsic and extrinsic structure which progressively restrict the phenotypes that can emerge. The distinction between these two approaches has also been noted by Gottlieb (1992) who refers to them as "predetermined epigenesis" and "probabilistic epigenesis." Predetermined epigenesis assumes that there is a unidirectional causal path from genes to structural brain changes to brain function and experience. In contrast, probabilistic epigenesis views the interactions between genes, structural brain changes, and function as bidirectional:

Predetermined epigenesis
(unidirectional structure-functional development)
genes → brain structure → brain function → experience

Probabilistic epigenesis
(bidirectional structure-functional development)
genes ↔ brain structure ↔ brain function ↔ experience
(*Source*: Gottlieb, 1992)

Thus, by the predetermined epigenesis view, the infant mind is seen as being comparable to adults with focal brain injury. That is, specific cognitive mechanisms are either present or absent at a given age. For example, parallels have been drawn between infants and patients with frontal lobe deficits (e.g. Diamond, 1991; Johnson, 1995). This view shares assumptions with the "marker task" method discussed earlier, and is commonly associated with a maturationist viewpoint. Circuits that support components of the adult system are assumed to come "on-line" at various ages. While this approach is likely to provide a reasonable first approximation for normal developmental events, it is unlikely to provide a full account in the long run.

An alternative approach to investigating the relation between the developing brain and cognition is associated with a probabilistic epigenesis approach to biological development. This viewpoint assumes that development involves the progressive restriction of fate. Early in development, a system, such as the brain/mind, has a range of possible developmental paths and end states. The developmental path and end state that results is dependent on the particular sets of constraints that operate. This type of analysis of ontogenetic development derives from work on the development of body structure by D'Arcy Thompson (1917) and C. H. Waddington (1975) among others.

Waddington (whose work greatly influenced Piaget) proposed that there are developmental pathways, or necessary epigenetic routes, which he termed "chreods." Chreods can be conceptualized as valleys in an epigenetic landscape such as that shown in figure 1.3. Self-regulatory processes (which Waddington called "homeorhesis") ensure that the organism (conceptualized as a ball rolling down the landscape) returns to its channel following small perturbations. Large perturbations, such as being reared in darkness, can result in a quite different valley route being taken, especially when these occur near a decision point. These decision points are regions of the epigenetic landscape where a perturbation can lead to a different route being taken. Thus, while for the "normal" child the same end point will be reached despite the small perturbations that arise from slightly different rearing environments, a deviation from the normal path early in development (high up the hill), at a decision point, or a major

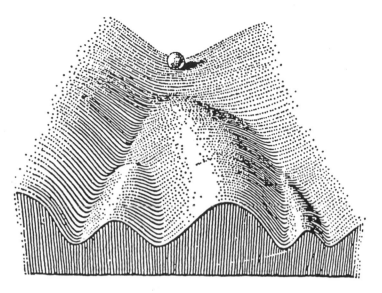

Figure 1.3 The epigenetic landscape of Waddington (1975).

perturbation later in development, may cause the child to take a different developmental path and reach one of a discrete set of possible alternative end states (phenotypes).

Aside from Waddington's informal conceptualization, the constructivist (probabilistic epigenesis) approach to development is currently more difficult to work with since we have few theoretical tools for understanding emergent phenomena in complex dynamic systems. On this view, developmental disorders are possible developmental trajectories that are responses to different sets of constraints. This implies that from the moment when the developmental trajectory deviates from the normal one, a variety of new factors and adaptations will come into play making it likely that some reorganization of brain functioning takes place. In contrast to the current developmental neuropsychology approach (causal epigenesis), therefore, applying the mapping between brain regions and functions found in normal adults to such cases may be only partially informative. It should be stressed that the constructivist view just outlined does not seek to downplay the role of genetic factors. Rather, it seeks to understand the emergence of new structures and functions through the complex interactions between genes and their multi-leveled environments.

Currently, developmental neuropsychology is largely dominated by the causal epigenesis view. However, in my view, there will be a gradual transition to constructivist (probabilistic epigenesis) models over the next decade. Some of the directions for this approach are sketched out in this book. However, until we have adequate models for understanding emergent phenomena, the more static view will continue to provide a useful preliminary sketch of the relation between the developing brain and cognition.

1.6   An outline of the book

The next chapter will review the current state of our knowledge of the pre- and postnatal development of the human brain. While the sequence of developmental events is very similar between man and other mammals, the timing of development, and especially postnatal development, is stretched out in humans. This extended period of postnatal development is associated with a greater extent of area of cerebral cortex, in particular the prefrontal regions. The more extended postnatal development observed in humans reveals differential rates of development in aspects of brain structure (e.g. different cortical areas and layers). The more differentiated picture of postnatal brain development in humans can be used to make predictions about the emergence of function.

Focusing on the cerebral cortex, neurobiological and brain imaging studies indicate that the cortex probably does not possess innate representations. That is, regions of neocortex do not appear to be intrinsically predestined to support particular classes of representations such as faces or language. Rather, the fairly consistent structure–function relations observed in the cortex of the normal human adult appear to be the consequence of multiple constraints both intrinsic and extrinsic to the organism. In the following chapters, a number of domains of cognitive development that have been associated with neural development are reviewed. In each of these domains I attempt to reveal some of the sources of constraint on the representations that emerge within cortical circuits. Examples of combinations of constraints from the correlational structure of the external environment, the basic architecture of the cortex, and the influence of subcortical circuits are discussed.

Although abnormal development is not the focus of this book, throughout the review of normal development evidence from abnormal development is discussed where relevant. Focusing on three developmental disorders (dyslexia, autism, and Williams syndrome), we see that specific neurocognitive deficits can result from diffuse damage to multiple brain systems. Brain damage in prenatal development can divert the child from one developmental path to another. However, it is possible that different types of brain damage can result in the same end state (phenotype), somewhat like the discrete number of valleys in Waddington's epigenetic landscape. In contrast to this, brain damage in later life (perinatal and early postnatal) is commonly compensated for by other parts of the brain. Thus, at this later stage, a focal brain lesion may have only mild diffuse cognitive consequences, resembling Waddington's self-organizing adaptation, keeping the organism within a certain chreod and resulting in the same general phenotype.

In chapter 9, a number of mechanisms and types of changes in representations during human postnatal development are discussed. The general assumption underlying this chapter is that the mechanisms responsible for cognitive changes can best be understood at a neurocomputational level, and specifically as transformations in cortical representations. A number of factors that influence the emergence of new representations are described, and I speculate on a neurocomputational mechanism for representational redescription (Karmiloff-Smith, 1992) during postnatal cortical development. Several authors have proposed selectionist theories in which selective patterns of synapse loss provide a basis for interactions with the external environment to shape neural circuitry. One of the specific outcomes of this process of selective synapse loss can be the parcellation of neural circuits into encapsulated modules. I suggest that this parcellation process leads to a number of apparent regressions in performance at the behavioral level. Another aspect of representational transformation during postnatal development concerns the gradual increase in "strength" of a representation with increased experience. A weak representation may be sufficient to drive a simple output, such as looking, but not sufficient to drive a more complex output, such as reaching. In chapter 10, some conclusions and recommendations for future research are made.

chapter two

Building a Brain

This chapter describes several aspects of the pre- and postnatal development of the brain, with specific reference to humans where data permits. In the first section, some of the stages of prenatal brain development are outlined, including the proliferation, migration, and differentiation of cells such that they give rise to particular brain structures. Next, a basic overview of primate brain anatomy is provided with specific emphasis on the neocortex. A distinction is made between two dimensions of the cortex: its areal or regional structure, and its laminar (layered) structure. The following section on postnatal development reports that while human brain volume quadruples between birth and adulthood, this is due to increases in fiber bundles, dendrites, and myelinization, and not to additional neurons. Further, some measures of structural and neurophysiological brain development, such as the density of synaptic contacts, show a characteristic "rise and fall" during postnatal development. Following this, the question of the extent to which the differentiation of neocortex into areas or regions is prespecified is addressed. The "protomap" hypothesis states that the areal differentiation of the cortex is determined by intrinsic molecular markers or prespecification of the proliferative zone. In contrast, the "protocortex" hypothesis suggests that an initially undifferentiated protocortex is divided up largely as a result of input through projections from the thalamus. A review of evidence proves more consistent with the latter view. It is concluded that while cortical networks impose architectural constraints on the representations that emerge within it, there is little evidence for innate representations. Further evidence in support of this conclusion comes from a variety of studies on cortical plasticity in neonatal rodents. In some of these studies, thalamic inputs to cortical areas are diverted to other regions, or pieces of cortex are transplanted from one region to another. In both of these cases, cortical tissue acquires representations according to the nature of the thalamic input, rather than its developmental origins. In some cases these representations can even be used to guide the behavior of the animal. With some caveats, I suggest that similar conclusions can be drawn about primate cortical development and plasticity. The next section focuses on a clear area of difference between human cortical development and that of other primates: its very extended period of postnatal development. This greatly extended period reveals two differential aspects of cortical development not as clearly evident in other primates: an inside-out pattern of development of layers, and gradients of differential timing of development of cortical regions. These differential aspects of human cortical development will provide the basis for associations between brain and cognitive development described in later chapters. The chapter concludes with discussion of the postnatal development of some subcortical structures, and with a brief review of our knowledge of the development of neurotransmitters and modulators. The developmental levels of several neurotransmitters mirror aspects of the differential structural development of cortex.

2.1   Prenatal brain development

The sequence of events during the prenatal development of the human brain closely resembles that of many other vertebrates. Shortly after conception, a fertilized cell undergoes a rapid process of cell division, resulting in a cluster of proliferating cells (called the blastocyst) that somewhat resembles a bunch of grapes. Within a few days, the blastocyst differentiates into a three-layered structure (the embryonic disk). Each of these layers will further differentiate into a major organic system. The endoderm (inner layer) changes into the set of internal organs (digestive, respiratory, etc.); the mesoderm (middle layer) turns into the skeletal and muscular structures; and the ectoderm (outer layer) gives rise to the skin surface and the nervous system (including the perceptual organs).

The nervous system itself begins with a process known as *neurolation*. A portion of the ectoderm begins to fold in on itself to form a hollow cylinder called the *neural tube*. The neural tube differentiates along three dimensions: length, circumference, and radius. The length dimension gives rise to the major subdivisions of the central nervous system, with the forebrain and midbrain arising at one end and the spinal cord at the other. The end which will become the spinal cord differentiates into a series of repeated units or segments, while the front end of the neural tube organizes differently with a series of bulges and convolutions forming (see figure 2.1). By around 5 weeks after conception these bulges can be identified as protoforms for major components of the mammalian brain. Proceeding from front to back: the first bulge gives rise to the cortex (telencephalon), the second gives rise to the thalamus and hypothalamus (diencephalon), the third turns into the midbrain (mesencephalon), and others to the cerebellum (metencephalon), and to the medulla (myelencephalon).

The circumferential dimension in the neural tube is critical, because the distinction between sensory and motor systems develops along this dimension: dorsal corresponds roughly to sensory cortex, ventral corresponds to motor cortex, with the various association cortices and "higher" sensory and motor cortices aligned somewhere in between. Within the brain stem and the spinal cord, the corresponding alar (dorsal) and basal (ventral) plates play a major role in the organization of nerve pathways into the rest of the body.

Differentiation along the radial dimension gives rise to the complex layering patterns and cell types found in the adult brain. Across the radial dimension of the neural tube the bulges grow larger and become further differentiated. Within these bulges cells *proliferate, migrate,* and *differentiate into particular types*. The vast majority of the cells that will compose the brain are born in the so-called *proliferative zones*. These zones are close to the hollow of the neural tube (which subsequently becomes the ventricles of the brain). The first of these proliferation sites, the *ventricular zone*, may be phylogenetically older (Nowakowski, 1987). The

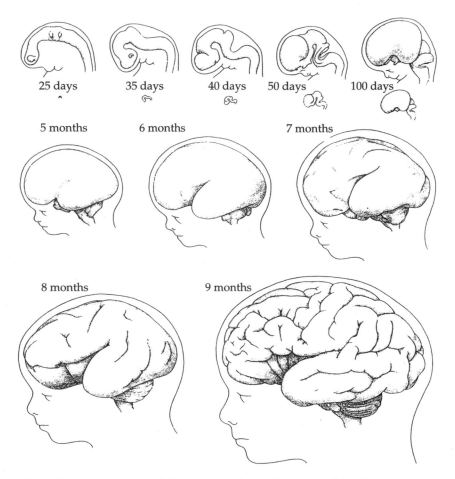

Figure 2.1   A sequence of drawings of the embryonic and fetal development of the human brain. The forebrain, midbrain, and hindbrain originate as swellings at the head end of the neural tube. In primates, the convoluted cortex grows to cover the midbrain, hindbrain, and parts of the cerebellum. Prior to birth, neurons are generated in the developing brain at a rate of more than 250,000 per minute.

second, the *subventricular zone*, only contributes significantly to phylogenetically recent brain structures such as the neocortex (i.e. "new" cortex). These two zones yield separate glial and neuron cell lines and give rise to different forms of migration. But first we will consider how young neurons are formed within these zones.

Neurons and glial cells are produced by division of proliferating cells within the proliferation zone to produce clones (a clone is a group of cells which are produced by division of a single precursor cell – such a precursor cell is said to give rise to a lineage). *Neuroblasts* produce neurons, and *glioblasts* produce glial cells. Each of the neuroblasts give rise to a definite and limited number of neurons, a point to which I will return later. In at least some cases particular neuroblasts also give rise to particular types of cell. For example, less than a dozen proliferating cells produce all the Purkinje cells of the cerebellar cortex, with each producing about 10,000 cells (Nowakowski, 1987).

After young neurons are born, they have to travel or *migrate* from the proliferative zone to the particular region where they will be employed in the mature brain. There are two forms of migration observed during brain development. The first, and more common, is passive cell displacement. This occurs when cells that have been generated are simply pushed further away from the proliferative zone by more recently born cells. This form of migration gives rise to an outside-to-inside spatiotemporal gradient. That is, the oldest cells are pushed toward the surface of the brain, while the most recently produced cells are toward the inside. Passive migration gives rise to brain structures such as the thalamus, the dentate gyrus of the hippocampus, and many regions of the brain stem. The second form of migration is more active and involves the young cell moving past previously generated cells to create an "inside-out" gradient. This pattern is found in the cerebral cortex and in some subcortical areas that have a laminar structure (divided into parallel layers).

2.2 An overview of primate brain anatomy

The mammalian brain follows a basic vertebrate brain plan found in lower species such as salamanders, frogs, and birds. The major differences between these species and higher primates is in the dramatic expansion of the cerebral cortex together with associated structures such as the thalamus. The rapid expansion of the area of cortex has resulted in it becoming increasingly convoluted. For example, the area of the cortex in the cat is about 100 cm^2, whereas that of the human is about 2,400 cm^2. This suggests that the extra cortex possessed by primates, and especially humans, is related to the higher cognitive functions they possess. However, the basic relations between principal structures of the brain remain similar from mouse to man. The neocortex of mammals is basically a thin (about 3–4 mm) flat sheet. While complex, its general laminar structure is relatively constant throughout its extent (see figure 2.2).

Most of the sensory inputs to the cortex pass through a structure known as the thalamus. Each type of sensory input has its own particular nuclei within this region. For example, the lateral geniculate nucleus carries visual input to the cortex, while the medial geniculate nucleus carries information from the auditory modality. Because of the crucial role of the thalamus in mediating inputs to the cortex, some authors have hypothesized that it also plays a crucial role in cortical development – an idea which I will discuss at greater length later. The flow of information between thalamus and cortex is not unidirectional, however, since most of the projections from lower regions into the cortex are matched by projections from the cortex back down. Some output projections from the cortex pass to regions that are believed to be involved in motor control, such as the basal ganglia and the cerebellum. However, most of the projections from the cortex to other brain regions terminate in roughly the same regions from which projections arrived (such as the thalamus). In other words, the flow of information to and from the cortex is largely bidirectional. For this reason, it is important not to confuse the terms "input" and "output" with "sensory" and "motor." All sensory and motor systems make extensive use of both input and output fibers, with information passing rapidly in both directions along collateral pathways.

The brain has two general types of cells: neurons and glial cells. Glial cells are more common than neurons, but are generally

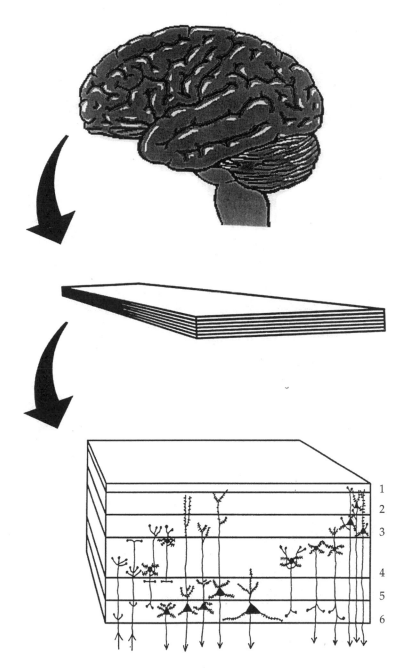

Figure 2.2 A simplified schematic diagram which illustrates that, despite its convoluted surface appearance (top), the cerebral cortex is a thin sheet (middle) composed of six layers (bottom). The convolutions in the cortex arise from a combination of growth patterns and the restricted space inside the skull. In general, differences between mammals involve the total area of the cortical sheet, and not its layered structure. Each of the layers possesses certain neuron types and characteristic input and projection patterns (see text).

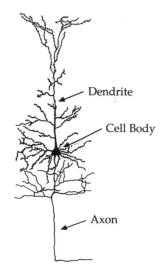

Figure 2.3 A typical cortical pyramidal cell. The apical dendrite is the long process that extends to the upper layers, and may allow the cell to be influenced by other neurons. An axon projects to subcortical regions.

assumed to play no direct role in computation. However, as we shall see later, they play a very important role in the development of the cortex. The computational unit of the brain has long been thought to be the neuron (Shepherd, 1972). Neurons come in many shapes, sizes and types, each of which presumably reflects a particular computational function. Currently, there appear to be approximately 25 different neuronal types within the cortex, although several of these types are relatively rare, and some are restricted to particular layers. About 80 percent of neurons found in the cortex are pyramidal cells, so-called because of the distinctive pyramid shape of the soma (cell body) produced by the very large apical dendrite (input process) which is always tangential to the surface of the cortex (figure 2.3). These are the neurons whose long axons (output processes) are so often found in the fibers feeding into other cortical and subcortical regions. While pyramidal cells are found in many of the layers of the cortex (generally they are larger in the lower layers and smaller in the upper layers), their apical dendrites often reach into the most superficial layer of the cortex, layer 1 (see below). This long apical dendrite allows the cell to be influenced by large numbers of cells from other (more superficial) layers and regions. This may be computationally important if the pyramidal cell is a very stable and inflexible class of cell whose output is modulated by groups of plastic and flexible inhibitory regulatory neurons. Figure 2.2 also shows a schematic section through an area of primate cortex cut at right angles to the surface of the cortex, revealing the layered structure. I will refer to this as the *laminar* structure of the cortex. As just noted, each of the laminae has particular cell types within it, and each layer has typical patterns of inputs and outputs.

Most areas of the neocortex (in all mammals) are made up of six layers. The basic characteristics that define each layer appear to hold in most regions of the cortical sheet. Layer 1 has few cell bodies. It is made up primarily of long white fibers running along the horizontal surface, linking one area of cortex to others some distance away. Layers 2 and 3 also contain horizontal connections, often projecting forward from small pyramidal cells to neighboring areas of cortex. Layer 4 is the layer where most of the input fibers terminate and it contains a high proportion of spiny stellate cells on which these projections terminate. Layers 5 and 6 have the major outputs to subcortical regions of the brain. These layers contain a particularly high proportion of large pyramidal cells, with long descending axons. There are also many neurons involved in intrinsic cortical circuits.

Although this basic laminar structure holds throughout most of the neocortex, there are some regional variations. For example, the input layer (layer 4) is particularly thick and well developed in sensory cortex. Indeed, in the visual system, it is possible to distinguish at least four 'sublayers' within layer 4. Conversely, layer 5 (one of the output layers) is particularly well developed in motor cortex, presumably due to its importance in sending output signals from the cortex. It is also clear that different parts of the cortex have different projection patterns to other parts of the cortex. While there may only be a small number of these characteristic projection patterns from one region of cortex to another, there is no single pattern that can be said to be characteristic of all cortical regions. Hence this is another dimension of variation that can contribute to regional specialization within the cortex. Further dimensions could include the presence of particular neurotransmitters, and the relative contribution of excitatory *v.* inhibitory neurotransmitters. Finally, as we will see later, regions may vary in the timing of key developmental events, such as the postnatal reduction in the number of synapses (Huttenlocher, 1990).

2.3 Postnatal brain development

There are a number of ways to study the postnatal development of neuronal structure in the brain. Traditionally, investigators have used neuroanatomical analysis of postmortem tissue. Such analysis tends to be based on relatively small numbers of children due to the extensive work involved and the difficulties associated in gaining such tissue. Furthermore, those children who come to autopsy have often suffered from trauma or diseases that complicate generalizations to normal brain development. *In vivo* studies using magnetic resonance imaging (Courchesne et al., 1987; Jernigan et al., 1990) and PET scanning of infants and adults (Chugani et al., 1987; Petersen et al., 1988) can inform us about the structural development of the brain. But these techniques are expensive, and are usually restricted to children with clinical symptoms that justify neural imaging. Hence generalizations to normal brain development must be made with caution in these cases as well. Despite these difficulties, a number of progressive and regressive neuroanatomical and neurophysiological changes have been observed during postnatal development in children. Specifically, a number of measures of brain anatomy and function show a characteristic "rise and fall" developmental pattern during this period. While the progressive and regressive processes should not be viewed as distinct stages, for the purposes of exposition I will discuss them in sequence.

Various lines of evidence indicate substantive additive changes during postnatal development of the brain. At the most gross level of analysis, brain volume quadruples between birth and adulthood. This increase comes from a number of sources, but, in general, not from additional neurons. The formation of neurons and their migration to appropriate brain regions takes place almost entirely within the period of prenatal development in the human. Except for a few brain regions that continue to add neurons throughout life (e.g. the olfactory bulbs), the vast majority of neurons are present by around the seventh month of gestation (Rakic, 1995). In contrast to the lack of new nerve cell bodies, there is dramatic postnatal growth of synapses, dendrites, and fiber bundles. Further, nerve fibers become covered in a fatty myelin sheath which adds further to the mass of the brain.

Perhaps the most obvious manifestation of postnatal neural development as viewed through the confocal microscope is the increase in size and complexity of the dendritic tree of most neurons. An example of the dramatic increase in dendritic tree extent during human postnatal development is shown in figure 2.4. While the extent and reach of a cell's dendritic arbor may increase dramatically, it also often becomes more specific and specialized. Less apparent through standard microscopes, but more evident with electron microscopy, is a corresponding increase in measures of the density of synaptic contacts between cells.

Huttenlocher and colleagues have reported a steady increase in synaptic density in several regions of the human cerebral cortex (Huttenlocher et al., 1982; Huttenlocher, 1990, 1994). While an increase in synaptogenesis begins around the time of birth for all cortical areas studied to date, the most rapid bursts of increase, and the final peak density, occur at different ages in different areas. In the visual cortex there is a rapid burst at 3–4 months, and the maximum density of around 150 percent of adult level is reached between 4 and 12 months. A similar time course is observed in the primary auditory cortex (Heschl's gyrus). In contrast, while synaptogenesis starts at the same time in a region of the prefrontal cortex, density increases much more

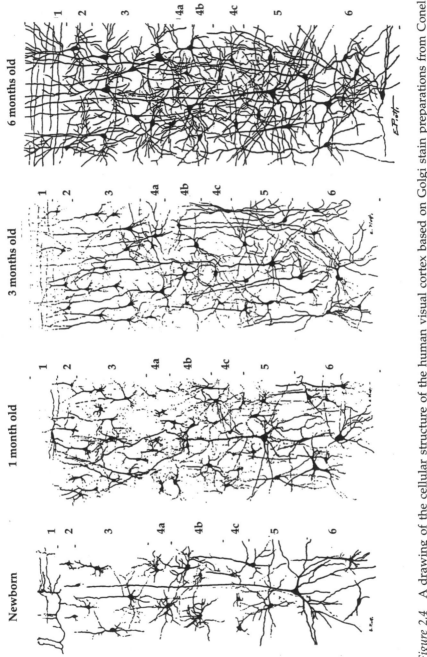

Figure 2.4 A drawing of the cellular structure of the human visual cortex based on Golgi stain preparations from Conel (1939–67).

slowly and does not reach its peak until after the first year. (It should be noted at this point that there are various possible measures of synaptic density: per cell, per unit dendrite, per unit brain tissue etc. Careful selection of measures is required so that factors such as increases in dendritic length do not unduly influence the results. Huttenlocher, 1990, discusses some of these issues of appropriate measurement.)

Another additive process is myelination. Myelination refers to an increase in the fatty sheath that surrounds neuronal pathways, a process that increases the efficiency of information transmission. In the central nervous system, sensory areas tend to myelinate earlier than motor areas. Cortical association areas are known to myelinate last, and continue the process into the second decade of life. Because myelination continues for many years after birth, there has been a great deal of speculation about its role in behavioral development (Yakovlev and Lecours, 1967; Parmelee and Sigman, 1983; Volpe, 1987). However, interest in the causal role of myelination has begun to wane in the past few years since it became clear that under-myelinated connections in the young human brain are still capable of transmitting signals.

A positron emission tomography (PET) study of human infants (Chugani et al., 1987) reported a sharp rise in overall resting brain metabolism (glucose uptake) after the first year of life, with a peak approximately 150 percent above adult levels achieved somewhere around 4–5 years of age for some cortical areas. While this peak occurred somewhat later than that in synaptic density, an adult-like *distribution* of resting activity within and across brain regions was observed by the end of the first year.

I now turn to regressive events during human postnatal brain development. Such events are commonly observed by those studying the development of nerve cells and their connections in the vertebrate brain (for reviews, see Cowan et al., 1984; Hopkins and Brown, 1984; Clarke, 1985; Purves and Lichtman, 1985; Janowsky and Findlay, 1986). That processes of selective loss have a significant influence on postnatal primate brain development is evident from a number of quantitative measures. For example, in the PET study just mentioned the authors found that the absolute rates of glucose metabolism rise postnatally until they exceed adult levels, before reducing to adult levels after about 9 years of age for most cortical regions.

Consistent with these PET findings, Huttenlocher (1990, 1994) reports quantitative neuroanatomical evidence from several regions of the human cortex that, following the increase in density of synapses described above, there is then a period of synaptic loss. Like the timing of bursts of synaptogenesis, and the subsequent peaks of density, the timing of the reduction in synaptic density varies between cortical regions. For example, synaptic density in the visual cortex returns to adult levels between 2 and 4 years, while the same point is not reached until between 10 and 20 years of age for regions of the prefrontal cortex. Huttenlocher (1990, 1994) suggests that this initial overproduction of synapses may have an important role in the apparent plasticity of the young brain, a matter which will be discussed in more detail later. There is no strong evidence for this pattern of rise and fall for either density of dendrites or for the number of neurons themselves in humans or other primates. However, in rodents and other vertebrates cell loss may be more significant.

One explanation for the decrease in glucose uptake observed in the PET studies is that it reflects the decrease in synaptic contacts. This hypothesis was investigated in a developmental study conducted with cats (Chugani et al., 1991). In this study, the peak of glucose uptake in cat visual cortex was found to coincide with the peak in overproduction of synapses in this region. However, when similar data from human visual cortex are plotted together (see figure 2.5), it is apparent that the peak of glucose uptake lags behind synaptic density. An alternative to the hypothesis that reduction of metabolic activity is the result of the elimination of neurons, axons, and synaptic branches is that the same activity may require less "mental effort" once a certain level of skill has been attained.

Most of the developments in the brain discussed so far concern aspects of the structure of the brain. However, there are

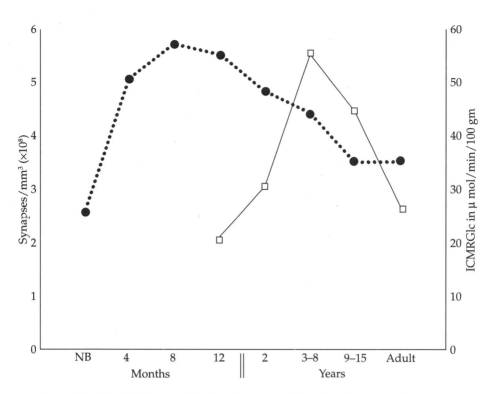

Figure 2.5 Graph showing the development of density of synapses in human primary visual cortex (dotted line: data taken from Huttenlocher, 1990), and resting glucose uptake in the occipital cortex as measured by PET (solid line: data taken from Chugani et al., 1987). ICMRGlc is a measure of the local cerebral metabolic rates for glucose.

also developmental changes in what has been known as the "soft soak" aspects of neural function, molecules involved in the transmission and modulation of neural signals. While these will be discussed in more detail in a later section, it is interesting to note at this point that a number of neurotransmitters in rodents and humans also show the rise and fall developmental pattern (see Benes, 1994, for review). Specifically, the excitatory intrinsic transmitter glutamate, the intrinsic inhibitory transmitter GABA (gamma-aminobutyric acid), and the extrinsic transmitter serotonin all show this same developmental trend.

Thus, the distinctive "rise and fall" developmental sequence is seen in a number of measures of structural and neurophysiological development in the human cortex. The number of measures and different laboratories in which this somewhat counter-intuitive developmental sequence has been observed leads to a degree of confidence in its validity. However, it should be stressed that (a) not all measures show this pattern (e.g. myelinization); (b) measures such as synaptic density are static snapshots of a dynamic process in which both additive and regressive processes are continually in progress: in other words, there are probably not distinct and separate progressive and regressive phases; and (c) models which are exclusively dependent on regressive processes are unlikely to be adequate.

In addition to these caveats, all of the additive and subtractive events just described for normal human brain development must be weighed against a growing literature on individual differences within the normal range. As more sophisticated brain-imaging techniques are developed, it becomes increasingly evident that there is considerable variation in structure and function in normal adult subjects. For example, Gazzaniga and his colleagues (Tramo et al., 1994) reconstructed the cortical areas of two identical twins from MRI scans. Even in the case of genetically identical individuals, the variation in cortical areas was striking, with the occipital lobe occupying 13–17 percent of cortical area in one individual, and 20 percent in the other. These differences between individuals in brain structure may also extend to brain functioning. For example, using functional MRI, Schneider and colleagues studied the areas of activation following upper or lower visual field stimulation. While it had classically been assumed that the upper and lower visual field mapped on to the regions above and below the sulcus, there is in fact a lot of variation with some normal subjects showing an upper/lower visual field cut that straddles this structure (Schneider et al., 1993). This new evidence of variability complements an older literature on individual differences in handedness and hemispheric organization for language (e.g. Kinsbourne and Hiscock,

1983; Hellige, 1993). In view of this variability in normal adults, efforts to construct a timetable for "normal" postnatal brain development in humans must be interpreted with caution.

2.4 The development of cortical areas: protomap or protocortex?

An ongoing debate among those who study the developmental neurobiology of the cortex concerns the extent to which its structure and function are prespecified, in the sense that they are the result of molecular and cellular level interactions prior to the effects of experience. Orthogonal to the laminar dimension of cortical structure is its differentiation into regions or areas, the "areal" structure. Figure 2.6 illustrates one of the best-known schemes for dividing the cerebral cortex into areas or regions. In the adult primate most of these cortical areas can be determined by very detailed differences in the laminar structure, such as the precise thickness of certain layers. Often, however the borderlines between regions are indistinct and controversial. It is commonly assumed that these anatomically defined areas are also functionally distinct, and generally speaking this has proved to be the case for sensory and motor areas. However, there are cases of functional regions or borders that do not neatly correspond to known neuroanatomical divisions. It should be stressed that the division of cortex into regions with differing functional specializations is not an exact science in that the detailed features of neuroanatomy relevant for supporting different functions are unknown.

Despite these caveats, a century of neuropsychology has taught us that the majority of normal adults tend to have similar functions within approximately the same regions of cortex. This observation has led to a common assumption that the division of the cerebral cortex into structural and functional areas is prespecified. However, as we will see this assumption is probably incorrect.

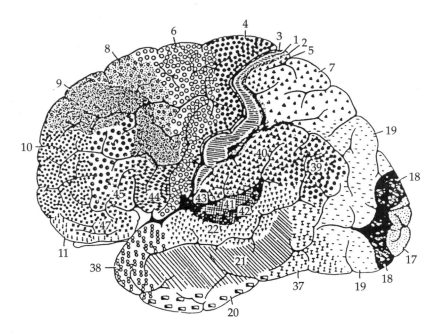

Figure 2.6 Cytoarchitectural map of the cerebral cortex. Some of the most important specific areas are as follows. Motor cortex: motor strip, area 4; premotor area, area 6; frontal eye fields, area 8. Somatosensory cortex: areas 3, 1, 2. Visual cortex: areas 17, 18, 19. Auditory cortex: areas 41 and 42. Wernicke's speech area: approximately area 22. Broca's speech area: approximately area 44 (in the left hemisphere) (from Brodmann, in Brodal, 1981).

The framework outlined in chapter 1 can be used to ask whether aspects of cortical structure are specified prior to postnatal experience. This question can be asked of both the laminar and the areal structure of cortex. Of course, the two dimensions of cortical structure are not entirely independent, since structural areal divisions are partly specified by detailed differences in laminar structure. However, the framework in chapter 1 allowed for the possibility that while the basic architecture of a network is innate (basic circuitry, learning rules, type, and number of cells etc.), the detailed patterns of (dendritic and synaptic) connectivity are dependent upon experience. In such a case we may say that while the *network imposes architectural constraints on the representations that emerge within it, there are no innate representations.*

In the review that follows I will suggest that the cerebral cortex has this general character since the differences between cortical areas are often in the detailed patterns of connectivity (rather than in the basic circuitry) and in many cases these differences are sensitive to postnatal experience. In contrast, the basic laminar structure of the cortex is relatively consistent between neocortical areas and is relatively insensitive to postnatal experience. I will suggest in what follows that the general laminar structure of the cortex contributes to the basic architecture of the cortical network, and is the product of interactions within the cortex prior to experience. In contrast, the areal differentiation of the cortex is partly the product of interactions with the external environment (for related arguments, see O'Leary, 1989; Killackey, 1990; Shatz, 1992). I begin by returning to the prenatal development of cortex, and arguably the most complete theory of the development of cortical structure: the radial unit model proposed by Pasco Rakic (1988).

As mentioned earlier, most cortical neurons in man are generated outside the cortex itself in a region just underneath what becomes the cortex, the "proliferative zone." This means that these cells must migrate to take up their locations within the cortex. How is this migration accomplished? Rakic has proposed a "radial unit model" of neocortical parcellation which gives an account of how *both* the areal and the layered structure of the mammalian cerebral cortex arise (Rakic, 1988). According to the model, the laminar organization of the cerebral cortex is determined by the fact that each proliferative unit (in the subventricular zone) gives rise to about 100 neurons. The progeny from each proliferative unit all migrate up the same radial glial fiber, with the latest to be born travelling past their older relatives. A radial glial fiber is a long process that stretches from top to bottom of the cortex and originates from a glial cell. Thus, radial glial fibers act like a climbing rope to ensure that cells produced by one proliferative unit all contribute to one radial column

within the cortex. Rakic's proposed method of migration is illustrated in figure 2.7.

There are some consequences of the radial unit model for the
role of genetic regulation in species differences. For example,
Rakic (1988) has pointed out that a single round of additional
symmetric cell division at the proliferative unit formation stage
would double the number of ontogenetic columns, and hence
the area of cortex. In contrast, an additional single round of
division at a later stage, from the proliferative zone, would only
increase the size of a column by one cell (about 1 percent). There
is very little variation between mammalian species in the layered structure of the cortex, while the total surface area of the
cortex can vary by a factor of 100 or more between different
species of mammal. It seems likely, therefore, that species differences originate (at least in part) in the timing of cell development (i.e. the number of 'rounds' of cell division that are allowed
to take place within and across regions of the proliferative zone).

A related view on the evolution of mammalian brain has been
put forward by Finlay and Darlington (1995). These authors
compared data on the size of brain structures from 131 mammalian species, and concluded that the order of neurogenesis is
conserved across a wide range of species and correlates with the
relative enlargement of structures as overall brain size increases.
Specifically, disproportionately large growth occurs in the late-
generated structures such as the neocortex. By this analysis, the
structure most likely to differ in size in the relatively slowed
neurogenesis of primates is the neocortex.

Rakic's model explains how cortical cells arrange themselves
into the thickness of the cortex, but how does the differentiation
into specific layers emerge? While we are far from being able to
answer this question definitively at this point, one view is that
differentiation into particular cell types occurs *before* a neuron
reaches its final location. That is, a cell "knows" what type of
neuron it will become (pyramidal, spiny stellate etc.) before it
reaches its adult location within the cortex. Some recent evidence suggests that cells do indeed begin to differentiate before

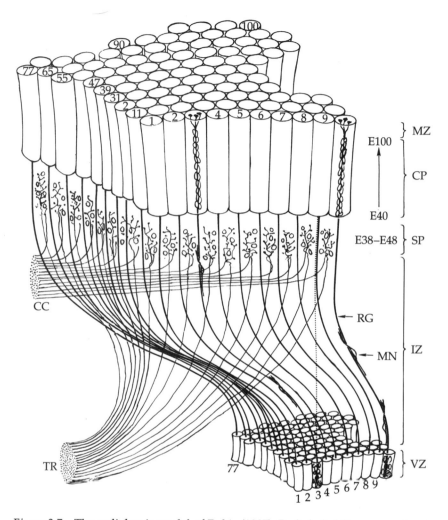

Figure 2.7 The radial unit model of Rakic (1987). Radial glial fibers span from the ventricular zone (VZ) to the cortical plate (CP) via a number of regions: the intermediate zone (IZ) and the subplate zone (SP). RG indicates a radial glial fiber, and MN a migrating neuron. Each MN traverses the IZ and SP zones that contain waiting terminals from the thalamic radiation (TR) and corticocortico afferents (CC). As described in the text, after entering the cortical plate, the neurons migrate past their predecessors to the marginal zone (MZ).

they reach their final vertical location. For example, in genetic mutant "reeler" mice, cells that acquire inappropriate laminar positions within the cortex still differentiate into neuronal types according to their time of origin, rather than the types normally found at their new location. This implies that the information required for differentiation is present at the cell's birth in the proliferative zone; it is not dependent upon its distance from the proliferative zone, nor on the characteristics of the neighborhood in which that cell ends up. That is, in the proliferative zone for the neocortex, some cell types may be determined at the stage of division.

Although in many cases a cell's identity may be determined before it leaves the proliferative zone, some of the properties that distinguish among cell types may form later on. Marin-Padilla (1990) has proposed that the distinctive apical dendrite of pyramidal cells, which often reaches into layer 1, is a result of the increasing distance between this layer and other layers resulting from the inside-out pattern of growth. Specifically, the increasing separation between layer 1 and the subplate zone, which results from young neurons moving into what will become layers 2–6, means that cells which have their processes attached to layer 1 will become increasingly "stretched" – that is, their leading dendrite will become stretched tangential to the surface of the cortex resulting in the elongated apical dendrite so typical of cortical pyramidal cells. As mentioned earlier, this long apical dendrite allows the cell to be influenced by large numbers of cells from other (more superficial) layers.

Another aspect of the laminar structure of cortex that appears to be regulated by intrinsic cellular and molecular interactions concerns the major connections between cells, in particular the inputs from the thalamus. As mentioned earlier, the main input layer in the cortex is layer 4. A series of experiments by Blakemore and colleagues established that the termination of projections from thalamus in layer 4 is governed by molecular markers. Slices of brain tissue are able to survive and grow in a Petri dish for several days under the appropriate conditions. Indeed, pieces of thalamus of the appropriate age will actually innervate other pieces of brain placed nearby. Molnar and Blakemore (1991) investigated if and how a piece of visual thalamus (LGN) would innervate various types of cortical and non-cortical brain tissue.

In initial experiments, they established that when a piece of thalamus (LGN) and a piece of visual cortex were placed close together in the dish, afferents from the LGN not only invaded a piece of visual cortex of the appropriate age, but also terminated in the appropriate layer 4. Thus, layer 4 appears to contain some molecular stop signal that tells the afferents to stop growing and form connections at that location. Next, they conducted a series of choice experiments in which the visual thalamus had a piece of visual cortex and some other piece of brain placed nearby. The thalamic afferents turned out to dislike cerebellum, rarely penetrating it, but the afferents did grow into hippocampus. However, the growth into hippocampus (a piece of brain that is closely related to neocortex, see section 2.8) was not spatially confined the way it had been for visual cortex, suggesting that it was just a "growth-permitting substrate."

The evidence discussed so far indicates that the laminar structure of cortex probably arises from local cellular and molecular interactions, rather than being shaped as a result of thalamic and sensory input. That is, the identity and location of neurons are determined before birth. Similarly, incoming fibers "know" in which layer to stop and make synaptic contacts. I now turn to the question of whether the areal structure of the cortex is determined in a similar way.

There are several possibilities that have been put forward to account for the division of cortex into areas, including the following;

1   The areal differentiation of the cortex is due to a *protomap* (Rakic, 1988). The protomap involves prespecification of the proliferative zone which is then imposed on the cortex via the radial glial fiber pathway, and/or intrinsic molecular markers guide the division of cortex into particular areas. By this view, the areal structure of the cortex would be determined largely prior to postnatal experience.

2   The different areas of cortex arise out of an undifferentiated *protocortex* that is divided up into specialized areas as a result of input through projections from the thalamus (O'Leary, 1989; Killackey, 1990). On this view, the areal structure of cortex could be influenced to at least some degree by postnatal experience.

While the first of these options may initially seem attractive, there is surprisingly little evidence for it. The idea that there is a detailed protomap in the proliferative zone is difficult to defend against experimental evidence showing that the cortex is relatively equipotential and plastic early in life. This evidence will be reviewed in the next section. Nor is there any evidence to date for specific molecular markers or gradients that map onto the cortical areas that compose the areal structure of cortex (see Shatz, 1992), in contrast with the evidence that does exist for molecular determination of laminar structure. Further, there is recent evidence that neurons born from a particular proliferative unit can wander quite far from their original areal locations. Thus, there seems to be no reliable mechanism for imposing a protomap on the cortex from the proliferative zone.

An alternative way that a protomap could be manifest is by means of molecular markers within the cortex that guide particular inputs (from the thalamus) to particular regions. Thus, for example, the area destined to become auditory cortex could specifically attract inputs from the auditory part of the thalamus. When discussing the laminar structure of cortex, I described the experiments of Blakemore and colleagues (Molnar and Blakemore, 1991) which gathered evidence for specific molecular markers in layer 4 that indicate the termination location for projections from the thalamus. While these initial Petri dish experiments provided evidence for laminar structure prespecification, and for thalamic afferents being attracted to cortical tissue, further experiments of a similar kind indicated that thalamic projections do not innervate particular areas of cortex preferentially. In experiments in which a piece of visual thalamus (LGN) was placed close to a variety of pieces of cortex from

different areas, the visual thalamus did *not* preferentially innervate visual cortex: all cortical targets were equally acceptable to
all parts of the thalamus. Molnar and Blakemore tried several
different combinations of thalamic areas and cortical ones and
found that, regardless of the origin of the piece of thalamus or
cortex, equivalent innervation of layer 4 occurs. If these results
can be extended to the developing brain *in situ* (i.e. inside the
animal, as opposed to a dish), they, imply that, while the cortex
provides an attractive growth substrate for the thalamus, and a
stop signal at layer 4, there is no area-specific targeting. Thus,
for example, the visual thalamus is not specifically attracted to
the visual cortex by some molecular marker, and auditory
thalamus is not attracted to auditory cortex and so on.

Another version of the protomap theory might be that the cortex
sends connections to specific regions of thalamus that then guide
the afferents from the thalamus. In other words, the developing
cortex may send out location-specific "guidewires." Unfortunately for this hypothesis, however, Molnar and Blakemore (1991)
found that cortical projections to thalamus lacked regional
specificity in the same way as the reciprocal connections. Any
zone of embryonic cortex would innervate any zone of thalamus.
These experiments indicate that there are no region-specific
molecular signals available to guide thalamocortical projections.

Recent evidence indicates that there may be some exceptions
to the above conclusion, at least in primates: the primary visual
cortex and the entorhinal cortex. In the primary visual cortex
inputs from the visual thalamus may regulate the extent of cell
proliferation in the ventricular zone (see Kennedy and Dehay,
1993), ensuring that this area of cortex has a rate of neuron production nearly twice that in neighboring areas. The entorhinal
cortex, the region of cortex most closely associated with the hippocampus, shows some differentiation from surrounding cortex
as early as 13 weeks after gestation (Kostovic et al., 1990). These
two regions may be the exception rather than the rule since
areal specification in primates is generally thought to occur later
than in rodents.

Given that there is little evidence for a cortical protomap that provides different "targets" for different thalamic projections, and little evidence that thalamic afferents are prespecified to project a thalamic map to the cortex, how are we to account for thalamic specificity in which particular thalamic afferents normally innervate particular regions of cortex, but do not appear to be specifically or rigidly targeted? Molnar and Blakemore (1991) propose an account of thalamic innervation in which the regional specificity of projections between thalamus and cortex arises from a combination of timing and spatial constraints. Briefly, this account states that afferents grow from regions of the thalamus according to a particular spatiotemporal gradient. Different regions of thalamus grow projections at slightly different times, and as a new afferent grows it always grows on top of, or beside, existing afferents. By following these existing afferents, the newly grown axons terminate an adjacent location to those that grew just before. Thus, there is a chronotopic innervation of cortex by thalamus which uses the physical presence of other afferents as a spatiotemporal constraint on the pattern of innervation.

To summarize so far, the basic laminar structure of the cerebral cortex in mammals appears to be very general. Cellular and molecular level interactions determine many aspects of the layered structure of cortex and its patterns of connectivity. Cortical neurons are often differentiated into specific computational types before they reach their destination (although some of the characteristic features of cell types are shaped by their journey to that site, e.g. the long apical dendrite that typifies pyramidal cells reflects a literal "stretching" of processes during the migration process). However, this does not mean that cells in a particular area are prespecified to process certain kinds of information. The division of cortex into distinct areas takes place along the areal dimension. This areal differentiation is heavily influenced by the thalamic (experiential) inputs to each region. There is as yet little evidence for the suggestion that cortex emerges from a protomap in the proliferative zone. In other words, neurons do not appear to be predestined to carry visual or auditory information. There is also little evidence to support the notion of an internal molecular marker to guide inputs from the thalamus (i.e. the way-station that conveys sensory input to each cortical region). Indeed, as Blakemore and his colleagues have shown, axons from an occipital thalamic source will happily invade and innervate slabs of frontal or auditory cortex, in patterns that are indistinguishable from those that the same axons produce in a slab of occipital cortex. Current evidence suggests that there are few intrinsic, predetermined areal maps in either the cortex or the thalamus; instead, both develop their area specializations as a consequence of their inputs and the temporal ("chronotopic") dynamics of neural growth. This means that normal cortical development (i.e. the basic vertebrate brain plan) permits a considerable degree of cortical plasticity. That is, cortical regions could support a number of different types of representations depending on their input.

A good example of how a region of cortex can become differentiated comes from work on the so-called "barrel-fields" that develop in the somatosensory cortex of rodents. Each barrel-field is an anatomically definable functional grouping of cells that responds to a particular whisker on the animal's snout (see figure 2.8). Barrel-fields are an aspect of the areal structure of cortex that emerges postnatally, and which are sensitive to whisker-related experience over the first days of life. For example, if a whisker is removed then the barrel-field that normally corresponds to that whisker does not emerge, and neighboring ones may occupy some of the cortical space normally occupied by it (for review, see Schlagger and O'Leary, 1993). Figure 2.8 illustrates how the areal divisions of the cortex arise as a result of similar divisions in structures closer to the sensory surface. In this case, it is almost as if the sensory surface *imposes* itself on to the brain stem, thence to the thalamus, and finally on to the cortex itself. The barrel-field compartments emerge in sequence in these areas of the brain, with those closest to the sensory surface forming first, and the cortex patterns emerging last. While there is little evidence that barrel-fields are prespecified in the cortex (but see Cooper and Steindler, 1986), a map of sensory space comes to occupy the somatosensory cortex in a reliable and replicable way.

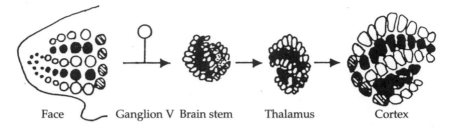

Face   Ganglion V Brain stem   Thalamus   Cortex

Figure 2.8   Patterning of areal units in somatosensory cortex. The pattern of "barrels" in the somatosensory cortex of rodents is an isomorphic representation of the geometric arrangement of vibrissae found on the animal's face. Similar patterns are present in the brain stem and thalamic nuclei that relay inputs from the face to the barrel cortex.

Many of the experiments demonstrating that the areal divisions of the cortex are not intrinsically prespecified have been conducted on rodents, and it is clear that there are at least some differences in developmental timing between rodents and primates. In particular, while in the rodent thalamic input plays a major role in the areal specification of an undifferentiated protocortex, as mentioned earlier, in the primate there are a few cases of areal specification in which thalamic input influences earlier stages of corticogenesis (see Kennedy and Dehay, 1993, for review). However, while it remains possible that some structural areal divisions in the primate cortex are regulated in this way, it is clear that most aspects of areal differentiation occur much later in primates than in rodents, suggesting that there is even greater scope for influence by postnatal experience.

In this section I have reviewed some of the literature on laminar and areal specification of cortex during normal development, concluding that while laminar organization is largely specified by intrinsic prenatal cellular and molecular interactions, areal organization is more heavily influenced by postnatal experience. In the next section I review a number of studies concerned with the extent to which different pieces of cortical tissue can support the same types of representations.

2.5   Cortical plasticity

Experiments have shown that the mammalian cerebral cortex can support a variety of representations early in development. In other words, there is a surprising amount of support for some degree of equipotentiality in neocortex. The evidence for this includes the following:

1   Reducing the extent of thalamic input to a region of cortex early in life influences the subsequent size of that region (Rakic, 1988; Dehay et al., 1989; O'Leary, 1989).
2   When thalamic inputs are "re-wired," such that they project to a different region of cortex from normal, the new recipient region develops some of the properties of the normal target tissue (e.g. auditory cortex takes on visual representations; Sur et al., 1988, 1990).
3   When a piece of cortex is transplanted to a new location it develops projections characteristic of its new location, rather than its developmental origin (e.g. transplanted visual cortex takes on the representations that are appropriate for somatosensory input; O'Leary and Stanfield, 1989).
4   When the usual sites for higher cortical functions are bilaterally removed in infancy (i.e. the temporal region with primary responsibility for visual object recognition in monkeys), regions at a considerable distance from the original site can take over the displaced function (i.e. the parietal regions that are usually responsible for detection of motion and orientation in space; Webster et al., 1995).

I will now consider each of these in more detail.

(1)   The effect on the cortex of manipulating the extent of sensory input (via the thalamus) to an area has been investigated in experiments where the thalamic input to an area of cortex is surgically reduced (Dehay et al., 1988). Surgical intervention in newborn macaque monkeys can reduce the thalamic projections

to the primary visual cortex (area 17) by 50 percent. This reduction results in a corresponding reduction in the extent of area 17 in relation to area 18. That is, the border between areas 17 and 18 shifts such that area 17 becomes much smaller. Despite this drastic reduction in the extent of area 17, it is important to note that its laminar structure remains normal. Further, the area which is still area 17 looks identical to its normal structure, and the region which becomes area 18 has characteristics normally associated with that area, and none of those unique to area 17 (Rakic, 1988; see also O'Leary, 1989, ref. 4). Thus, there is (surprisingly) little effect of reducing the extent of sensory projections to area 17 on the subsequent laminar structure of areas 17 and 18. The specific effect of this manipulation is to reduce the *area* of 17 relative to 18, despite the evidence of some prespecification of neuron numbers in this region discussed earlier. This indicates that even those cortical areas for which there is some evidence of prespecification can be subsequently modified.

Even the outputs characteristic of areas 17 and 18 follow the shift in border between them. For example, while area 18 normally has many callosal projections to the other hemisphere, area 17 does not. The region which is normally area 17, but becomes area 18 in the surgically operated animals, has the callosal projection pattern characteristic of normal area 18. A reasonable conclusion reached on the basis of these observations is that the region of cortex that would normally mature into area 17, develops properties that are characteristic of the adjacent area 18 as a result of reducing its thalamic input. Thus, at least some of the area-specific characteristics of cortex appear to be regulated by extrinsic factors.

(2)   Cross-modal plasticity of cortical areas has now been demonstrated at the neurophysiological level in several mammalian species (for review, see Sur et al., 1990). For example, in the ferret, projections from the retina can be induced to project to auditory thalamic areas, and thence to auditory cortex. Following a technique initially developed by Frost (1990), this is done by placing lesions in the normal visual cortex and in the lateral geniculate (the thalamic target of retinal projections). Lesions

are also placed such that auditory inputs do not innervate their normal thalamic target, the medial geniculate. Under these pathological conditions, retinal projections will re-route to innervate the medial geniculate nucleus (MGN). Projections from the MGN then project to the auditory cortex as normal. The experimental question concerns whether the normally auditory cortex becomes visually responsive (i.e. in accord with its input,) or whether it retains features characteristic of auditory cortex. The answer turns out to be that auditory cortex does become visually responsive. Furthermore, cells in what would have been auditory cortex also become orientation and direction selective, and some become binocular.

While these observations are provocative, they do not provide evidence that the auditory cortex as a whole becomes functionally similar to the visual cortex. It is possible, for example, that the visually driven cells in the auditory cortex would fire in isolation from the activity of their colleagues. That is, there may be no organization above the level of the individual neuron. In order to address this issue, evidence that there is a spatial map of the visual world formed across this area of cortex is needed. In order to study this issue, Sur and colleagues recorded from single neurons in a systematic way across the re-wired cortex (Sur et al., 1988; Roe et al., 1990). These experiments revealed that the previously auditory cortex had developed a two-dimensional retinal map. In normal ferrets, the primary auditory cortex contains a one-dimensional representation of the cochlea. Along one axis of the cortical tissue, electrode penetrations revealed a gradual shift from responses to low frequencies to responses to high frequencies (see figure 2.9). Along the orthogonal dimension of cortex, frequency remains constant (the isofrequency axis). In contrast, the visual representation developed in the re-wired animals occupies both dimensions (elevation and azimuth). The authors conclude: "Our results demonstrate that the form of the map is not an intrinsic property of the cortex and that a cortical area can come to support different types of maps" (Roe et al., 1990: 818).

Although this neuroanatomical and neurophysiological data

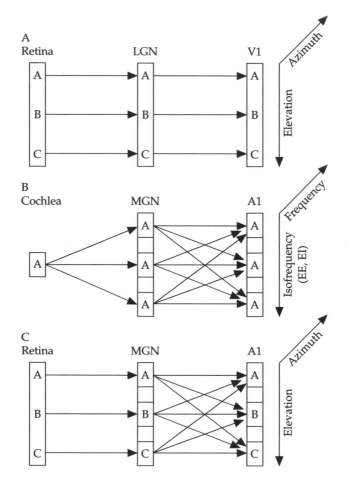

Figure 2.9 Schematic representation and summary of projections from the sensory receptor surface through the thalamus to cortex in (A) the normal visual system, (B) the normal auditory system, and (C) lesioned ferrets with retinal projections induced into the auditory pathway.

support the idea that the auditory cortex can support visual representations, it remains to be established whether these representations can be used to guide the behavior of the animal in the normal way. Sur and colleagues have recently begun a series of behavioral studies to determine what use the ferret can make of visual input to auditory cortex. They trained adult ferret's, re-wired in one hemisphere at birth, to discriminate between visual and auditory stimuli presented to the normal hemisphere. After this they probed the functioning of the re-wired hemisphere by presenting visual stimuli that activated only the re-wired pathway. The ferrets reliably interpreted the visual stimulus as visual rather than auditory (see Sur, 1993). If these results prove replicable, they provide support for Sur's conclusions concerning the relative functional equipotentiality of cortical regions early in life.

(3) Additional evidence for cortical plasticity comes from studies on rodents in which pieces of cortex are transplanted from one region to another early in development. These experiments allow neurobiologists to address the question of whether transplanted areas take on representations appropriate for their *developmental origins*, or the function of the *new location* in which they find themselves.

Pieces of fetal cortex have been successfully transplanted into other regions of newborn rodent cortex. For example, visual cortex neurons can be transplanted into the sensorimotor region and vice versa. Experiments such as these, conducted by O'Leary and Stanfield (1985, 1989) among others, have revealed that the projections and structure of such transplants develop according to their new spatial location rather than their developmental origins. For example, visual cortical neurons transplanted to the sensorimotor region develop projections to the spinal cord, a projection pattern characteristic of the sensorimotor cortex, but not the visual cortex. Similarly, sensorimotor cortical neurons transplanted to the visual cortical region develop projections to the superior colliculus, a subcortical target of the visual cortex, but not characteristic of the sensorimotor region. Thus, the inputs and outputs of a transplanted region take on the characteristics of their new location.

A further question concerns the internal structure of the transplanted region. As discussed earlier, the somatosensory cortex of the rat (and other rodents) possesses characteristic internal structures known as "barrel-fields". Barrel-fields are an aspect of the areal structure of the cortex, and are clearly visible under the microscope. Each of the barrels corresponds to one whisker on the rat's face. Barrels develop during postnatal growth, and can be prevented from appearing in the normal cortex by cutting the sensory inputs to the region from the face. Furthermore, barrel structure is sensitive to the effects of early experience such as repeated whisker stimulation, or whisker removal (see Schlagger and O'Leary, 1993, for recent review). The question then arises whether transplanted slabs of visual cortex take on the barrel-field structures that are typical of somatosensory cortex in the rat.

Schlagger and O'Leary (1991) conducted a study in which pieces of visual cortex were transplanted into the part of the somatosensory cortex that normally forms barrel-fields in the rodent. They found that when innervated by thalamic afferents, the transplanted cortex developed barrel-fields very similar to those normally observed. Thus, not only can a transplanted piece of cortex develop inputs and outputs appropriate for its new location, but the inputs to that location can organize the internal structure of the cortical region.

Two caveats to the conclusion that the majority of cortical tissue is largely equipotent early in life should be mentioned at this stage. First, most of the transplant and re-wiring studies have involved primary sensory cortices. Some authors have argued that primary sensory cortices may share certain common developmental origins that other types of cortex do not. Specifically, some neuroanatomists have argued that the detailed cytoarchitecture of the cortex is consistent with there being three fields of cortex, sometimes referred to as "root," "belt," and "core" (Galaburda and Pandya, 1983; Pandya and Yeterian, 1985, 1990). These lineages of cortex differ slightly in the thickness of particular layers, the shapes of certain cell types, and also in their layered projection patterns to neighboring cortical regions. While the details of this theory are complex and remain somewhat controversial, it is worth noting that each of these cortical fields is claimed to facilitate a particular type of processing. For example, the "core" band of cortex is associated with primary sensory cortices, the "root" with "secondary" sensory areas, and the "belt" field with association cortices. Assuming that the structural differences between the putative lineages is due to phylogenetic, rather than ontogenetic, factors (and this is far from clear since these hypotheses are reached following study of adult brains), it is possible that levels of stimulus processing may be attracted to certain subtypes of cerebral cortex. Thus, it is possible that certain lineages of cortex which differ in detailed ways from other areas of cortex may be more suited for dealing with certain types of information processing. With regard to the transplant experiments discussed earlier, it may be that cortex is only equipotential within a lineage (e.g. primary-to-primary or secondary-to-secondary).

The second caveat to the conclusion that cortex is equipotential is that, while transplanted or re-wired cortex may look very similar to the original tissue in terms of function and structure, it is rarely absolutely indistinguishable from the original. For example, in the re-wired ferret cortex studied by Sur and colleagues, the mapping of the azimuth (angle right or left) is at a higher resolution (more detailed) than the mapping of the elevation (angle up or down) (Roe et al., 1990). In contrast, in the normal ferret cortex, azimuth and elevation are mapped in equal detail. I also note that, with the exception of the study mentioned earlier, there is still very little behavioral evidence indicating that the transplanted tissue shows the same functional properties that the host region normally does. Hence, even though visual cortex can take on a barrel-field structure, and auditory cortex can take on a retinotopic structure, these unusual preparations may not be as optimal as the default case. That is, they may never function in quite the same way as the cortical representations that would have occurred under normal conditions.

(4) When there is bilateral damage to a cortical region, sometimes other cortical regions can take over the function of the original region. As one example of this, Webster et al. (1995) have compared the effects of bilateral lesions in infant and adult monkeys trained in the visual non-match-to-sample task. ("Pick the one that's different from the object you saw before, and you will get a reward.") Based on many years of work on higher

visual centers in primates, most researchers in this area con-
cur that a particular region of temporal cortex called TE plays
a critical role in visual object recognition. By contrast, the parietal regions of cortex appear to mediate spatial action. In adult
monkeys, bilateral removal of area TE results in serious deficits
in object recognition, as measured by the visual non-match-to-
sample task. By contrast, infant monkeys with homologous
lesions perform very well on the same object recognition task
(although their performance is reduced by approximately 5–10
percent compared with unoperated infant monkeys). Based on
these results, Webster et al. (1995) conclude that other areas of
cortex seem to have taken over the function of visual object
recognition in the lesioned infants. But what areas are responsible, and what is the mechanism that permitted this transfer to
take place?

The most obvious candidate is an area adjacent to TE called
TEO, which receives the necessary visual inputs and could take
over the default functions of TE if exuberant connections were
retained and/or additional sprouting took place to replace the
missing circuitry. This form of "local" plasticity could involve
new growth, retention of exuberant connections and/or repro-
gramming of spared tissue. But it would still constitute a relatively conservative form of general plasticity, within a region
that is presumably well suited to support the "what is it" function. In fact, some of the neuroanatomical evidence provided
by Webster and colleagues does suggest that TEO receives
atypical innervation in infant monkeys after bilateral lesions to
TE. However, after a subsequent operation to produce bilateral
lesions to TEO (so that the infant monkeys are now missing
both area TE and area TEO), performance on the non-match-to-
sample task was still very good (although it was reduced somewhat compared with performance after TE lesions only). In other
words, area TEO may have made some contribution to the task,
but apparently it has not taken over all responsibility for visual
object recognition. The authors then investigated a further possibility: parietal areas that receive visual input, but which are ordinarily thought to play no role in visual object recognition, and

are not adjacent to the damaged temporal zones (i.e. areas STP, PG, and TF). When these parietal areas are bilaterally removed in adult monkeys, their loss normally has no significant effect on performance in the visual non-match-to-sample task. What would happen in monkeys who lost area TE in infancy? The infant monkeys then underwent a third operation involving bilateral lesions of the dorsal–parietal regions. This lesion finally managed to reduce performance on the non-match-to-sample task to the low levels observed in adult animals after a lesion restricted entirely to TE. They reached the tentative conclusion that distant (non-adjacent) areas that would ordinarily specialize in the "where" function have been recruited to assist in performance of the "what" function.

Thus, cognitive functions like visual object recognition can be organized in a variety of ways. The mechanisms that underlie behavioral plasticity in the infant primate include "local" effects (i.e. sparing or growth of connections in adjacent areas), but they also include broad-scale forms of reorganization in which non-adjacent areas are recruited to serve a function for which they may be only minimally qualified (i.e. they do receive visual input of some kind).

2.6 Differential development of human cortex

The main phylogenetic changes in cortical development in primates appear to be in the extent of cortical tissue and the more prolonged period of development in primates and man. Even between *Homo sapiens* and other primates there is a wide difference in timing, with human postnatal cortical development being extended (roughly by a factor of four) longer than other primates. This prolonged postnatal development in humans stretches out differential laminar and regional cortical development that is more compressed in time in other species.

In the case of laminar development, although most cortical neurons are in their appropriate locations by the time of birth in

the primate, the "inside-out" pattern of growth observed in prenatal cortical development extends into postnatal life. Extensive
descriptive neuroanatomical studies of cortical development in
the human infant by Conel over a 30-year period lead him to the
conclusion that the postnatal growth of cortex proceeds in an
"inside-out" pattern with regard to the extent of dendrites, dendritic trees, and myelinization (Conel, 1939–67). Conel's general
conclusions have been largely substantiated with more modern
neuroanatomical methods (e.g. Purpura, 1975; Rabinowicz, 1979;
Becker et al., 1984). In particular, the maturation of layer 5
(deeper) in advance of layers 2 and 3 (superficial) seems to be
a very reliably observed sequence for many cortical regions in
the human infant (Rabinowicz, 1979; Becker et al., 1984). For
example, the dendritic trees of cells in layer 5 of primary visual
cortex are already at about 60 percent of their maximum extent
at birth. In contrast, the mean total length for dendrites in layer
3 is only at about 30 percent of their maximum at birth. Furthermore, higher orders of branching in dendritic trees are observed
in layer 5 than in layer 3 at birth (Becker et al., 1984; Huttenlocher,
1990). Interestingly, this inside-out pattern of growth is not
evident in the later occurring rise and fall in synaptic density.
For this measure, there are no clear differences between cerebral
cortical layers.

Differential development in human postnatal cortical growth
is also evident in the areal dimension. Huttenlocher (1990, 1994)
reports clear evidence of a difference in the timing of postnatal
neuroanatomical events between the primary visual cortex, the
primary auditory cortex, and the frontal cortex in human infants, with the latter reaching the same developmental landmarks considerably later in postnatal life than the first two. It is
worth noting that this differential development within the cerebral cortex has not been reported in other primate species (Rakic
et al., 1986). Rakic et al. (1986) report that all areas of cortex
appear to reach their peak in synaptic density about the same
time: around 2–4 months in the rhesus monkey, roughly corresponding to 7–12 months in the human child. Contrary to Huttenlocher's findings, this suggests that there may be a common

genetic signal to regulate connectivity across all brain regions, simultaneously, regardless of their current maturational state. A sudden event of this kind stands in marked contrast to known region-by-region differences in the time course of cell formation, migration, myelination, and metabolism in the human cortex (Conel, 1939–67; Yakovlev and Lecours, 1967). The most likely difference between the human results and those from the macaques is that the stretched out postnatal development of humans means that regional differences are more evident. In the macaque, however, possible regional differences are compressed into a much shorter time, making them harder to detect (Huttenlocher, 1994). However, Goldman-Rakic (1994) suggests that the differences between the macaque and human results may be due to the neuroanatomical techniques used.

Consistent with the reports from human postmortem tissue, a study in which the functional development of the human brain was investigated by positron emission tomography (PET) has also found differential development between regions of cortex (Chugani and Phelps, 1986; Chugani et al., 1987). In infants under 5 weeks of age glucose uptake was highest in sensorimotor cortex, thalamus, brain stem and the cerebellar vermis. By 3 months of age there were considerable rises in the parietal, temporal, and occipital cortices, basal ganglia, and cerebellar cortex. Maturational rises were not found in the frontal and dorsolateral occipital cortex until approximately 6–8 months. These developments are shown in figure 2.10.

The differential laminar and regional development observed in the human, as described in this section, provides the basis for many of the associations between brain growth and cognitive change to be described later. But first I will review some other aspects of postnatal brain development.

2.7 The hippocampus and subcortical structures

This chapter has focused primarily on the neocortex since this is the part of the brain that shows most protracted postnatal

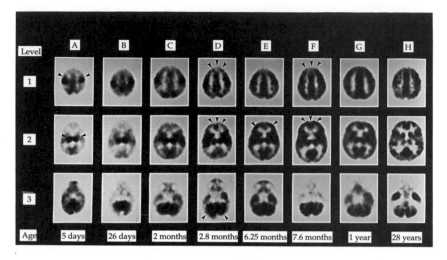

Figure 2.10   PET images illustrating developmental changes in local cerebral metabolic rates for glucose (ICMRGlc) in the normal human infant with increasing age. Level 1 is a superior section, at the level of the cingulate gyrus. Level 2 is more inferior, at the level of caudate, putamen, and thalamus. Level 3 is an inferior section of the brain, at the level of cerebellum and inferior position of the temporal lobes. Gray scale is proportional to ICMRGlc with black being highest. Images from all subjects are not shown on the same absolute gray scale of ICMRGlc: instead, images of each subject are shown with the full gray scale to maximize gray scale display of ICMRGlc at each age. (A) In the 5-day-old, ICMRGlc is highest in sensorimotor cortex, thalamus, cerebellar vermis (arrows), and brain stem (not shown). (B,C,D) ICMRGlc gradually increases in parietal, temporal, and calcarine cortices; basal ganglia; and cerebellar cortex (arrows), particularly during the second and third months. (E) In the frontal cortex, ICMRGlc increases first in the lateral prefrontal regions by approximately 6 months. (F) By approximately 8 months, ICMRGlc also increases in the medial aspects of the frontal cortex (arrows), as well as the dorsolateral occipital cortex. (G) By 1 year, the ICMRGlc pattern resembles that of adults (H).

development. However, other brain structures, such as the hippocampus and cerebellum, also show some postnatal development and, as we will see, have been associated with cognitive changes in infancy and childhood. The postnatal development of some subcortical structures (such as the hippocampus, cerebellum, and thalamus) poses something of a paradox; on the one hand, there is much behavioral and neural evidence to indicate that these structures are functioning at birth, while, on the other, they all show some evidence of postnatal development and/or functional reorganization. One explanation for this is that as the neocortex develops postnatally, its interactions with subcortical regions undergoes certain changes. Thus, while some subcortical structures are capable of functioning relatively independently of the cortex early in life, the increasing development of the cortex requires some structural and functional adjustment.

The limbic system is normally taken to include the amygdala, the hippocampus, and the limbic regions of cortex (cingulate gyrus and parahippocampal gyrus (entorhinal cortex)). While these latter cortical regions follow the same developmental timetable as other regions of the cortex, they are differentiated from the rest of cortex at an early stage, and are therefore unlikely to show the same degree of plasticity. As discussed earlier, gyral development (folding) does not necessarily indicate architectural specificity. Nevertheless, the gyral folding associated with the cingulate region is discernible as early as 16–19 weeks of gestational age in humans and the parahippocampal gyrus within the temporal lobe at 20–23 weeks gestational age (Gilles et al., 1983). In contrast, other prominent gyri in the cortex do not emerge until 24–31 weeks. The major nuclear components of the limbic system, such as the hippocampus, start to differentiate from the developing temporal lobe around the third and fourth months of fetal development. After this, further differentiation of the hippocampus takes place, resulting in it becoming a rolled structure tucked inside the temporal lobe and surrounded by tissue known as the dentate gyrus. In rodents, neurogenesis continues into postnatal life in the dentate gyrus region (Wallace et al., 1977), but this may not be the case in primates (Eckenhoff and Rakic, 1988).

The cerebellum is a brain structure thought to be involved in motor control, but which probably also plays a role in some aspects of "higher" cognitive functioning. Within 2 months of conception, the cerebellum has formed its three primary layers, the ventricular (V), intermediate (I), and marginal (M) layers.

However, its development is prolonged, and neurogenesis in this region continues postnatally with only about 17 percent of the final number of granule cells present at birth, and neurogenesis possibly continuing until 18 months (Spreen et al., 1995). Despite being one of the few regions of the human brain to show postnatal neurogenesis, cerebellar functional development as measured by resting PET shows high glucose metabolic activity as early as 5 days old (postnatal), the same schedule as other sensory motor regions such as the thalamus, brain stem, and sensorimotor cortex (Chugani, 1994).

2.8   Neurotransmitters and neuromodulators

The aspects of brain development discussed so far have mainly concerned its neurons and "wiring." However, there are also developmental changes in what has been referred to as "soft soak" aspects of neural function. Soft soak refers specifically to the chemicals involved in the transmission and modulation of neural signals. Neurons and their dendrites can be thought of as lying in a bath composed of various chemicals that modulate their functioning. In addition, other chemicals play a vital role in the transmission of signals from one cell to another. Neurotransmitters in the cerebral cortex may be classified into those that arise within the cortex (intrinsic), and those that arise from outside the cortex (extrinsic) (see Benes, 1994). The intrinsic transmitters can be further divided according to whether they have an excitatory or inhibitory effect on postsynaptic sites.

The intrinsic excitatory transmitter glutamate is thought to play an important role in the axons of pyramidal cells that project to intrinsic cortical microcircuits, projections to other cortical regions, and projections to subcortical regions (Streit, 1984). In rats, the developmental time course of different glutamatergic pathways varies considerably. In general, however, it is the receptors for the transmitter, rather than the quantity of the transmitter, that increases with postnatal age. This development seems to follow the rise and fall pattern seen in other aspects of neural development. Specifically, in the rat, between postnatal days 10 and 15, the amount of glutamate binding in cortical regions increases rapidly and reaches a peak around ten times the level observed in adults (Schliebs et al., 1986). By day 25 these levels have reduced drastically.

GABA (Gamma-aminobutyric acid) is probably the most important intrinsic inhibitory transmitter in the mammalian brain. While there is a variety of ways to measure GABA activity which sometimes gives differing results (see Benes, 1994), in the human the same overall pattern of rise and fall seen for glutamate is also observed for GABA. Specifically, the density of GABA receptors increases rapidly in the perinatal period and doubles over the first few weeks, before later declining (Brooksbank et al., 1981). The extent to which the rise and fall in these intrinsic neurotransmitters mirrors that observed in the structural measures such as glucose uptake and synaptic density discussed earlier, is currently unclear and requires further research. It is clear, however, that the levels of GABA can be influenced by the extent of sensory experience (Fosse et al., 1989).

Extrinsic neurotransmitters arise from a number of different subcortical locations. One of these transmitters, acetylcholine, originates mainly from the basal forebrain (Johnston et al., 1979). Interestingly, the innervation of cortex by cholinergic fibers follows the "inside-out" pattern of growth described earlier, with the deeper cortical layers being innervated before the more superficial ones. In humans, this cholinergic innervation begins prenatally, though adult levels are not reached until about 10 years old (Diebler et al., 1979). However, the binding sites within the cortex for this transmitter decrease from birth onwards, possibly due to synaptic pruning (Ravikumar and Sastry, 1985).

Another neurotransmitter with origins outside the cortex is norepinephrine (or noradrenaline), which originates in a nucleus called the locus coeruleus. As well as its role as a neurotransmitter, norepinephrine has been associated with cortical plasticity (Kasamatsu and Pettigrew, 1976). In several mammals there is an extensive network of noradrenergic fibers in the cortex at birth which may be more dense than that seen in adults (Coyle and Molliver, 1977). Currently, little developmental information is available on this transmitter in primates (Benes, 1994).

Serotonin originates in the raphe nuclei, and in both rats and primates the level increases rapidly over the first few weeks of life (Johnston, 1988). In rhesus monkeys the adult pattern of projection of serotonin fibers is reached by the sixth postnatal week, though levels continue to rise after this (Goldman-Rakic and Brown, 1982). There is some evidence (from specific binding sites) of a later decrease in serotonin in human cortex and hippocampus (Marcusson et al., 1984). Like acetylcholine, serotonin is found mainly in the deeper cortical layers at birth, consistent with the structural inside-out gradient of development discussed earlier.

The fourth main extrinsic cortical transmitter, dopamine (which originates in the substantia nigra) likewise shows an inside-out pattern around the time of birth, at least in rats (Kalsbeek et al., 1988). Dopaminergic fibers show the adult pattern of projection into the frontal and cingulate cortex through extended postnatal development in rats (Bruinink et al., 1983).

In summary, it appears that:

- Most intrinsic and extrinsic transmitters are present in the cortex at birth, at least in rats and probably also in humans, but show changes in distribution and overall levels for some time after birth.
- Several transmitters of both intrinsic and extrinsic origins show the characteristic rise and fall evident in some measures of structural neuroanatomical development. Due to a paucity of human data, it is currently not possible to say to what extent these developmental patterns overlap.
- Several transmitters of extrinsic origin show the same inside-out gradient of cortical laminar development observed in structural measures.
- Neurotransmitters may play multiple roles during development. For example, noradrenaline may also regulate cortical plasticity.

- Some transmitters show a differential distribution through-out the cortex. This differential distribution may play some role in the subsequent specialization of regions of cortex for certain functions.

chapter three

Vision, Orienting, and Attention

This chapter reviews a number of topics in vision, visual orienting, and visual attention for which attempts have been made to relate brain development to behavioral change. The contribution of peripheral systems (retinal) development in the emergence of basic visual functions is briefly alluded to, before discussion of the neural basis of the development of binocular vision. Neuroanatomical and computational modeling evidence highlights the importance of the segregation of inputs to layer 4 cells in the primary visual cortex. This increased segregation of inputs from the two eyes can be viewed as the result of a self-organizing neural network constrained by certain intrinsic and extrinsic factors. A compelling behavioral test of the increased segregation hypothesis is discussed. Moving on from sensory processing to sensorimotor integration, an attempt to use the developmental neuroanatomy of the cortex to make predictions about transitions in orienting behavior in infants is described. Specifically, the postnatal inside-out dendritic development of visual cortex is argued to constrain the outputs from this region to other cortical pathways in a partially sequential manner. This restricts the pathways that can influence eye movement control at certain ages. A number of marker tasks for cortical regions involved in oculomotor control are reviewed. Later developing pathways tend to be (a) more sensitive to the effects of experience, and (b) able to control or regulate earlier developing pathways. Finally, experiments concerned with the development of covert (internal) attention shifts in infants and children are described. A number of changes in the flexibility and speed of shifting attention are shown to originate in infancy but continue into childhood.

3.1   The development of binocular vision

Attempts have been made to relate transitions in a number of domains of cognitive development to aspects of postnatal brain growth. The following chapters review this literature selectively. I have emphasized research in areas in which there are some theoretical propositions to relate evidence from brain and cognitive development. Since relatively few aspects of cognitive development have been related to a neural basis, the following chapters should not be regarded as a general review of cognitive development (for such a review the reader is referred to Bremner, 1988; Siegler, 1991; Karmiloff-Smith, 1992).

Visual pathways, and especially the visual cortex, are among the most studied regions of the brain. More than 20 visual areas of the primate cortex have been identified and, by means of single-cell recording, neuroimaging, and neuropsychological studies, attempts have been made to understand the functions of these regions. On the behavioral side, much is known about visual psychophysics, and our knowledge about visual cognition is rapidly expanding. Vision would therefore seem to be a good starting place for studying the functional consequences of the developing brain.

Immediately we start to consider this matter it becomes obvious that it might be hard to determine whether a change in visual abilities during development is due to limitations in the periphery, such as the structure of the eye, lens, or eye muscles, or whether it is due to central changes in the brain. It is clear that immaturities in peripheral sensory systems place limits on the perceptual capacities of young infants. For example, it is well known that immaturity of the retina limits spatial acuity. The issue remains, however, whether peripheral limitations provide the major constraints on the development of perception as some have argued, or whether development of the central visual pathways of the brain is the primary limiting factor. While this issue remains controversial, Banks and colleagues (e.g. Banks and Shannon, 1993) have conducted an "ideal observer" analysis in which the morphology of neonatal photoreceptors and optics

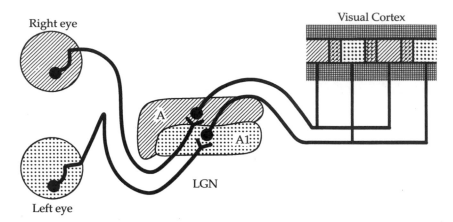

Figure 3.1 Simplified schematic diagram illustrating how projections from the two eyes form ocular dominance columns in the visual cortex.

were compared with those of adults. From this analysis, estimates of the contribution of optical and receptor immaturity, as opposed to central immaturities, to deficits in infant spatial and chromatic vision were generated. Observed differences in these aspects of vision between adults and infants turn out to be significantly greater than would be predicted on the basis of peripheral limitations only, indicating that central nervous system pathway development is an important contributing factor in the development of vision. Given that central nervous system factors play an important role even in the development of spatial acuity, we can enquire further into the nature and source of these constraints. As an example of this approach, I will discuss binocular vision.

The central visual field of most primates is binocular, requiring integration of information between the two eyes. This integration is thought to be achieved in the primary visual cortex. Functional and anatomical structures observed in layer 4 of the primary visual cortex, so-called ocular dominance columns, are thought to be important for binocular vision (see figure 3.1). These columns arise from the segregation of inputs from the two eyes. In other words, neurons in a single ocular dominance column are dominated by input from one eye in adult mammals.

Ocular dominance columns are thought to be the stage of processing necessary to achieve binocular vision and, subsequently, detection of disparities between the two retinal images. Due to the fact that ocular dominance columns are known to have a sensitive period for their formation, and to be sensitive to the differential extent of input from the two eyes, they have become a popular model system for developmental neurobiology (e.g. Kasamatsu and Pettigrew, 1976; Rauschecker and Singer, 1981; Bear and Singer, 1986).

Held (1985) reviewed converging evidence that binocular vision develops at approximately the end of the fourth month of life in human infants. One of the abilities associated with binocular vision, stereoacuity, increases very rapidly from the onset of stereopsis, such that it reaches adult levels within a few weeks. This is in contrast to other measures of acuity, such as grating acuity, which increase much more gradually. Held suggested that this very rapid spurt in stereoacuity requires some equally rapid change in the neural substrate supporting it. On the basis of evidence from animal studies, he proposed that this substrate is the development of ocular dominance columns found in layer 4 of the primary visual cortex. While Held's proposal was initially based on a simple causal association between the formation of ocular dominance columns and the onset of binocularity, more recent research in his laboratory has been concerned to describe a link between the process of change at the two levels.

As mentioned in chapter 2, processes of selective loss commonly contribute to the sculpting of specific pathways in the cortex. Neurophysiological evidence indicates that the geniculocortical afferents from the two eyes are initially mixed so that they synapse on common cortical neurons in layer 4 (see figure 3.2). These layer 4 cells project to disparity selective cells (possibly in cortical layers 2 and 3). During ontogeny, geniculate axons originating from one eye withdraw from the region, leaving behind axons from the other eye. Held suggested that it is these events at the neural level that give rise to the sudden increase in stereoacuity observed by behavioral measures at around 4 months of age in the human infant.

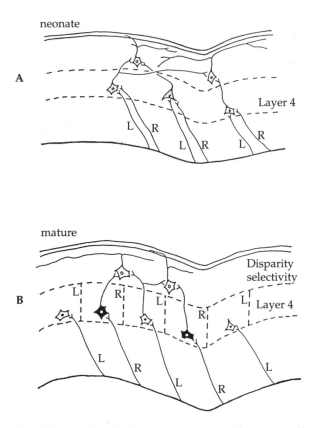

Figure 3.2   (A) Afferents from both eyes synapse on the same cells in layer 4, thereby losing information about the eye of origin. (B) Afferents are segregated on the basis of eye origin (R and L), and consequently recipient cells in layer 4 may send their axons to cells outside of that layer so as to synapse on cells that may be disparity selective.

This process of selective loss has the information-processing consequence that information from the two eyes which was previously combined in layer 4 of the primary visual cortex becomes segregated (Held, 1993). Specifically, there will be a certain degree of integration between the eyes that will decline once each neuron receives innervation from only one eye. Held and colleagues elegantly demonstrated this increasing segregation of information from the two eyes by showing that infants under 4 months can perform certain types of integration between the two eyes that older infants cannot. In this experiment, Held and his colleagues presented a grating to one eye of an infant, and an orthogonal grating to the other eye (Shimojo et al., 1983). Infants under 4 months perceived a single gridlike representation instead of two sets of gratings that were orthogonal to each other. This is because, presumably, synaptic inputs from the individual eyes have not segregated into ocular dominance columns. As a result, a given cortical layer 4 neuron may have synaptic inputs from each eye and will effectively "see" the image from each eye simultaneously. That is, information from the two eyes would be summed in layer 4, resulting in an averaging of the two signals. Since the inputs from each eye summate, in the case of the orthogonal gratings a grid was perceived. Older infants (older than 4 months of age) do not perceive this grating because neurons in cortical layer 4 of striate cortex only receive inputs from one eye. The inputs to layer 4 have been segregated from one another, and a given layer 4 neuron will receive input from one eye or the other.

The loss of these connections is probably due to the refinement of synapses by selective loss. This refinement most likely occurs through activity-dependent neural mechanisms since it has been shown that the formation of ocular dominance columns can be experimentally blocked by reducing neuronal activity (Stryker and Harris, 1986). Monocular deprivation (Wiesel and Hubel, 1965) also results in abnormal ocular dominance columns; in this case, the eye that is preserved takes over more than its normal share of cortical area.

In chapter 1 a distinction between causal epigenesis (maturationist) and probabilistic epigenesis (constructivist) approaches was discussed. While at first sight the rapid onset of binocular function and its hypothesized neural basis makes it seem an attractive candidate for the former approach, some recent computational modeling efforts suggest that even in this case the constructivist approach may be more appropriate. For example, Miller and his colleagues (Miller et al., 1989; Miller, 1990) developed a neural network model of ocular dominance column development. The model is based on four key features that they suggest play a critical role in organizing ocular dominance patches:

1   The patterns of initial connectivity of the afferents from the LGN to cells in layer 4 of the primary visual cortex (the "arbor function.")
2   The patterns of activity in the afferents. In other words, the extent to which the information within one eye projection, or between the two eye projections, is correlated ("correlation functions.")
3   Influences acting laterally within the cortex, such that synapses on one layer 4 cortical cell can influence neighboring cells ("cortical interaction function.")
4   Constraints limiting the total synaptic strength supported by an afferent or cortical cell.

Using these key features, Miller and colleagues modeled the projection from the LGN to the primary visual cortex, including some intrinsic connections within layer 4. They found that "ocular dominance columns" emerged robustly under a variety of starting conditions and learning rules (see figure 3.3). The purpose of such modeling is to understand the core requirements or constraints for the formation of a structure. In this case, Miller and colleagues identified several critical factors for the formation of this pattern. The first of these was the arbor function. Specifically, the projection pattern from each LGN cell to cortical cells is such that cortical cells at the center of the projection fan receive stronger input than do those at the edge of the projection. The width of the arbor function (projection fan) also determines the periodicity of the dominance columns. The second critical factor identified by Miller and colleagues was that the intrinsic corticocortico projections need to be locally excitatory and inhibitory for longer distances. Intuitively, it is obvious that this arrangement will ensure that cells that respond to similar inputs will cluster together and "push apart" from those that have different response properties. The third critical factor is that correlations of firing from LGN cells within each eye must

A

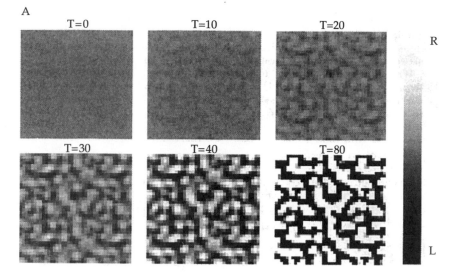

Figure 3.3 Typical development of ocular dominance patches of cortex at timesteps T = 0, 10, 20, 30, 40, 80. Each pixel represents a single cortical cell. The shades represent ocular dominance of each cell, that is, the difference between the total (summed) strength of right eye and of left eye geniculate inputs to the cell. White indicates complete dominance by the right eye; black indicates complete dominance by the left eye; and gray represents equality of the two eyes.

be greater than between the two eyes. In other words, inputs from within one eye tend to correlate more highly in their activity than those between the two eyes. Miller and colleagues suggest that this is the case because spontaneous activity (firing) in the retina and LGN is likely to be more correlated within each eye than between the two eyes.

To generalize the conclusions of the work of Miller and colleagues: for the ocular dominance columns to develop, critical factors from three sources must all be present. First, the correlational structure of the input is important (in this case to ensure that the correlations within an eye projection are greater than those between the two eyes); second, is the intrinsic microcircuitry of cortex (in this case the relative distribution of excitatory and inhibitory projections); and, third, the constraints imposed by subcortical circuitry (in this case the projections patterns from the LGN). We will see that these three sources of constraint play a role in shaping the representations and areal structures that emerge in other examples of cortical development. While ocular dominance columns and binocular vision may seem at first sight like a prime example of the maturation of the brain causing a behavioral change, on closer inspection we have seen that viewing the process as a constrained self-organizing system may be more fruitful.

3.2   The development of visual orienting

In the previous section, attempts to relate brain development to an aspect of sensory processing were discussed. In this section we move to a domain, visual orienting, in which the effects of brain development on the integration between sensory input and motor output can be studied. Most of the tasks to be described involve stimuli which are well within the visual capacities of infants, and involve a form of action (eye-gaze shifts) which infants can readily accomplish. Thus, while there is continuing development of both sensory and motor processing throughout infancy, through carefully designed experiments we are able to focus more on the integration between input and output.

There are other reasons for studying the development of visual orienting. One of these is that over the first 6–8 months of life the human infant's primary method of gathering information from its environment involves shifts of eye gaze. These shifts of gaze allow the infant to select particular aspects of the external world for further study and learning. For example, and as we will see in the next section, simply by shifting the head and eyes infants can ensure that they are exposed to faces more than to other stimuli. In addition, most of what we have learned about mental processes in infants has come from tasks in which some measure of looking behavior, such as preferential looking or habituation to a repeatedly presented stimulus, is used.

Despite the importance of shifts of eye gaze in early infancy, however, until recently very little was known about how the development of the brain relates to changes in visual orienting abilities. This was despite a substantial literature on the neural basis of saccades (eye movements) which comes from neuro-psychological and neuroimaging studies of human adults, as well as single-cell recording and lesion studies in non-human primates (see Posner and Peterson, 1990, for review).

In one of the first attempts to relate brain development to behavioral change in the human infant, Gordon Bronson (1974, 1982) argued that the development of vision and visual orienting over the first few months of life could be attributed to a shift from subcortical visual processing to processing in cortical visual pathways over the first 6 months of life. Specifically, Bronson cited evidence from electrophysiological, neuroanatomical, and behavioral studies that the primary (cortical) visual pathway is not fully functioning until around 3 months postnatal age (for more recent reviews, see Atkinson, 1984; Johnson, 1990). More recently, it has become evident that there is some, albeit limited, cortical activity in newborns, and that the onset of cortical functioning probably proceeds by a series of graded steps, rather than in an all-or-none manner. Meanwhile, neurophysiological research on monkeys and neuropsychological research with human adults has revealed that there are multiple pathways involved in oculomotor control and attention shifts in the primate brain. Some of the structures and pathways involved in oculomotor control in primates are illustrated in figure 3.4.

Most of the pathways and structures illustrated in figure 3.4 are known to be involved in particular types of information processing related to the planning of eye movements. When considering the integration between sensory inputs and motor outputs it is important that the pathways discussed can be traced from the source of the input (the eye) to the muscles that shift the eyes. A diagram of such pathways may look different from one that just shows pathways for sensory processing, for example.

Four oculomotor pathways will be discussed here. First, the pathway from the eye to the superior colliculus. This subcortical pathway has stronger input from the temporal visual field (the

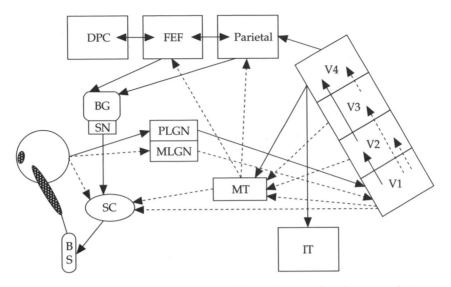

Figure 3.4   Diagram representing some of the main neural pathways and structures involved in visual orienting and attention. The solid lines indicate primarily parvocellular input, while the dashed lines represent magnocellular. V1–V4, visual cortex; FEF, frontal eye fields; DPC, dorsolateral prefrontal cortex; BG, basal ganglia; SN, substantia nigra; LGN, lateral geniculate (magno and parvo portions); MT, middle temporal area; IT, inferotemporal cortex; SC, superior colliculus; BS, brain stem.

peripheral or outer half of the field of each eye), and is involved in the generation of rapid reflexive eye movements to easily discriminated stimuli. The other three pathways to be discussed here share a projection from the eye to cortical structures via the midbrain (thalamic) visual relay, the lateral geniculate nucleus (LGN), and the primary visual cortex (V1). The first of these goes both directly to the superior colliculus from the primary visual cortex and also via the middle temporal area (MT). Some of the structures on this pathway are thought to play an important role in the detection of motion and the smooth tracking of moving objects. The next pathway proceeds from V1 to other parts of the visual cortex and thence to the frontal eye fields (FEF). As we will see later, this FEF pathway is thought to be involved in more complex aspects of eye movement planning such as anticipatory saccades and learning sequences of scanning patterns. Finally, there is a more complex and less well-understood pathway that involves tonic (continual) inhibition of the superior colliculus (via subcortical structures called the substantia nigra and basal ganglia). Schiller (1985) proposed that this pathway ensures that the activity of the colliculus can be regulated. More recent findings suggest that this oculomotor pathway forms an integrated system with the frontal eye fields and parietal lobes (e.g. Alexander et al., 1986) and that it plays some role in the regulation of the subcortical oculomotor pathway by the other cortical pathways.

The challenge has been to relate the development of these various pathways to the visuomotor competence of the infant at different ages. To date, this has involved two complementary approaches: predictions about the sequence of development of the pathways from developmental neuroanatomy (Atkinson, 1984; Johnson, 1990), and the administration of marker tasks (see chapter 1) to ascertain the functional development of particular structures or pathways.

An example of the first approach was an analysis that I presented a number of years ago (Johnson, 1990). In this analysis I suggested that, first, the characteristics of visually guided behavior of the infant at particular ages is determined by which of the pathways (shown in figure 3.4) is functional, and, second, which of these cortical pathways is functional is influenced by the developmental state of the primary visual cortex. The basis of this claim at the neuroanatomical level lies in three sets of observations. First, that the primary visual cortex is the major (though not exclusive) "gateway" for input to most of the cortical pathways involved in oculomotor control (Schiller, 1985). Second, the primary visual cortex shows a postnatal continuation of the prenatal 'inside-out' pattern of growth of the cortex described in chapter 2, with the deeper layers (5 and 6) showing greater dendritic branching, length, and extent of myelinization than more superficial layers (2 and 3) around the time of birth. Third, there is a restricted pattern of inputs and outputs from the primary visual cortex (e.g. the projections to V2 depart from the

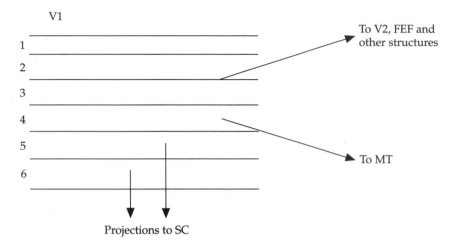

Figure 3.5   A schematic diagram illustrating that different projections from V1 depart from different layers (FEF, frontal eye fields; MT, middle temporal area; SC, superior colliculus).

upper layers, see chapter 2). By combining these observations with information about the developmental neuroanatomy of the human primary visual cortex, I hypothesized the following sequence of development of cortical pathways underlying oculomotor control: the subcortical pathway from the eye directly to the superior colliculus (probably including cortical projections from the deeper layers of V1 to superior colliculus), followed by the cortical projection which inhibits the superior colliculus pathway, followed by the pathway through cortical structure MT, and finally the pathway involving the frontal eye fields and related structures. This is illustrated as a schematic diagram in figure 3.5.

Following these predictions derived from developmental neuroanatomy, one can return to the behavioral level to see if the transitions here support the sequence of development of pathways predicted. Beginning with the newborn infant, evidence from measures of the extent of dendritic arborization and myelinization indicate that only the deeper layers of the primary visual cortex are likely to be capable of supporting organized information-processing activity in the human newborn. Since the majority of feed-forward intracortical projections depart from outside the deeper layers (5 and 6) most of the cortical pathways involved in oculomotor control will only be receiving weak or disorganized input at this stage. However, evidence from various sources, such as visually evoked potentials, indicate that information from the eye is entering the primary visual cortex in the newborn. Thus, while some of the newborn's visual behavior can be accounted for in terms of processing in the subcortical pathway, I argued in my 1990 paper that there is also information processing occurring in the deeper cortical layers at birth. At least two characteristics of visually guided behavior in the newborn are consistent with predominantly subcortical control: saccadic pursuit tracking and preferential orienting to the temporal visual field. To review these in more detail:

- The ability of infants to track a moving stimulus in the first few months of life has two characteristics (Aslin, 1981). The first is that the eye movements follow the stimulus in a "saccadic" or step-like manner, as opposed to the smooth pursuit found in adults and older infants. The second characteristic is that the eye movements tend to lag behind the movement of the stimulus, rather than predicting its trajectory. Therefore, when a newborn infant visually tracks a moving stimulus, it could be described as performing a series of saccadic eye movements. Such behavior is consistent with subcortical control of orienting.
- Newborns much more readily orient toward stimuli in the temporal, as opposed to the nasal (the half of the visual field of each eye closer to the nose), visual field (e.g. Lewis et al., 1979). Posner and Rothbart (1980) suggest that midbrain structures such as the colliculus can be driven most readily by temporal field input. This proposal has been confirmed in studies of adult "blindsight" patients by Rafal et al. (1990), who established that distracter stimuli placed in the temporal "blindfield" had an effect on orienting into the good field, whereas distracter stimuli in the nasal "blindfield" did not.

Recent evidence from studies of infants in which a complete cerebral hemisphere has been removed (to alleviate epilepsy) indicate that the subcortical (collicular) pathway alone is capable of generating saccades toward a peripheral target in the cortically "blindfield" (Braddick et al., 1992).

Around 1 month of age infants show "obligatory attention" (Stechler and Latz, 1966; Johnson et al., 1991; Hood, 1995). That is to say, they have great difficulty in disengaging their gaze from a stimulus in order to make a saccade to another location. Sometimes an infant around 1 month of age can spend as long as several minutes fixedly gazing at a seemingly uninteresting aspect of the environment, such as a section of carpet, before bursting into tears! Although this phenomenon is still poorly understood, I have suggested that it is due to the development of tonic inhibition of the colliculus via the substantia nigra (see figure 3.4). Since this pathway projects from the deeper layers of the primary visual cortex to the colliculus, it is hypothesized to be the first strong cortical influence on oculomotor control. This (as yet) unregulated tonic inhibition of the colliculus has the consequence that stimuli impinging on the peripheral visual field no longer elicit an automatic exogenous saccade as readily as in newborns.

By around 2 months of age infants begin to show periods of smooth visual tracking, although their eye movements still lag behind the movement of the stimulus. At this age they also become more sensitive to stimuli placed in the nasal visual field (Aslin, 1981) and also more sensitive to coherent motion (Wattam-Bell, 1990). I proposed that the onset of these behaviors coincides with the functioning of the pathway involving structure MT. The enabling of this route of eye movement control may provide this cortical stream with the ability to regulate activity in the superior colliculus.

Associated with further dendritic growth and myelinization within the upper layers of the primary visual cortex, strengthening the projections from V1 to other cortical areas, around 3 months of age the pathways involving the frontal eye fields may become functional. This development may greatly increase the infant's ability to make "anticipatory" eye movements and to learn sequences of looking patterns, both functions associated with the frontal eye fields. With regard to the visual tracking of a moving object, infants now not only show periods of smooth tracking, but their eye movements often predict the movement of the stimulus in an anticipatory manner. Experiments by Haith and colleagues have demonstrated that anticipatory eye movements can be readily elicited from infants by this age. For example, Haith et al. (1988) exposed 3.5-month-old infants to a series of picture slides which appeared either on the right or on the left-hand side of the infant. These stimuli were either presented in an alternating sequence with fixed inter-stimulus interval (ISI), or with an irregular alternation pattern and ISI. It was observed that the regular alternation pattern produced more stimulus anticipations, and faster reaction times to make an eye movement than in the irregular series. Haith and colleagues concluded from these results that infants of this age are able to develop expectancies for non-controllable spatio-temporal events. Canfield and Haith (1991) tested 2- and 3-month-old infants in an experiment which included more complex sequences (such as left-left-right, left-left-right etc). Consistent with the predictions from developmental neuroanatomy, while they failed to find significant effects with 2-month-olds, 3-month-olds were able to acquire at least some of the more complex sequences.

Given that this survey of the behavioral evidence pertaining to the development of visual orienting was broadly consistent with the predictions from developmental neurobiology (see table 3.1 for a summary), the next step is to develop and consider marker tasks for some of these and other parts of the cortex with a role in oculomotor control. Table 3.2 shows a number of marker tasks that have recently been developed for the functioning of structures involved in oculomotor control and visual attention (next section) shifts.

Marker tasks for several cortical regions thought to play a role in oculomotor control, the parietal cortex, frontal eye fields

Table 3.1   Summary of the relation between developing oculomotor pathways and behavior

Age	Functional anatomy	Behavior
Newborn	SC pathway + layer 5 and 6 pyramidal output to LGN and SC	Saccadic pursuit tracking Preferential orienting to temporal visual field "Externality effect"
1 month	As above + inhibitory pathway to SC via BG	As above + "obligatory" attention
2 months	As above + MT (magnocellular) pathway to SC	Onset of smooth pursuit tracking and increased sensitivity to nasal visual field
3 months and over	As above + FEF (parvocellular) pathway to SC and BS	Increase in "anticipatory" tracking and sequential scanning patterns

SC, superior colliculus; LGN, lateral geniculate; BG, basal ganglia; MT, middle temporal area; FEF, frontal eye fields; BS, brain stem.

(FEF), and dorsolateral prefrontal cortex (DLPC) have recently been developed, and show rapid development between 2 and 6 months of age in human infants. Starting with marker tasks for the frontal eye fields (FEF), frontal cortex damage in humans results in an inability to suppress involuntary automatic saccades toward targets, and an apparent inability to control volitional saccades (Guitton et al., 1985; Fischer and Breitmeyer, 1987). For example, Guitton et al. (1985) studied normal subjects and patients with frontal lobe lesions or temporal lobe lesions in a so-called "anti-saccade" task. In this task subjects are instructed *not* to look at a briefly flashed cue, but rather to make a saccade in the opposite direction (Hallett, 1978). Guitton et al. (1985) reported that while normal subjects and patients with temporal

Table 3.2 Marker tasks for the development of visual orienting and attention

Brain region	Marker task	Studies
Superior colliculus	Inhibition of return	Clohessy et al. (1991); Simion et al. (1995)
	Vector summation saccades	Johnson et al. (1995)
Middle temporal area	Coherent motion detection; structure from motion	Wattam-Bell (1991)
	Smooth tracking	Aslin (1981)
Parietal cortex	Spatial cueing task	Hood and Atkinson (1991); Hood (1993); Johnson (1994); Johnson and Tucker (in press)
	Eye-centered saccade planning	Gilmore and Johnson (1995a)
Frontal eye fields	Inhibition of automatic saccades	Johnson (1995)
	Anticipatory saccades	Haith et al. (1988)
Dorsolateral prefrontal cortex	Oculomotor delayed response task	Gilmore and Johnson (1995b)

lobe damage could do this task with relative ease, patients with frontal damage, in particular those with damage around the FEF, were severely impaired. Patients with frontal damage had particular difficulty in suppressing unwanted saccades toward the cue stimulus.

I have developed a version of the anti-saccade task for use with infants (Johnson, 1995). Clearly, one cannot give verbal instruction to a young infant to look in the opposite direction from where the cue stimulus appears. Instead, infants require to be motivated to look at the second of two opposite peripheral stimuli more than at the first stimulus. This can be done by making the second stimulus reliably more dynamic and colorful than the first. Thus, after a number of such trials, infants may learn to inhibit their tendency to make a saccade to the first stimulus (the cue) when it appears, in order to respond as rapidly as possible to the more attractive second stimulus (the target). A group of 4-month-old infants showed a significant decrease in their frequency of looking to the first (cue) stimulus over a number of such trials (Johnson, 1995). A second experiment demonstrated that this decrement was not due to differential habituation to the simpler stimulus. Since 4-month-olds are able to inhibit saccades to a peripheral stimulus, it is reasonable to infer that their frontal eye field circuit is functioning by this age. Similar experiments are currently being run with younger infants.

Other tasks recently conducted with infants are consistent with an increasing prefrontal cortex endogenous control over shifts of attention and saccades around 6 months of age. For example, Goldman-Rakic and colleagues (Funahashi et al., 1989, 1990) devised an oculomotor delayed response paradigm to study the properties of neurons in the dorsolateral prefrontal cortex (DLPC) of macaque monkeys. In this task the monkey plans a saccade toward a particular spatial location, but has to wait for a period (usually between 2 and 5 seconds) before actually executing the saccade. Single-unit recording in the macaque indicates that some cells in the DLPC code for the direction of the saccade during the delay. Further, reversible microlesions to the area result in selective amnesia for saccades to a localized part of the visual field. A recent PET study on human subjects has confirmed the involvement of DLPC (and parietal cortex) in this task (Jonides et al., 1993).

Gilmore and Johnson (1995b) devised an infant version of the oculomotor delayed response task: a marker task for DLPC (see figure 3.6). The results obtained to date indicate that 6-month-old human infants can perform delayed saccades successfully with delays of up to at least 5 seconds, suggesting some influence of the prefrontal cortex on eye-movement control by this

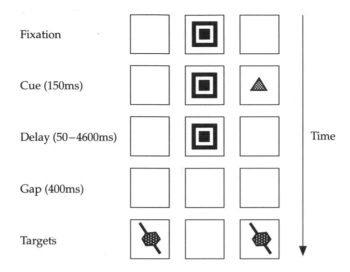

Figure 3.6 The oculomotor delayed response task as designed for use with infants. Infant subjects face three computer screens on which brightly colored moving stimuli appear. At the start of each trial a fixation stimulus appears on the central screen. Once the infant is looking at this stimulus, a cue is briefly flashed up on one of the two side screens. Following the briefly flashed cue, the central stimulus stays on for between 1 and 5 seconds, before presentation of two targets on the side screens. By measuring delayed looks to the cued location prior to the target onset, Gilmore and Johnson (1995b) established that infants can retain information about the cued location for several seconds.

age. As an aside, these findings with infants cast some doubt on claims that the dorsolateral prefrontal cortex is not sufficiently developed to support tasks which require both inhibition and working memory until around 10 months (chapter 7), but may be consistent with a more graded account of the development of these abilities (see chapter 9).

In general, the work relating brain development to advances in visual orienting has provided evidence for the view that multiple brain pathways are involved in even apparently simple aspects of sensorimotor integration, such as making a saccadic eye movement. Further, these pathways have a hierarchical arrangement, such that some pathways (usually the later developing ones) have some degree of control over others. While these

multiple, hierarchically arranged pathways may be very difficult to dissociate using standard cognitive and cognitive neuroscience techniques, studying their sequential development can
illuminate both their existence and their interrelationships. By
now it should be evident that the stages identified above are
not meant to be sudden steps, but should rather be viewed as a
series of graded transitions in which behavior at a given age is a
product of the dynamic interactions between several pathways.
Related to this point is the question of whether the approach
illustrated above comes from a causal epigenesis (maturational)
or a probabilistic epigenesis (constructivist) view (see chapter
1). While the approach as described so far has been of the causal
epigenesis type, some recent lines of investigation have sought
to investigate the effects of experience of the external world on
the emergence of representations for controlling eye movements.
One of these lines of investigation has centered on marker tasks
for the parietal cortex.

The parietal cortex is a region of the primate cortex which has
been implicated in aspects of saccade planning in monkey cellular recording studies, human functional neuroimaging studies, and neuropsychological studies of brain-damaged patients.
It is also a region of cortex that undergoes marked developmental changes between 3 and 6 months of age as demonstrated in
both neuroanatomical studies of postmortem brains (Conel, 1939–
67) and PET (Chugani et al., 1987). Anderson and colleagues
have recorded from single cells in parts of the macaque monkey
parietal cortex, and many of these cells code for saccades within
an eye- or head-centered frame of reference. In other words, their
receptive fields respond to combinations of eye or head position,
on the one hand, and retinal distance from the fovea to the
target, on the other. This is in contrast to parts of the superior
colliculus in which cells commonly only respond according to the
retinal distance and direction of the target from the fovea.

Zipser and Anderson (1988; Anderson and Zipser, 1988) constructed a connectionist model in which the hidden-layer units
developed response properties which closely resembled those
observed within regions of the primate parietal cortex. While

the details of this neuroconnectionist model need not concern us here, the take-home point is that the representations for generating saccades within an eye- or head-centered frame of reference emerged as a result of training, and did not require to be "hard-wired" into the network. (Some readers might object that the Anderson and Zipser network used a learning algorithm, back propagation, in which the network is "tutored" with the correct answer until its errors are reduced. However, the types of representations that emerge in the hidden layer of back propagation nets are often very similar to those that appear in a similar network that uses self-organizing, e.g. Hebbian, learning rules.) An important question that remains is whether infants only develop the ability to use extra-retinal coordinates to plan saccades during postnatal life. If they do, this would be consistent with the assumption underlying the model that representations controlling eye- or head-centered action need to be constructed postnatally, and result from constraints imposed by the network structure and its interaction with the external environment.

In collaboration with Rick Gilmore, I have conducted several experiments designed to ascertain whether the ability of infants to use extra-retinal frames of reference to plan saccades emerges over the first few months of life. In one of these experiments we exposed 4- and 6-month-old infants to two simultaneously flashed targets on a large monitor screen. The targets were flashed so briefly that they were gone before the infant started to make a saccade to them. We then studied the saccades which infants made in response to these targets (see figure 3.7). In many trials they made two saccades, the first of these being to the location of one of the two targets. Having made a saccade to one of the two targets, we examined whether the second saccade that they made was to the actual location of the second target, or whether it was to the retinal location (the location on the retina at which that target had originally appeared). To make the second saccade to the correct spatial location requires infants to be able to take into account the fact that their eyes had shifted position, and then compute the saccade necessary given the new eye position. The results indicated that for 4-month-olds the majority of second

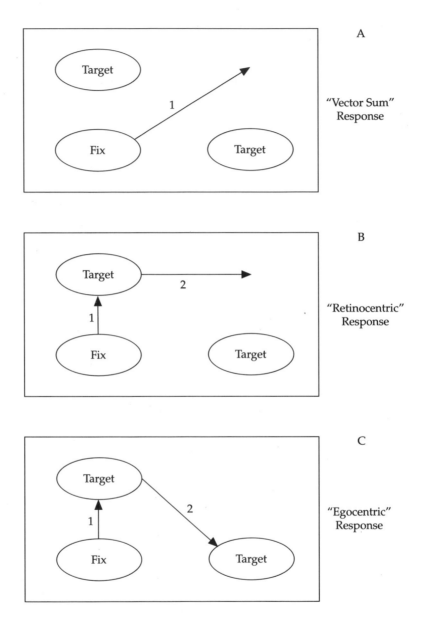

Figure 3.7 Three types of saccades made by young infants in response to two targets briefly flashed as shown. (A) A "vector summation" saccade in which eye movement is directed between the two targets. (B) A "retinocentric" saccade in which the second saccade is directed to the location corresponding to the retinal error when the flash occurred. (C) An "egocentric" saccade which corresponds to the use of extra-retinal information to plan the second saccade. Between birth and 6 months, infants shift from the first two types of response to the third.

saccades were directed to the retinal location in which the target had appeared. In contrast, for the 6-month-olds, the majority of second saccades were made to the correct spatial location for the other target. These preliminary results suggest that the ability to use extra-retinal cues to plan saccades emerges through the first 6 months of life. However, saccades based on retinal location (and thought to be subcortical in origin) are probably present from birth.

3.3 Visual attention

Our discussion so far has concerned overt shifts of attention due to eye and head movements. It is evident that adults are also capable of shifting their attention *covertly* (without moving the eyes or other sensory receptors). One way in which evidence for covert attention has been provided in adults is by studying the effect on detection of briefly cueing a particular spatial location. A briefly presented cue serves to draw covert attention to the location, resulting in the subsequent facilitation of detection of targets at that location (Posner and Cohen, 1980; Maylor, 1985). While *facilitation* of detection and responses to a covertly attended location occurs if the target stimulus appears very shortly after the cue offset, with longer latencies between cue and target *inhibition* of saccades toward that location occurs. This latter phenomenon, referred to as "inhibition of return" (Posner et al., 1985), may reflect an evolutionarily important mechanism which prevents attention returning to a recently processed spatial location. In adults, facilitation is reliably observed when targets appeared at the cued location within about 150 ms of the cue, whereas targets appearing between 300 and 1,300 ms after a peripheral (exogenous) cue result in longer detection latencies (e.g. Posner and Cohen, 1980, 1984; Maylor, 1985).

Following lesions to the posterior parietal lobe, adults show severe neglect of the contralateral visual field. According to Posner and colleagues, this neglect is due to damage to the "posterior attention network." This refers to a brain circuit which includes not only the posterior parietal lobe, but also the pulvinar and superior colliculus (Posner, 1988; Posner and Peterson, 1990; see figure 3.4 for all but the pulvinar). Damage to this circuit is postulated to impair subjects' ability to shift covert attention to a cued spatial location. The involvement of these regions in shifts of visual attention has been confirmed by positron emission tomography (PET) studies. As mentioned above, both neuroanatomical (Conel, 1939–67) and PET (Chugani et al., 1987) evidence from the human infant indicate that the parietal lobe is undergoing substantive and rapid development between 3 and 6 months after birth. The question arises, therefore, as to whether infants become capable of covert shifts of attention during this time.

Since infants do not accept verbal instruction and are poor at motor responses used to study spatial attention in adults, such as a key press, the only response available to demonstrate facilitation and inhibition of a cued location is eye movements. That is, overt shifts are used to study *covert* shifts of attention by examining the influence of a cue stimulus (which is presented so briefly that it does not normally elicit an eye movement) on infants' subsequent saccades toward conspicuous target stimuli. Using these methods, Hood and Atkinson (1991; see Hood, 1995) reported that 6-month-old infants have faster reaction times to make a saccade to a target when it appears immediately after a brief (100 ms) cue stimulus than when it appears in an uncued location. A group of 3-month-old infants did not show this effect. Johnson (1994; Johnson and Tucker, in press) employed a similar procedure in which a brief (100 ms) cue was presented on one of two side screens, before bilateral targets were presented either 100 ms or 600 ms later. It was hypothesized, on the basis of the adult findings, that the 200 ms stimulus onset asynchrony (SOA) would be short enough to produce facilitation, while the long SOA trials should result in preferential orienting toward the opposite side (inhibition of return). This result was obtained with a group of 4-month-old infants, suggesting the possibility that infants are capable of covert shifts of attention at this age. Consistent with the previous findings, these effects were not observed in a group of 2-month-old infants.

At present it remains an open question whether the facilitation produced by the cue in these experiments is the result of direct priming of the eye-movement system, or whether the eye movements are following an independent covert shift of attention. While eye movement has also been used in some adult studies purporting to examine shifts of covert attention (e.g. Maylor, 1985; Posner et al., 1985), the use of this output measure raises alternative hypotheses regarding the facilitatory effects of the cue. There are at least three ways in which a spatial cue could have its effect on saccadic latency and direction:

1 The cue stimulus itself directly initiates the saccade.
2 The cue alters the threshold for planning a saccade to a particular location (motor priming).
3 The cue drives covert shifts of attention (independent of the mechanisms of saccade planning) which then subsequently influence eye movements.

A variety of evidence has ruled out the facilitatory effects observed being due to the cue directly driving eye movements (see Johnson, 1994; Johnson and Tucker, in press, for discussion of this point). The second possibility is that the facilitation effects observed are due to a spatially selective priming of the mechanisms which plan saccades. By this view, when the target appears, the cued location is responded to more rapidly and frequently since the earlier presence of the cue reduced the threshold to initiate a saccade to that spatial location. While such a mechanism may be considered an aspect of covert attention in the sense that a stimulus to which no overt response is made (the cue) influences subsequent responses to a later occurring target, it does not require the existence of a covert attention system which is partially or wholly independent of eye-movement planning and control. Currently, there is no behavioral data with infants that will allow us to dissociate this possibility from an independent covert orienting system. Indeed, the relation between covert shifts of attention and saccade planning remains controversial in the adult literature (e.g. Rizzolatti et al., 1987, 1994; Klein et al., 1992).

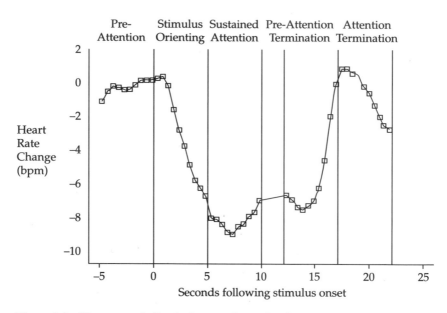

Figure 3.8   Heart-rate defined phases of sustained attention.

Another manifestation of covert attention concerns so-called "sustained" attention. Sustained attention refers to the ability of subjects to maintain the direction of their attention toward a stimulus even in the presence of distracters. Richards (1989a, b) has developed a heart-rate marker for sustained attention in infants. The heart-rate defined period of sustained attention usually lasts for between 5 and 15 seconds after the onset of a complex stimulus (see figure 3.8).

In order to investigate the effect of sustained attention on the response to exogenous cues, Richards (1989a, b) used an "interrupted stimulus method" in which a peripheral stimulus (a flashing light) is presented while the infant is gazing at a central stimulus (a TV screen with a complex visual pattern). By varying the length of time between the onset of the TV image and the onset of the peripheral stimulus, he was able to present the peripheral stimulus either within the period of sustained covert attention, or outside it. Richards found that during the periods when heart rate was decreased (sustained endogenous attention) it took twice as long for the infants to shift their gaze toward the peripheral stimulus as when heart rate had returned to pre-stimulus levels (attention termination). Further, those saccades that are made to a peripheral stimulus during sustained attention are less accurate than normal, and involved multiple hypometric saccades, characteristic of collicular generated saccades (Richards, 1991). Thus, the lack of distractibility during periods of sustained attention is likely to be due to cortically mediated pathways inhibiting collicular mechanisms.

Several studies have traced developments in visual attention during childhood using purely cognitive methods, but have described the continuation of similar transitions to those observed in early infancy. Three transitions that have been described are the greater ability to expand or constrict a field of attention (e.g. Chapman, 1981; Enns and Girgus, 1985), the greater ability to disengage attention from distracting information or invalid cueing (Akhtar and Enns, 1989; Enns and Brodeur, 1989), and a faster speed of shifting attention (Pearson and Lane, 1990).

Enns and Girgus (1985) tested school-age children and adults in speeded classification tasks involving a stimulus composed of two elements that varied in distance (visual angle). Subjects had to classify stimuli on the basis of one of the two elements. Younger children (6–8 years) experienced more interference when the elements were closely spaced than older children (9–11 years) and adults. The same stimuli were used for a second task in which both of the elements had to be taken into account. In this task the younger children had difficulty when the elements were separated by large visual angles. The authors conclude that younger children have problems in contracting and expanding the size of attentional focus. An ERP study of auditory attention also concluded that there is a development in the ability to narrow attentional focus during childhood (Berman and Friedman, 1995).

An observation which may be related is that older children and adults are often reported as being able to shift their attention more rapidly than younger ones. For example, Pearson and Lane (1990), using a spatial cueing paradigm, observed that younger infants took longer to covertly shift their attention to more peripheral targets, whereas they were almost as fast as adults to shift to targets very close to fixation. This indicates that it is the speed of shifting, rather than the latency to elicit a covert shift, that improves with age. The increasing speed of shifting attention with age has also been reported during infancy (Johnson and Tucker, in press), indicating that this developmental transition may be a gradual one that begins early in life.

In several studies, younger children and infants have been argued to have greater difficulty in disengaging from distracting stimuli or invalid spatial cues. For example, Enns and Brodeur (1989) used a spatial cueing paradigm to either cue neutrally (all locations cued), unpredictably (random cueing), or predictably (cue predicts target presentation). The results from subjects aged 6, 8, and 20 years indicated that, while all age groups automatically oriented attention to the cued location, the children processed targets in non-cued locations more slowly than adults, and did not take advantage of the predictability of the cues. Thus the costs and benefits of cueing were greater in the younger subjects due to an increased cost imposed by invalid cueing. Tipper et al. (1989) suggest that these deficits are due to the relative inability to inhibit irrelevant stimuli. Once again, similar developmental trends have been observed in infancy experiments where younger infants are more likely to fail to disengage from competing stimuli, such as obligatory attention described earlier.

Very little work has been done on the neural basis of the development of covert orienting in childhood. However, some authors have attempted to study the development of visual attention in developmental disorders such as attention deficit disorder (ADD) and autism (see chapter 4 for an introduction to autism), and to correlate these with hypothesized neural deficits. As one example of this approach, Courchesne and colleagues (Akshoomoff and Courchesne, 1994; Townsend and Courchesne, 1994) have tested autistic individuals on a variety of spatial cueing and attention switching tasks. They report, on the basis of autopsy and structural MRI data, that most autistic subjects have developmental damage to their cerebellum. In a number of tasks they have associated this damage with reduced ability to switch attention, and a slower shifting of covert spatial attention. Another neural deficit observed in at least some autistic subjects is bilateral parietal damage. Townsend and Courchesne (1994) have proposed that this damage gives rise to a narrowed focus of spatial attention, such that targets presented within the narrowed "spotlight" are detected more rapidly than normal. In contrast, targets presented at small eccentricities from fixation, that would be responded to rapidly by normal subjects, are responded to much more slowly by autistic subjects since they are outside the narrow attentional focus.

chapter four

Face Recognition and Social Cognition

An apparent conflict in the data on the development of face-recognition abilities in infants is outlined. On the one hand, there is evidence that newborns will preferentially orient to face-like patterns, while, on the other hand, other studies have failed to show a face preference until 2 or 3 months of age. The first line of data, when taken together with cognitive neuroscience evidence for the involvement of specific cortical structures in face processing, has been interpreted in terms of innate cortical representations for face processing. In contrast to this, the second body of evidence has been interpreted in terms of the gradual acquisition of face specificity through experience. In order to shed light on this conflicting data in human infants, I turn to evidence from a simpler species, the domestic chick. Research from this species indicates that there are two independent brain systems operating to allow the young animal to learn about individual conspecifics: a predisposition to orient to faces present from shortly after hatching, and a gradual learning process. The latter process is associated with a particular region of the forebrain (cortex), and the neuroanatomy of this region has been used to construct a neurocomputational model. This model accounts for a number of aspects of early visual learning in the chick. We then return to the human infant and a similar two-process model, which accounts for both sets of data outlined above, is presented. This model states that newborn preferential responses to faces are not controlled by the cortical structures involved in adult face processing, but at least partly by subcortical visuomotor pathways. By ensuring that the infant frequently orients to faces, this system enables certain cortical microcircuits to develop representations for processing this class of stimuli. It is suggested that the basic architecture of the cortex interacts with the input (faces) to generate representations for face processing, rather than representations for face processing being innate. The final section of the chapter addresses the issue of whether there is an "innate social module" within the brain that comes to process information about the thoughts and intentions of others. Evidence from two developmental disorders, autism and Williams syndrome, initially appears to provide support for a social module that can be selectively impaired (autism) or spared in the face of other deficits (Williams syndrome). On closer inspection, however, it becomes apparent that such a clean dissociation is not borne out by the evidence, and that a social information-processing module emerges as a result of constraints from interactions with other conspecifics, initial biases toward social stimuli, and the basic architecture of the brain. A corollary of this is that a variety of types of deficits in social cognition can be observed.

4.1 Face recognition

The ability to detect and recognize faces is commonly considered to be a good example of human perceptual abilities, as well as being the basis of our adaptation as social animals. While there is a long literature on the development of face recognition in young infants, extending back to the studies of Fantz more than 30 years ago (e.g. Fantz, 1964), only recently has there been speculation about the neural basis of these abilities. Specifically, de Schonen and Mathivet (1989) and Johnson and Morton (1991; Morton and Johnson, 1991) have hypothesized that the preferential responses to faces observed in newborn infants is controlled primarily (though not exclusively) by subcortical visuomotor pathways, whereas later developing abilities to recognize individual faces (on the basis of internal features) and facial expressions are influenced more by developing cortical visuomotor pathways, some of which were mentioned in chapter 3.

Face-recognition skills may be divided into a number a components, including the ability to recognize a face as such, the ability to recognize the face of a particular individual, the ability to identify facial expressions, and the ability to use the face to interpret and predict the behavior of others. The theory which I put forward with Morton attempted to account for the literature on the first two of these aspects of face processing in infants (Johnson and Morton, 1991; Morton and Johnson, 1991). Two apparently contradictory bodies of evidence emerged from a survey of this literature; while the prevailing view, and most of the evidence, supported the idea that infants gradually learn about the arrangement of features that compose a face over the first few months of life (for reviews, see also Maurer, 1985; Nelson and Ludemann, 1989), the results from at least one study indicated that newborn infants, as young as 10 minutes old, will track a face-like pattern further than various "scrambled" face patterns (Goren et al., 1975). Evidence that newborns showed a preferential response to faces was used by some to bolster nativist views of infant cognition. In contrast, the evidence for the graded development of face-processing abilities over several months tended to be cited by theorists who believed that such skills need to be learned, and result from experience of the world. To translate these views into the framework introduced in chapter 1, while some believed that the brain possesses innate representations of faces, others took the view that face representations resulted from the information structure of the environment.

Since the study with newborn infants remained controversial for methodological reasons, my colleagues and I attempted to replicate it with some minor changes to improve the methodology (Johnson et al., 1991a). As in the original study, newborn infants (this time around 30 minutes old) were required to track different stimuli. The visual tracking procedure used differs markedly from that employed by most other investigators in that the dependent measure is the extent to which the subject turns its head and eyes to keep a moving stimulus in view. This measure contrasts with more standard procedures in which the infant views one or more stimuli in static locations and the length of time spent looking at the stimuli is measured. In the first experiment we conducted, three of the four stimuli used in the original Goren et al. study were used: a schematic face pattern, a symmetric "scrambled" face, and a blank face outline stimulus.

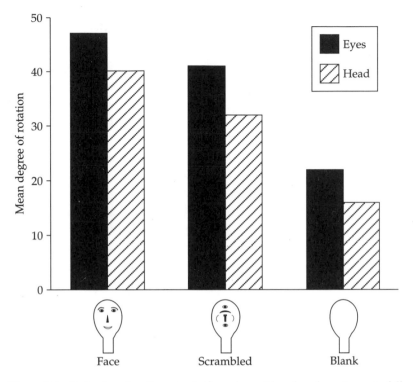

Figure 4.1   Data showing the extent of newborns' head and eye turns in follow-ing a schematic face, a scrambled face, and a blank (unpatterned) stimulus. The infants tracked the face significantly further than the other stimuli by the eyes measure (Johnson and Morton, 1991).

While we were unable to replicate preferential head turning to follow the face pattern, we did successfully replicate the prefer-ential response to the face using a measure of eye movements (see figure 4.1).

This experiment confirmed that the brain of the newborn human infant contains some information about the structure of faces. However, many other studies which used more conven-tional infant testing methods, such as preferential looking, have not found a preference for face patterns over others until 2 or 3 months after birth (for review, see also Maurer, 1985; Nelson and Ludemann, 1989). For example, Maurer and Barrera (1981) used a sensitive "infant control" testing procedure, in which subjects view a series of singly presented static stimuli, and established that while 2-month-olds looked significantly longer at a face-like pattern than at various scrambled face patterns, 1-month-olds had no such preference. Using the same method, Johnson et al., (1992a) replicated this result and extended the original findings by including in the stimulus set the "de-focused" face arrangement stimulus used in the newborn studies earlier. The results replicated entirely the previous findings: the face was looked at longer than any of the other stimuli by 10 week olds, but a group of 5-week-old infants showed no preference. This evidence was consistent with the alternative claim that infants gradually construct representations of faces as a result of repeated exposure to them over the first few months of life (Gibson, 1979). Clearly, these apparently contradictory findings raised a problem for existing theories of the development of face recognition which involved only one process (either learning or innate face representations). In an attempt to interpret this apparently conflicting behavioral data, Johnson and Morton (1991) turned to evidence from two areas of biology: ethology and brain development.

The primary source of evidence from other species (ethology) that Johnson and Morton used to interpret the human infancy results concerned filial imprinting in the domestic chick. Imprinting in chicks was selected because it is well studied both in terms of behavior and in terms of its neural basis. Filial imprinting is the process by which young precocial birds such as chicks recognize and develop an attachment for the first conspicuous object that they see after hatching (for recent reviews, see Johnson and Bolhuis, 1991; Bolhuis, 1991). While imprinting has been reported in the young of a variety of species including spiny mice, guinea pigs, chicks, and ducklings, only in precocial species (those that are mobile from birth) can we measure it using the conventional measure of preferential approach.

4.2 Filial imprinting in chicks

The domestic chick can be thought of as the "laboratory rat" of development (see Andrew, 1991), since it is an ideal species for addressing many developmental questions. For a variety of reasons, chicks are useful to the molecular biologist and geneticist, as well as possessing probably the simplest vertebrate brain to show cognitive abilities of interest to the psychologist such as object recognition (Horn, 1985; Johnson, 1991; O'Reilly and Johnson, 1994). In the laboratory, chicks will imprint onto a variety of objects such as moving colored balls and cylinders. After even a few hours of exposure to such a stimulus, chicks develop strong and robust preferences for the training object over novel stimuli. In the absence of a mother hen, this learning is relatively unconstrained; virtually any conspicuous moving object larger than a matchbox will serve as an imprinting stimulus, and will come to be preferred over any other.

A particular region of the chick forebrain (thought to correspond to mammalian cortex) has been shown to be critical for imprinting, a region known as the intermediate and medial part of the hyperstriatum ventrale (IMHV) (for reviews, see Horn, 1985; Horn and Johnson, 1989). Lesions to IMHV placed before or after training on an object severely impairs preference for that object in subsequent choice tests, but does not affect several other types of visual and learning tasks (McCabe et al., 1982; Johnson and Horn, 1986, 1987). Similar size lesions placed elsewhere in the chick forebrain do not result in significant impairments of imprinting preference (McCabe et al., 1982; Johnson and Horn, 1987).

The next step in analyzing the neural basis of imprinting was to study the microcircuitry of the region involved. Although the bird forebrain lacks the laminar organization of mammalian cortex (but see Karten and Shimizu, 1989), the relation of the forebrain to subcortical structures is similar, following the basic higher vertebrate brain design (chapter 2). Evidence from a variety of vertebrate species supports the suggestion that the avian forebrain is a site of plasticity, and not the location of inbuilt, automatic types of behavior which are located in other structures (MacPhail, 1982; Ewert, 1987).

Figure 4.2 illustrates the location of IMHV within the chick brain. It is worth noting that this region corresponds to, or overlaps with, regions critical for auditory imprinting and song

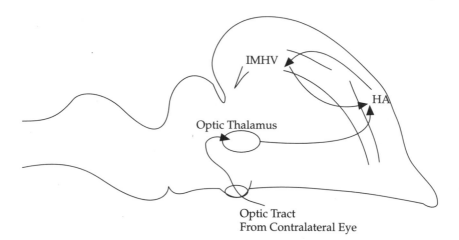

Figure 4.2 Outline sagittal view of the chick brain showing the main visual pathway to IMHV (HA, hyperstriatum accessorium). There are other routes of visual input to IMHV which are not shown in this figure (see Horn, 1985). The brain of a 2-day-old chick is approximately 2 cm long.

learning (e.g. Maier and Scheich, 1983). The area occupies about 5 percent of total forebrain volume. Its main inputs come from visual projection areas (hyperstriatum accessorium and the optic tectum) and some of its projections go to regions of the bird brain thought to be involved in motor control (such as the archistriatum). Thus, the area is well placed to integrate visual inputs and motor outputs.

While regions of the bird forebrain may have analogous functions to the mammalian cerebral cortex (see Horn, 1985), recent cytoarchitectonic studies of IMHV have revealed that it is much simpler in structure. In contrast to the six-layered laminar structure found in the mammalian cerebral cortex, there is no clear laminar structure of IMHV, and, to date, only four distinctive types of cells have been classified (Tombol et al., 1988). Figure 4.3 illustrates the basic intrinsic microcircuit as described by Tombol and colleagues (Tombol et al., 1988).

Without going into the details of the four cell types identified, two of them are classified as projection neurons (PNs), somewhat similar to mammalian pyramidal neurons (although they

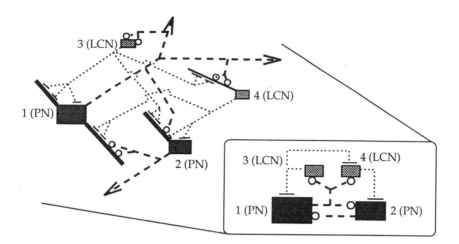

Figure 4.3 Schematic drawing summarizing the circuitry of IMHV at two levels of detail (simplified version in the box). Excitatory contacts are represented by open circles and inhibitory ones by flat bars. Shown are the local circuit inhibitory neurons (LCN) and their reciprocal connectivity with the excitatory principal neurons (PN), and the recurrent excitatory connectivity between the principal neurons. In the detailed diagram, the thick solid lines are dendrites, while the axons are dashed or dotted lines. Both the inhibition and recurrent excitatory connectivity are used in the simplified model to produce hysteresis in the activation state of IMHV (adapted from Tombol et al., 1988).

lack true apical dendrites). These cell types are probably excitatory. These two types of PN cells are interconnected such that they form a characteristic excitatory feedback loop. The other two types of cells observed in the chick IMHV are medium and small local circuit neurons (LCNs). These cell types are probably inhibitory. They receive input from the PNs and project inhibitory input back to them. Since the positive feedback loops involving the PNs can be intrinsically unstable, the LCNs may act to ensure stability in these loops.

After identifying features of the basic microcircuitry of IMHV, the next step was to take a synthetic approach and build a computational model of the circuit concerned (Bateson and Horn, 1994; O'Reilly and Johnson, 1994). In one of these models, Randall O'Reilly and I constructed a connectionist model based on two characteristics of the cytoarchitectonics of IMHV: the existence of positive feedback loops between the excitatory principle neurons, and the extensive inhibitory circuitry mediated by the local circuit neurons. The detailed architecture of the model is shown in figure 4.4.

To simulate the chick being trained by exposure to an object, we trained the model by presenting it with "objects" composed of combinations of features that moved across the input layer. The strength of links (synapses) in the model were adjusted during the training phase according to an associative Hebbian learning rule. The general properties of a learning rule that are important for this model, and most other self-organizing neural network models, such as the model of Miller et al. (1989) described in chapter 3, are that while coactive nodes have their links strengthened, nodes that do not have correlated activation have their links weakened.

Another important feature of the model concerns the degree of hysteresis. Hysteresis is the influence of previous activation states on later ones. The hysteresis in the model caused units that were active for a given position of an "object" to remain active for subsequent positions. In combination with the Hebbian associative learning rule, this resulted in the development of units which would respond to a particular set of features in any of a certain range of different locations, depending on how long that unit was able to remain active. In the top layer of the model the nodes learn to become active to a particular "object" regardless of the spatial location in which it appears. That is, they are location-invariant object detectors.

To get an intuitive sense of how the model works, imagine moving a pen laterally across your visual field. As the pen moves it is still clearly recognizable as a pen. The neural network model learns to "bind" together the features of an object such as a pen by detecting that the same features (the nib, the top, the barrel, of the pen) move together as one in time. Nodes that are able to integrate information over several points in time are able to detect that a particular set of features co-occur, and therefore respond to it anywhere in the visual field.

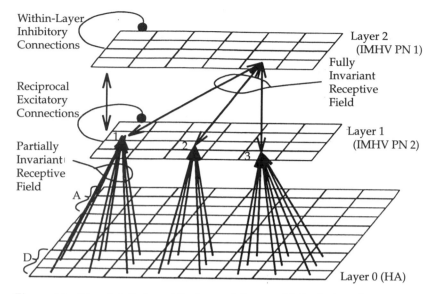

Within-Layer Inhibitory Connections

Reciprocal Excitatory Connections

Partially Invariant Receptive Field

Layer 2 (IMHV PN 1)

Fully Invariant Receptive Field

Layer 1 (IMHV PN 2)

Layer 0 (HA)

Figure 4.4 The detailed architecture of the model is designed around the anatomical connectivity of IMHV and its primary input area, the hyperstriatum accessorium (HA). The model is based on a set of layers, each of which has lateral inhibition within it. The "input" layer of the network, layer 0, represents HA. HA then projects to one subpopulation of IMHV PN cells, which we assume to be type 1 PNs. This is layer 1 of the IMHV component of the model. Note that the laminar distinction in the model between these two component cells of IMHV is not intended to suggest that the cells are arranged as such in the IMHV itself, but rather serves to reflect the functional distinction between the two types of PN. The axons from the type 1 neurons project to the type 2 projection neurons, as well as onto the local inhibitory neurons. This comprises the second layer of the model's "IMHV" component. The type 2 PNs then send a bifurcating axon both back to the type 1 PNs and the inhibitory cells (layer 2), and to other areas, which are not modeled. Within each layer of the model, strong lateral inhibition exists in the form of relatively large negative weights between all units in the layer. This reflects the presence of a large number of GABAergic inhibitory interneurons in IMHV (Tombol et al., 1988), and its relatively low levels of spontaneous activity. The strong inhibition in this layer of the model resulted in only one unit in each layer becoming active at any time.

Using this model, O'Reilly and Johnson (1994) were able to successfully simulate a range of phenomena associated with imprinting in the chick. These included:

- The extent to which an imprinted preference can be "reversed" by exposure to a second object is dependent on a combination of the length of exposure to the first object and the exposure to the second object (for review, see Bolhuis and Bateson, 1990; Bolhuis, 1991). In other words, the sensitive period is self-terminating.
- Exposing a chick, or the network, to two rapidly alternating stimuli results in a preference for a hybrid (combined features) object. Unlike the simulations of reversal experiments just mentioned, with rapidly alternating stimuli nodes in the upper layer of the network become responsive to both objects. The network "blends" the two objects into one.
- Like the chick, the network will generalize from a training object to one that shares some features, such as color or shape. Further, by gradually changing the features of the object, preferences can be shifted even after the termination of the "sensitive period."

In the laboratory, a wide range of objects, such as moving red boxes and blue balls, are as effective for imprinting as more naturalistic stimuli, such as a moving stuffed hen. However, in the wild, precocial birds such as chicks invariably imprint on their mother, and not on other moving objects. These observations raise the question as to what constraints ensure that this plasticity in the chick brain is normally guided to encode information about conspecifics (the mother hen), rather than other objects in its environment.

An answer to this question became evident from the results of a series of experiments in which stimulus-dependent effects of IMHV lesions were observed (Horn and McCabe, 1984). Groups of chicks trained on an artificial stimulus, such as a rotating red box, were severely impaired by IMHV lesions placed either before or after training on an object. However, groups of

Table 4.1   Stimulus-dependent effects of neurophysiological manipulations

Treatment	Hen-trained chicks	Box-trained chicks
Bilateral IMHV lesions	Mild impairment	Severe impairment
DSP4 treatment	Mild impairment	Severe impairment
Plasma testosterone levels	Correlated with preference	No correlation with preference
Multicellular recording in IMHV	No correlation	Correlated

chicks exposed to a stuffed hen were only mildly impaired in their preference. Other neurophysiological manipulations also show differences between the hen-trained and box-trained birds (see table 4.1). For example, administration of the neurotoxin DSP4, which depletes forebrain levels of the neurotransmitter norepinephrine (see chapter 2), resulted in a severe impairment of preference in birds trained on the red box, but only a mild impairment in birds trained on the stuffed hen (Davies et al., 1985). In contrast, plasma levels of the hormone testosterone correlate with preference for the stuffed hen, but not preference for the red box (Bolhuis et al., 1986).

These results led Johnson and Horn (1988) to seek experimental evidence for an earlier suggestion (Hinde, 1961) that naturalistic objects such as hens may be more effective at eliciting attention in young chicks than are other objects. A series of experiments were therefore conducted in which dark-reared chicks were presented with a choice between a stuffed hen and a variety of test stimuli created from cutting up and jumbling the pelt of a stuffed hen. Johnson and Horn (1988) concluded from these experiments that chicks have a untrained tendency, or predisposition, to attend toward features of the head and neck region of the hen. While this untrained preference seemed to be specific to the correct arrangement of features of the face/head, it was not specific to the species. For example, the head of a duck was as attractive as that of a hen.

The results of these and several other experiments led to the proposal that there are two independent brain systems that control filial preference in the chick (Horn, 1985; Johnson et al., 1985). The first of these controls a specific predisposition making newly hatched chicks orient toward objects resembling a mother hen. In contrast to non-specific color and size preferences in the chick (see Johnson and Bolhuis, 1991), this predisposition system appears to be specifically tuned to the correct spatial arrangement of elements of the head and neck region. While the stimulus configuration triggering the predisposition is not species or genus specific, it is sufficient to pick out the mother hen from other objects the chick is likely to be exposed to in the first few days after hatching. Although the neural basis for this predisposition is currently unknown, the optic tectum, the homologue of the mammalian superior colliculus, is one likely candidate.

The second brain system acquires information about the objects to which the young chick attends and is supported by the forebrain region IMHV. In the natural environment, it has been argued, the first brain system guides the second system to acquire information about the closest mother hen. Biochemical, electrophysiological, and lesion evidence all support the conclusion that these two brain systems have largely independent neural substrates (for review, see Horn, 1985). For example, while selective lesions to IMHV impair preferences acquired through exposure to an object, they do not impair the specific predisposition (Johnson and Horn, 1986).

There are, of course, a number of different ways that the predisposition could constrain the information acquired by the IMHV system. For example, the information in the predisposition could act as a sensory "filter" or template through which information had to pass before reaching the IMHV system. This possibility, and a variety of other alternatives, has been rejected on the basis of recent experiments (Bolhuis et al., 1989; Bolhuis and Johnson, 1990; Johnson and Bolhuis, 1991). The evidence available at present is consistent with the view that the two systems influence the preference behavior of the chick independently, i.e. there is no internal informational exchange between them. Instead, it appears that the input to the IMHV system is selected simply as a result of the predisposition biasing the chick to orient toward any hen-like objects in the environment. Given that the species-typical environment of the chick includes a mother hen in close proximity, and that the predisposition includes adequate information to pick the hen out from other objects in the early environment, the input to the learning system will be highly selected.

4.3   Brain development and face recognition

The other source of biological data which Johnson and Morton used to generate an account of human infant face recognition came from the postnatal development of the cerebral cortex. As discussed in chapter 3, both neuroanatomical and neurophysiological data indicate that visually guided behavior in the newborn infant is largely (though not exclusively) controlled by subcortical structures such as the superior colliculus and pulvinar, and that it is not until 2 or 3 months of age that cortical circuitry comes to regulate subcortical circuits. Consistent with these arguments is the position that visually guided behavior in human infants, like that in domestic chicks, is based on activity in two or more distinct brain systems. If these systems have distinct developmental time courses then they may differentially influence behavior in infants of different ages.

There is much evidence that the recognition of individual faces in adults involves cortical structures and pathways. This evidence comes from three main sources: (a) neuropsychological patients with brain damage who are unable to recognize faces (prosopagnosia); (b) neuroimaging studies of face perception; and (c) single and multi-cellular recoding studies with non-human primates. To briefly review this literature, prosopagnosia commonly results from damage to the region of cortex that lies between the temporal and occipital (visual) cortex, although the exact neuro-pathology required is still controversial and may vary between subjects. Some cases have suggested that only a right-hemisphere lesion is necessary, while others suggest bilateral lesions are required (see Farah, 1990, for a review). The deficit resulting from these lesions can be fairly specific. Although prosopagnosic patients have difficulty recognizing individual faces, they some-times do not have agnosia for other objects (i.e. they seem to be able to identify other objects). Of course, exceptions to this have been noted, with some patients having difficulty identifying other complex objects. However, all face processing is not entirely abolished in these patients. For example, some prosopagnosic patients seem to have intact facial emotion processing (e.g. Bruyer et al., 1983), and many show "covert" recognition of familiar faces as indicated by sensitive measures such as galvanic skin responses (Tranel and Damasio, 1985). Evidence from neuroimag-ing studies of human adults has demonstrated the involvement of a number of regions of cortex. For example, in one magneto encephalography (MEG) study, activity in the superior and middle temporal gyrus and at the occipitotemporal junction was detected following presentation of unfamiliar faces (Lu et al., 1991).

Neurons responsive to face stimuli have been found in the tem-poral cortex, and especially the superior temporal sulcus (STS) region, of the macaque cortex by a number of different labor-atories (for review, see Desimone, 1991). Neurons responsive to faces are also found in some other regions of the brain with connections to the temporal cortex such as the amygdala and the frontal cortex. However, they are more common in the temporal region where they can constitute up to 20 percent of visually responsive cells. Many of these cells do not respond to other visually complex stimuli such as food types, and they are often relatively insensitive to changes in the size or spatial frequency composition of faces. Single-unit recording studies in infant macaques indicate a developmental onset of face-sensitive cells in the temporal lobe also at around 2 months of age (Rodman et al., 1993). In adult macaques these face-sensitive cells are known to alter their response properties as a result of training with new faces (e.g. Rolls, 1989), suggesting that they are "tuned" in response to their inputs. The relative importance of exposure to faces over the first few months of life for the establishment of face-sensitive cells in the temporal lobe is currently unknown. However, one important point to note from all of the above cognitive neuroscience studies of face processing is that the specificity of the neural substrate for face processing observed in adults does not imply that these brain circuits are prespecified (de Schonen and Mathivet, 1989; Johnson and Morton, 1991), a point to which I will return later.

Thus, there is considerable evidence for specific cortical involvement in face processing in adults. However, there is also evidence for a face preference in newborn infants whose behavior, as discussed in chapter 3, is thought to be guided largely by subcortical sensorimotor pathways. Consideration of this evidence led Morton and myself to propose a two-process theory of infant face preferences analogous to that in chicks. We argued that the first process consists of a system accessed via the subcortical visuomotor pathway (but possibly also involving some of the deeper, earlier developing, cortical layers) that is responsible for the preferential tracking of faces in newborns. However, the influence of this system over behavior declines (possibly due to inhibition by developing cortical circuits) during the second month of life. The second brain system depends upon cortical maturity, and exposure to faces over the first month or two, and begins to control infant orienting preferences from around 2 or 3 months of age.

By extension with the evidence on chicks, we (Johnson and Morton, 1991) argued that the newborn preferential orienting system biases the input set to developing cortical circuitry. This circuitry is configured in response to a certain range of input, before it starts to gain control over the infant's behavior. Once this occurs, the cortical system has acquired sufficient information about the structure of faces to ensure that it continues to acquire further information about them. As in the chick, the proposal is that a specific, early developing brain circuit acts in concert with the species-typical environment to bias the input to later developing brain circuitry. While this theory is far from proven, a number of strands of evidence are consistent with it. First, let us consider two lines of evidence, in addition to that discussed in chapter 3, that the preferential tracking of faces in newborn infants occurs without full functioning of the cortical face-processing pathways:

- *Its developmental time course.* The preferential tracking of faces declines sharply between 4 and 6 weeks after birth (Johnson et al., 1991a, experiment 3). The time course of this response is similar to that of other newborn responses thought to be mediated by subcortical circuits such as pre-reaching (von Hofsten, 1984). It has been suggested that the disappearance of these early reflex-like behaviors in the second month of life is due to inhibition by developing cortical circuits (see Muir et al., 1989).

- *The testing procedures that elicit it.* Why should visual tracking be sensitive to the face preference of newborn infants, while standard preference test procedures with static stimuli are ineffective? The temporal visual field feeds more into the subcortical (collicular) pathway, while the nasal field feeds mainly into cortical visual pathways. In tracking tasks, the stimulus is continually moving from the nasal into the temporal field of the leading eye. This is especially true of newborns since they tend to make saccades to re-foveate the stimulus, rather than showing smooth tracking. The movement into the temporal field initiates a saccade to re-foveate the stimulus in newborns (for details see chapter 3). This presentation of the stimulus in the temporal field would not arise with static presentations in the central visual field, and therefore I suggest that preferences will rarely be evident. Thus, the tracking task may more effectively tap into the capacities of subcortical structures such as the superior colliculus than the conventional infant testing procedures such as preferential looking at static stimuli. Note that predictions of this account are that (a) static bilateral presentations of stimuli that are spaced far enough apart to impinge on the temporal visual field should also elicit the newborn preference; and (b) if one eye of a newborn is covered, the discriminative response to faces should only be observed in the temporal visual field. Both of these predictions have recently been confirmed (Simion et al., unpublished manuscript; Valenza et al., in press).

Clearly, the above lines of evidence are indirect, and do not bring us any closer to a detailed specification of the neural basis of newborn preferential tracking. Different possibilities remain open, however, including the involvement of superior colliculus, pulvinar, deeper layers of the cortex, or any combination of these. Only direct methods, such as neuroimaging, will enable further progress to be made on this issue.

Turning now to the second system hypothesized by Johnson and Morton (1991), several lines of evidence support the view that these circuits start to influence behavior toward faces from around 2 or 3 months after birth. First, there is evidence, discussed in chapters 2 and 3, from developmental functional neuroanatomy to indicate that many cortical visual pathways have, at best, very impoverished input over the first few months of life. Second, a PET study was conducted on 2-month-old infants scanned for medical reasons (see de Schonen and Mancini, 1995). This study involved the "subtraction" of the activation resulting from a complex dynamic stimulus from that elicited by photographs of the female face. The resulting areas of activation corresponded to those regions activated by face processing in adults. Namely, bilateral activation of the superior and middle temporal gyrus (though the regions activated in infants may be more anterior than those in adults). Despite a low baseline of overall metabolic activity in the frontal lobes (in agreement with the study by Chugani et al., 1987, reviewed in chapter 2), there was a significant increase in activity in left orbito-frontal cortex and Broca's area in the face condition. Similar orbitofrontal cortex and temporal cortex activation has been observed in a PET study with adults by Sargent et al. (1992). The third source of evidence comes from single-cell recording experiments with non-human primates which demonstrate that face-sensitive cells in the STS are only observed in monkeys more than 6 weeks of age (Rodman et al., 1993). Finally, a marker task of cortical face processing, perceiving direction of eye gaze in a face, shows an emergence between 2 and 4 months of age in human infants (Vecera and Johnson, 1995).

Thus, several lines of evidence indicate that the emergence face preferences within the nasal visual field corresponds to the development of cortical face-processing pathways. There are two ways to view this developmental transition. The first is to assume that innate representations for face-processing are enabled as a result of increased input from the visual cortex. The second is that certain cortical circuits are configured as a result of experience with faces. In terms of the framework introduced in chapter 1, we may say that, while the basic architecture of the cortex is established prior to interaction with the external input, the details of synaptic and dendritic contacts are established as a result of the interaction between the basic architecture and the input (in this case, faces). Indeed, one adaptive reason for the delayed developmental input to certain cortical circuits may be the necessity for inputs to shape the microcircuity appropriately. These points can be illustrated more concretely by reference to the chick IMHV discussed above.

The sources of information that constrained the representations (related to recognizing the face of individual members of the species) that emerged in the chick IMHV model were (a) the statistical regularities from the input; (b) the architecture of the network (hysteresis giving rise to spatially invariant object recognition); and (c) the subcortical (tectal in the chick) pathway selecting the appropriate input for developing cortical (forebrain) circuitry. It seems likely that similar, though more complex, constraints will operate on face-specific representations in the primate temporal cortex.

Before leaving the topic of face and individual face recognition, I should note that there is some evidence that infants in the first week of life are able to identify their mother (Pascalis et al.,

1995). At first sight this evidence seems to conflict with the view that cortical face processing does not emerge until at least the second month. However, this discriminative ability in newborns is based only on the general shape of the head and hair, and not on facial configuration or features. De Schonen and Mancini (1995) argue that this "third system" is a non-specific visual pattern learning ability which has also been evident from studies with visual patterns of many other kinds. This early visual recognition memory will be discussed in chapter 5.

Another caveat to the two-process account of the development of face recognition is that additional brain pathways may be involved in identifying facial expressions such as sad and happy. As noted above, the identification of expressions from faces is sometimes intact in prosopagnosic patients despite deficits in other aspects of face processing. In a review of the development and neural basis of the perception of facial expressions, Nelson and de Haan (in press) present evidence that, as well as regions of the temporal lobe, the amygdala has an important role in this ability. They note that physiological and anatomical evidence implies that the amygdala is adult-like between 6 and 12 months postnatal, the same ages at which behavioral studies indicate the development of the ability to identify expressions from faces.

4.4 Social cognition

Brothers and Ring (1992) and others have discussed evidence for a dedicated and encapsulated brain system devoted to processing socially relevant information, such as predicting the behavior of conspecifics, the beliefs of others, and the dynamics of social interactions. In adult primates (including humans), they proposed that this modular social information system involves the limbic system (especially the amygdala and a region of the frontal lobes connected to it, the orbital frontal cortex) and "higher-order association" cortex that feeds into the amygdala (particularly parts of the temporal lobe). Supporting evidence for this view has come from developmental disorders in which this putative social module is either apparently selectively impaired (autism), or, selectively intact amidst otherwise impaired cognition (Williams syndrome).

Autism is a relatively rare developmental disorder (with an incidence of around 5 in 10,000 births). While there is evidence for some genetic contribution to the disorder, there may be several possible genetic disorder "routes" to autism, and there is also clearly an interaction with environmental factors (see Happe and Frith, in press, for review). Most of the core deficits of this developmental disorder lie in the domain of social relations with others, though there are many non-social cognitive deficits as well. Major behavioral symptoms include avoidance of eye contact, an apparent unawareness of the existence and thoughts of others, a reluctance to be held or touched by others, repetitive behaviors such as rocking or hand flapping, and commonly a fascination for certain objects or other inanimate aspects of their environment. Alongside these deviant behaviors are often deficits in other cognitive and language skills, such as echolalia (repeating words and sentences heard previously). A related disorder which shares many of the same symptoms is Asperger syndrome, though these subjects have a normal verbal IQ (Happe, 1994; Pennington and Welsh, 1995).

Many different laboratories have attempted to locate specific brain deficits in autism. Applying the adult neuropsychology model (see the causal epigenesis view in chapter 1), it was initially assumed that there would be a focal structural deficit somewhere in the brain, and that this "hole" in the brain could be associated with a particular pattern of cognitive deficits. As we will see, although developmental deficits can result in seemingly quite specific profiles of cognitive deficit, the corresponding structural damage to the brain can be elusive, diffuse, and/ or inconsistent across different individuals. In the case of autism, structural brain imaging and postmortem neuroanatomical studies have variously implicated the brain stem, cerebellum, limbic system, the thalamus, and the frontal lobes (for review, see Happe and Frith, in press). Several studies have reported enlargement of the ventricals, indicating atrophy in adjacent limbic and frontal structures (for review, see Pennington and Welsh, 1995). However, like several of the brain abnormalities that have been reported in autism, ventricular enlargement is not specific to autism, since it is also observed in schizophrenia.

Another deficit observed in several studies on autism is in the cerebellum (e.g. Courchesne et al., 1988). At present it is unclear whether this is a postnatal effect (recall from chapter 2 that cell migration in this region continues into postnatal life) or whether, as Courchesne et al. (1988) argue, it is caused by abnormal cell migration between 3 and 5 months of gestation. Some evidence for migrational failures in cortex has also been observed, though these do not appear to be restricted to any particular area (Piven et al., 1990). One problem in determining developmental brain damage is that it is difficult to ascertain which abnormalities are the root cause, and which are subsequent consequences of earlier abnormal development. In general, it is likely that structures and areas that develop latest are most likely to be affected by earlier deviations from the normal developmental trajectory. For example, in autism the abnormalities sometimes observed in the cortex, hippocampus, and cerebellum could all possibly be the consequences of a primary deficit in the thalamus.

The latest region of the cortex to show structural changes in postnatal development, the frontal cortex, has been a favorite region of focus for autism and other developmental disorders such as PKU (see chapter 7). While abnormalities in this region may be responsible for some of the cognitive deficits observed, this does not mean that autistic subjects can be equated with patients with acquired prefrontal cortex damage.

While the brain damage that gives rise to autism may be diffuse and variable, the resulting cognitive profile presents a clearer picture. Many social processes observed in infancy appear to be intact in children with autism. However, they show clear deficits in a later developing aspect of social cognition called "theory of mind." Despite its grand title, theory of mind is a relatively basic and essential function for our understanding of, and interactions with, other people. Specifically, theory of mind refers to the ability most of us have to comprehend other people's thought processes, such as their feelings, beliefs, and knowledge. One type of task that can be used to study theory of mind abilities is the so-called "false-belief" task. For example, the following scenario can be demonstrated with dolls, puppets, or human actors (Wimmer and Perner, 1983).

> Sally has a marble that she puts in a basket. Sally then goes away for a walk. While Sally is away, Anne comes in and moves the marble from the basket to a box. The subject viewing this scenario is then asked "When Sally returns, where will she look for her marble?" If the subject simply tries to predict Sally's response on the basis of his/her own personal knowledge, then he or she will answer "the box." If, on the other hand, he or she predicts Sally's response on the basis of Sally's (false) belief, then the subject will correctly predict that Sally will look in the basket for the marble.

Another false-belief scenario involves showing the subject a container that normally holds candy well known to the child (e.g. M&Ms), and asking the child what is in the container. The subject will reply with the name of the appropriate candy. The box is then opened and the child shown that it contains a pencil, and not candy. The child is then told that a friend will come in a moment and be shown the closed container and asked what is in it. The subject is asked what the friend will say. Once again, only if the child can infer the friend's inevitable false belief will he or she reply with the name of the candy rather than a pencil.

Baron-Cohen, Leslie, Frith and their collaborators have shown in a series of studies that most autistic subjects, unlike Downs syndrome, fail these and other theory of mind tasks (for reviews, see Frith, 1989; Happe, 1994; Baron-Cohen, 1995), while they are relatively unimpaired (compared to mental age matched controls) on a variety of related tasks. This pattern of deficit would explain why autistic people often seem to regard others as little different from inanimate objects. Thus, many believe that a deficit in theory of mind is a central cognitive deficit in autism. While there is some agreement on the nature of this cognitive deficit, there are some detailed variants of this view that are currently being tested. Leslie (1987) proposed that the development of theory of mind and symbolic play (which is largely absent in children with autism) are dependent on the maturation of the capacity for "metarepresentation" in the brain around 18 months of age. However, the propositional/symbolic nature of this theory makes it difficult to relate to any neural substrate.

Other theoreticians have proposed more developmental accounts, arguing that a lack of theory of mind arises from deficits in precursors such as the infant's capacity for imitation (Rogers and Pennington, 1991) or the perception of emotion (Hobson, 1993). Thus, these authors believe that a social cognitive deficit from birth, or very shortly thereafter, results in the later deficit of theory of mind. However, whether children subsequently diagnosed as autistic show clear deficits before 18 months of age remains controversial. One recent population study suggests that failure to show pretend play and joint attention at 18 months can predict children diagnosed as autistic at 30 months (Baron-Cohen et al., in press). However, in another study, Johnson et al. (1992c) examined the medical screening records of a small sample of infants subsequently diagnosed with autism. The records of these screening tests included a section on social development. Infants with general developmental delay commonly had problems noted under the categories of motor and cognitive development from the first test (usually 6 months of age). In contrast, the autistic subjects only showed problems under the social category at the 18 months' test or later. Since this study was retrospective and based on a relatively small sample size, further research on this issue is clearly required.

Given the somewhat mixed structural neuroimaging and neuroanatomical evidence, some research teams have tried to use the pattern of cognitive deficits to infer which brain pathways and structures are damaged in autism. Perhaps the most commonly held neuropsychological view is that the pattern of cognitive deficits observed is consistent with damage to the frontal cortex (e.g. Damasio and Maurer, 1978; Pennington and Welsh, 1995). For example, even high functioning autistics fail on a number of "executive function" tasks thought to be markers for frontal lobe functioning, such as the Tower of Hanoi planning task and the Wisconsin card sorting task (Ozonoff et al., 1991). At present it is unclear whether these deficits are primary to those in theory of mind, independent of theory of mind, or dependent on the same underlying computations (see Pennington and Welsh, 1995).

The view that the deficit in theory of mind is one of several cognitive deficits which share common underlying computations is also held by those who argue for the importance of the abnormalities observed in the cerebellum (e.g. Courchesne, 1991). By this view, theory of mind is disrupted because the cerebellum is important for the processing of complex context-dependent sequential information that unfolds over time. It is likely that future studies involving functional neuroimaging will allow the dissociation between these different neuropsychological hypotheses.

In contrast to the specific social deficit seen in autism, Williams syndrome subjects appear to have the putative "social module" intact. Williams syndrome (WS) (also known as infantile hypercalcemia) is a relatively rare disorder of genetic origin effecting approximately 1 in 20,000–50,000 births (Greenberg, 1990). The disorder can now be diagnosed in early infancy through genetic or metabolic markers, and is typified by a number of physical and cognitive characteristics. While WS is genetic in origin, the exact genes and mode of transmission remains controversial. One hypothesis is that there is a defect in the gene involved in production of a modified version of the calcitonin gene-related peptide (CGRP) (Culler et al., 1985). However, the most recent family studies have linked a vascular system defect characteristic of WS to the elastin gene on the long arm of chromosome 7 (Ewart et al., 1993). This defect can either occur through familial transmission or through *de novo* mutation (Bellugi and Morris, in press). The pathway from the genetic abnormality to the characteristic facial dismorphology and neurocognitive profile is unknown, but transient elevation of calcium levels and/or disturbances in the balance of neurotransmitter systems are likely mediators (Bellugi and Morris, in press).

Calcium is crucially involved in a number of aspects of brain plasticity, such as regulation of neurotransmitter release at synapses, and the firing threshold of neurons. Therefore, a transient elevation of calcium during development is likely to alter the emergence of representations within cortex and other regions. Evidence also indicates that elevated calcium levels may delay cell death. It is unknown, however, whether the characteristic decrease in synaptic density observed in normal postnatal development (chapter 2) is also observed in Williams syndrome.

Evidence from structural neuroimaging indicates that WS brains are only about 80–85 percent of the overall volume of normal brains, but there are no obvious gross abnormalities or lesions (Jernigan and Bellugi, 1994). Currently, the only evidence for a specific focus of damage is that they show a relative increase in volume in particular lobules on the cerebellum. This cerebellar abnormality contrasts with autism in which the same lobules are relatively smaller than normal (Jernigan and Bellugi, 1994). At the cytoarchitectonic level, a preliminary analysis by Galaburda et al. (1994) found disturbances within cortical layers and decreased myelinization. Given the lack of evidence for any discrete focal lesions, the specificity of the neurocognitive profile that WS subjects present is striking.

Alongside surprising linguistic abilities (see chapter 6), WS subjects perform as well as controls in a face discrimination task (the Benton test; Bellugi et al., 1992), and better than normal adults on the face recognition component of a standard memory test (the Rivermead Behavioral Memory Test; Udwin and Yule, 1991). This pattern of sparing suggests approximately the opposite of deficits described earlier for autism, and raises the possibility that WS subjects have intact a functional brain system corresponding to a "social module."

One preliminary hypothesis is that the social module remains intact in WS, while being specifically damaged in autism. As discussed earlier, one prominent account of the cognitive deficit in autism is that autistic subjects lack a theory of mind. Karmiloff-Smith and colleagues (1995: 197) carried out a series of experiments with WS subjects to test the hypothesis that there is "a broad cognitive module for representing and processing stimuli relevant to other individuals, including face processing, language, and theory of mind." While only about 20 percent of autistic subjects pass theory of mind tasks such as that described earlier, 94 percent of the WS subjects passed these tasks, indicating that theory of mind is intact alongside aspects of language and face processing. From this result, along with some others, it is tempting to portray WS as showing approximately the opposite neurocognitive profile to autism (while acknowledging that both groups may show some general retardation). This hypothesis is enhanced by the differential cerebellar abnormalities.

However, Karmiloff-Smith et al. (1995) cite evidence from other developmental disorders that is contrary to the simplest view of an impaired or intact prespecified module. For example, in Down syndrome, a serious deficit in face processing and in the use of morphology in language can co-occur with relatively good performance on theory of mind tasks (Baron-Cohen et al., 1985, 1986). Conversely, in a subject with hydrocephalus with associated myelomeningocele, very competent language output coexists with serious deficits in face processing and theory of mind (Cromer, 1992; Karmiloff-Smith, 1992). These different patterns of dissociation clearly challenge the notion of a predetermined social module in the brain.

An alternative view, and that advanced by Karmiloff-Smith and colleagues (1995), is that some degree of modularization is a result of postnatal development, and not a precursor to it (see also chapter 9). Specifically, domain-specific biases in the newborn (such as the face preference discussed earlier in this chapter and the speech discrimination abilities discussed in chapter 6) ensure that cortical circuits are preferentially exposed to socially relevant stimuli like language and faces. With prolonged exposure to such stimuli, plastic cortical circuits develop representations appropriate for processing these inputs, eventually giving rise to an emergent superordinate system for the pragmatics of social interaction in general.

Thus, there is probably not an innate module for social cognition, or innate representations relating to these functions that "mature" in the cortex during postnatal life. Rather, complex representations for processing information about other people, their probable thoughts, and likely future actions, emerge in the brain as a result of at least three sets of factors: initial biases to attend to socially relevant stimuli such as faces and language, complex interactions with other people, and the basic architecture of the cortex and relevant subcortical structures. Abnormalities in any of these factors could send the infant into a deviant path in which only components of normal social cognitive abilities develop.

chapter five

Memory

A distinction has been made between two types of memory: a cognitive, declarative, or explicit form of memory system, and a procedural or habit memory system. An initial hypothesis was that while the latter system was present from birth, the former took longer to develop due its dependency on the development of the limbic system, and particularly the hippocampus. However, recent evidence favors the view that there is (a) a more graded development of explicit memory; and (b) a variety of different implicit learning systems. One recent proposal is that there is a gradual expansion from a hippocampally mediated pre-explicit memory system present shortly after birth, to an "adult" explicit memory system toward the end of the first year of life. The expansion of cortical involvement in the neural basis of explicit memory may be due to an experience-dependent increasing specialization of cortical regions related to the hippocampus. A further similarity with the domains reviewed in other chapters is that several brain systems may be engaged by most memory tasks.

Learning is clearly a fundamental aspect of human cognitive development, and is represented in many of the other chapters in this book, especially with regard to the development of face recognition, object properties, and language acquisition. A number of authors have, however, taken a cognitive neuroscience approach to the development of memory systems that are assumed to be dissociable from the plasticity of developing neural circuitry. This developmental cognitive neuroscience approach to memory faces a number of difficulties:

- Behavioral development in a memory task may be due to the emergence of function in non-memory related brain systems. Further, at the molecular and cellular level, development and learning often share common mechanisms, making the distinction between them sometimes difficult to make.
- It has become clear from behavioral neuroscience and neuropsychological investigations that there are multiple brain systems supporting different types of memory. Even in the adult these various systems have proved difficult to disentangle.
- Some forms of "explicit" memory in human adults involve conscious awareness of information, something that is difficult to ascertain in non-verbal infants.

Despite these difficulties, in this chapter we will see that considerable progress has been made by adopting a cognitive neuroscience approach to the development of memory. As a starting point, most researchers have turned to studies of the neural basis of various memory systems in adults and animals. They have then attempted to develop marker tasks for the functioning of these systems, often speculating that deficits in memory abilities in young infants and children may be due to the differential development of neural systems supporting particular types of memory function.

There have been a number of attempts to characterize a dissociation between two types of memory systems: one of which is variously described as "explicit," "declarative," or "cognitive," and the other of which is "procedural," "implicit," or "habit" memory. While there are some differences in the exact definitions of these terms, the same data are often used to dissociate the two putative systems (see Janowsky, 1993, for review). Explicit, declarative, or cognitive memory refers to memory that can be brought to mind as an image or proposition, whereas implicit or procedural memory refers to memory that is embedded in a skill or procedure and of which the subject is not consciously aware (Squire, 1986). One source of data that provides the impetus for this dissociation comes from the much-studied neuropsychological patient called H.M. H.M. had the anterior

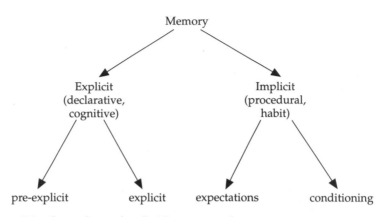

Figure 5.1   One scheme for dividing types of memory.

part of both his temporal lobes (including the hippocampus and amygdala) removed to cure severe seizures. While the seizures were much reduced by this operation, he suffers from a severe memory impairment in which he is unable to form new explicit or declarative memories, while being relatively unimpaired in procedural or implicit memory tasks (Scoville and Milner, 1957; Squire, 1986). Thus, memory for information which involves conscious recall or recognition of previously learned material requires the limbic temporal lobe including hippocampus. These structures are not essential for information acquired through skilled motor activity. This commonly accepted dissociation into two systems is sometimes subdivided further. Figure 5.1 shows one possible classification of memory systems, based on the analysis of Nelson (1995), which I will use to structure this review.

One of the first cognitive neuroscience hypotheses about memory development was put forward by Schacter and Moscovitch (1984) who speculated that the brain mechanisms necessary for the long-term storage of information, most probably in the limbic system, are not functional for the first year or two of life. A related hypothesis was put forward by Bachevalier and Mishkin (1984), who pointed out similarities between the amnesic syndrome, in which limbic system damage in adults results in deficits in recognition memory but no deficits in learning stimulus–response "habits", and the profile of memory abilities in infants. Mishkin and colleagues had earlier demonstrated that a similar pattern of deficits to that observed in human amnesic syndrome patients could be seen in adult monkeys following surgical lesions to portions of the limbic system. These observations led to the proposal that infant memory abilities reflected the more delayed postnatal maturation of limbic circuits.

To test the hypothesis that the putative "cognitive memory" and "habit" systems show a different ontogenetic timetable, Bachevalier and Mishkin (1984) tested infant monkeys aged 3, 6, and 12 months on two types of tasks. The first task was a visual recognition task that involved the infant monkey learning to identify the novel object of a pair following the earlier presentation of the familiar one (delayed non-match to sample: DNMS). This task was thought to require a "cognitive memory" system. In the second task, a visual discrimination habit task, the infant monkey was sequentially exposed to 20 pairs of objects every day. Every day the same object of each pair was baited with a food reward, even though their relative positions were varied. The monkeys had to learn to displace the correct object in each pair.

Infant monkeys failed to learn the "cognitive memory" task until they were approximately 4 months old, and did not reach adult levels of proficiency even by the end of the first year. In contrast, infant monkeys of 3 or 4 months old were able to learn the visual "habit" as easily as adults. Bachevalier and Mishkin (1984) suggested that this dissociation in memory abilities in infant monkeys is due to the prolonged postnatal development of the limbic system delaying the ability of recognition and associative ("cognitive") memory relative to sensorimotor habit formation. This explanation could be extended to human infants since they are also unable to acquire the delayed non-match-to-sample task in early infancy (until around 15 months), and still have not reached adult levels of performance at 6 years old (Overman et al., 1992).

More recent evidence from both cognitive and neuroscience studies has indicated that this initial two systems view of the ontogeny of memory is not sufficient to explain the data. The cognitive evidence comes from studies indicating that human infants can recall experiences from the first year of life several years later (for review, see Rovee-Collier, 1993). These findings suggest some continuity of memory mechanisms from early infancy to later life. Further, other behavioral experiments on memory processes in infants suggest that differences between infant and adult memory processes are quantitative (retrieval time, memory span) rather than qualitative (see Rovee-Collier, 1993). Thus, at least some prominent researchers believe that there is not a transition from one form of memory to another during infancy, but rather just a change in the characteristics of memory storage.

Another issue is that human infants are successful at the DNMS task at much younger ages if the response required is for the subject to merely *look* at the novel stimulus, rather than manually displacing it (to obtain the reward). This suggests that the standard manual version of DNMS requires some additional ability, such as the ability to inhibit a previously rewarded action (Diamond, 1991). Consequently, other tasks which tap into "cognitive" or "explicit" memory need to be studied in infants.

Even more damaging for Bachevalier and Mishkin's original hypothesis is evidence that lesions to the limbic system impair recognition memory abilities in infant monkeys in the first month of life (Bachevalier et al., 1993), indicating that even from this early age the limbic system plays some role in memory processes. Bachevalier and colleagues measured recognition memory by a paired comparison preferential looking task similar to one used with human infants. In this task the subject is shown an object for 30 seconds. After a short delay, the subject is presented with a pair of objects, one of which is novel, and the extent of looking at each of the objects is recorded. Between 15 and 30 days of age, normal infant rhesus monkeys develop a strong preference for looking toward the novel stimulus, indicating recognition of the familiar one. This preference was not found in monkeys that received medial temporal lobe lesions, including the hippocampus, in early infancy. These surprising results suggest that limbic structures make a significant contribution to visual recognition memory even at this very early age, and that other neurocognitive systems that mature more slowly may be responsible for the developments in memory ability observed in other tasks. More recent studies have indicated that damage to the hippocampus itself, rather than the related cortex (area TE), is responsible for the deficit in novelty preference in infant monkeys.

To summarize so far, the original two systems view argued that deficiencies in infants' memory was due to the lack of a cognitive or explicit memory system mediated by the limbic/hippocampal system. However, this account is not adequate for the following reasons:

1   Cognitive evidence suggests that the development of memory involves the graded increase of existing systems, rather than the maturation of independent systems (implying that memory development entails overlapping as opposed to dissociable systems).
2   When direction of looking rather than a manual reaching measure is used, there is evidence of a form of explicit memory from shortly after birth.
3   The hippocampus seems to play a role in this form of explicit memory from shortly after birth.

After reviewing much of this literature, Nelson (1995) proposes that there are more than two types of memory system that develop from infancy (see figure 5.1). Further, he views the development of some memory systems in terms of the expansion of a neural system to include additional structures and capacities, as opposed to the *de novo* appearance of a new system(s) dissociable from others. The systems outlined by Nelson (1995) are as follows:

• An implicit memory system involved in visual expectations, such as the tasks described in chapter 3 by Haith and colleagues (1988). This type of procedural memory is dependent on the striatum, and not the temporal lobe or cerebellum. Visual expectancies can readily be elicited from the human infant by around 3 months of age.

- An implicit memory system involved in tasks that require conditioning, such as the contingent leg-kicking response studied by Rovee-Collier (1993) and colleagues. Nelson suggests that this system may depend on the cerebellum and deep nuclei of the brain stem, and possibly also the hippocampus, in tasks that require retrieval or visual recognition. Evidence suggests that conditioning can be acquired by 3 months of age in the human infant.

- A pre-explicit memory system which is responsible for infants showing novelty preferences in paired comparison tests with short delays. Nelson suggests that the hippocampus is critical for this behavior, and that it is present from birth or shortly thereafter.

- An explicit memory system which is involved in a variety of tasks involving recognition memory, the coordination of information across different sensory modalities, and the generation of action schemes based on prior information. This memory system involves an expansion of the neural substrate of the pre-explicit memory system with the additional involvement of the entorhinal cortex, and inferior temporal cortex (e.g. area TE). This "adult" form of explicit memory becomes functional around the end of the first year of life.

- A working memory system which starts to develop between 6 and 12 months of age, but which may show a more protracted development throughout childhood. The dorsolateral prefrontal cortex is a critical component of the neural substrate for this form of memory, and it is discussed further in chapter 7.

The proposal that there is a graded development from a pre-explicit to an "adult" explicit memory system can account for most of the findings that are discrepant with the original two-process account in the following ways. The notion of the expanding involvement of brain structures in explicit memory is more consistent with the cognitive data implying a graded change in memory abilities, rather than the emergence of a dissociable new system(s). Nelson's graded account of the development of an explicit memory system implies that successful performance on looking versions of the DNMS task can be obtained from infants in the first few months of life due to the pre-explicit memory system being able to support novelty preference when no action planning (reaching) is required.

Between 8 and 18 months of age infants become able to perform reaching versions of DNMS and other tasks that serve as markers for explicit or cognitive memory. This form of "explicit" memory is dependent upon adequate development of the hippocampus and also related cortical areas, such as area TE. However, apparently successful performance can be elicited from infants younger than 8 months in tasks that depend solely on them showing a novelty preference, and do not require them to dissociate how often events were presented or do not involve a delay before the response is required. Nelson (1995) hypothesizes that this "pre-explicit" memory requires only the functioning of the hippocampus, and not related temporal cortex structures. Around 8 months of age the development of temporal cortical areas, or their integration with the hippocampus, correlates with a transition from pre-explicit to explicit memory.

In the explicit memory tasks, as outlined above, infants have been observed in tasks which are close analogs of the monkey and adult tasks. In contrast, with the implicit forms of memory, there has been little attempt to develop marker tasks for infants that closely correspond to tasks used with animals, neuropsychological patients, or functional brain imaging. Despite this, Nelson (1995) has suggested some similarities between types of learning that have been studied in infants, and cognitive neuroscience tasks. For example, the visual expectancies paradigm studied by Haith and colleagues (1988) (in which infants of 3 months and older start to anticipate the location of the next target in a fixed sequence) resembles some sequence learning tasks which may involve the striatum. While there is little evidence on the development of human striatum, it seems likely from the PET studies of Chugani et al. (1987, see chapter 2) that this structure is functional by around birth. A further constraint on the emergence of sequence learning abilities, however, may be the control of eye movements by the frontal eye fields (see chapter 3).

Another example of a form of implicit learning present from early infancy is contingent leg-kicking (Rovee-Collier, 1993). In this procedure infants lie on their backs and watch a mobile suspended above them. A ribbon is attached to the mobile at one end and to one of the infant's legs at the other. Thus, by kicking the relevant leg the infant can animate the mobile. Infants as young as 3 months will readily learn to associate their leg movement with the movement of the mobile, and will increase their leg movement to well above baseline levels. The infant is then removed from the test situation. After a time interval (which, in different studies, varies from minutes to weeks) the infant is returned to the experiment. When returned to the test a variety of things can be varied such as the nature of the mobile, the context of the crib etc. In many of the variants of this procedure, young infants show evidence of learning retained over periods of weeks.

Nelson suggests that a possible analogy to contingent leg-kicking in infants is the instrumentally conditioned limb flexion response in which animals learn to flex their legs when a tone predicts a shock. Lesions to parts of the cerebellum disrupt this form of learning, suggesting that the same brain structure may be critical for contingent leg-kicking in infants. However, the additional complexities of the infant leg-kicking task, such as the need to recognize the mobile and task context, make it likely that other memory circuits will be engaged. While further research is needed, some PET and myelinization evidence indicates that the human cerebellum approximates its adult state shortly after birth (see Nelson, 1995). The early development of this structure may also be responsible for the fact that between 10 and 30 days the human infant starts to show the conditioned eyeblink response (see Lipsitt, 1990).

Some of the memory systems discussed in this chapter can also be studied using event-related potentials (ERPs, see chapter 1).

Several laboratories have conducted ERP studies with infants using habituation paradigms (in which the subject is familiarized by repeated presentations of one stimulus prior to the introduction of a novel stimulus) and related paradigms, such as the "oddball" paradigm (in which an infrequent novel stimulus appears amidst repeated exposures to a familiar one). In a review of this literature, Nelson (1994) draws the conclusion that there are three major components of the ERP signal which emerge as important in these studies. These three components probably reflect distinct cognitive processes with different neural bases.

When infants are presented with a visual stimulus, even when it is repeated many times, a well-defined negative component of the ERP is observed. This negative component occurs regardless of whether the stimulus is familiar or novel, and Nelson (1994) suggests that it probably reflects an attentional process (and may be related to the N400 linked to attention in older subjects). A variable that influences the latency of this negative component is the age of the subjects; it has a longer latency in younger infants (around 800 ms after stimulus onset in 4 month olds) than in older infants (around 400 ms in 12 month olds).

Following this negative peak, there is often a sustained negative slow wave which Nelson suggests reflects the detection of novel stimuli. It generally occurs when an unfamiliar stimulus is detected after a sequence of familiar ones. In contrast, when a familiar stimulus is repeated, the initial negative peak discussed above quickly returns to baseline. This peak may reflect "attention load" (Nelson, personal communication, 13 September 1995). The third component is a late positive component that may be invoked by stimuli that are only partially encoded and require further processing or updating. In 6–8-month-olds it can be invoked by novel or rarely encountered stimuli (see Nelson and Collins, 1992). This component has not been observed in infants under 6 months. This wave may be related in some respects to the P300 observed in adults and suggested to mark the updating of working memory.

While these components of ERPs in infants have not been related to particular brain structures, Nelson (personal communication

1995) speculates that the late positive component may be due to medial temporal lobe activity. Possibly the emergence of this component of the ERP corresponds to development of cortical regions related to the hippocampus (such as area TE), and the transition from "pre-explicit" to explicit memory systems.

From the discussion above it is evident that most memory tasks likely engage multiple memory systems, in a similar way to the partially independent brain pathways that are engaged in eye-movement control and attention shifts. A lack of maturity in one or other pathway may be masked in some tasks due to compensatory activity in other pathways. Possibly it is the extent of integration between different memory pathways that is the most significant change with postnatal development. If this is the case, it is not until we have a more integrative account of the relations between different brain memory pathways that we will be able to make sense of the developmental data.

In summary, it is clear that several types of procedural or habit memory, probably dependent on subcortical structures such as the cerebellum and hippocampus, are present from birth or shortly thereafter. There are currently few marker tasks which allow the direct comparison of cognitive neuroscience data to developmental findings, but this seems a promising area for future research. While there is some capacity for explicit memory in the newborn, this expands over the first year of life. At the neural level, this expansion may involve regions of the temporal cortex becoming coordinated with the hippocampus, possibly through a process of input-dependent increasing specialization. This graded development of explicit memory may be able to account for some of the previously discrepant findings in the field.

chapter six

Speech Recognition and Language

This chapter starts with the question of whether language is "biologically special." This issue refers to the extent to which the human infant's brain is predisposed to learn about language. In other words, does a region(s) of the cortex have innate representations for language, or are language representations the emergent result of a variety of constraints? A number of cognitive neuroscience approaches to this question are outlined. First, studies from early brain damage indicate that several regions of cortex are capable of supporting nearly normal language acquisition. Second, ERP studies with deaf subjects show that regions which normally support oral language can support other functions. While these two lines of evidence indicate that there are no innate language representations in the cortex, there is ERP evidence that some regions of cortex (left temporal lobe) may be particularly efficient at processing speech input from the first few months of life. Some have suggested that the ability to process the rapid temporal transitions that discriminate phonemes may be essential for normal language acquisition. In addition to the ERP work with neonates, children with specific language delay show deficits in rapid temporal processing. It has been hypothesized that in some cases this may lead to reading problems similar to those observed in dyslexia. Finally, a number of neural correlates of stages of normal language acquisition are outlined. In some developmental disorders, such as Williams syndrome, language can be relatively spared compared to other domains of cognition. While these apparent dissociations have sometimes been characterized as evidence for an "innate language module," they are also consistent with a more probabilistic epigenetic view.

6.1   Introduction

Several approaches have been taken to studying the neural correlates of language acquisition in the human infant. A general problem with this area of research in developmental cognitive neuroscience is that it is not possible to use animal models to study an aspect of cognition unique to humans (although some work on speech perception has been done with other species, such as the chinchilla, and work on song learning in birds may have some parallels, e.g. Marler, 1991). However, various other approaches have been taken, such as ERP studies, studies of infants with focal brain damage, studies of congenital abnormalities, and correlations between phases of language acquisition and neuroanatomical development. An implicit or explicit motivating question for many researchers in this field has been the extent to which language is "biologically special." This issue refers to the extent to which the human infant is predisposed to learn about language. To translate this question into the framework presented in chapter 1, does a region of the cortex have innate representations for language, or are language representations the emergent result of a variety of constraints?

Two cognitive neuroscience approaches to this question have been pursued. The first of these has been to investigate whether there are particular parts of the cortex critical for language processing or acquisition. If particular parts of the cortex are critical for language, it may be assumed that this region(s) contains innate language-specific representations. At the cellular level, this may be implemented as the specific prespecification of microcircuits and patterns of synaptic connectivity. In contrast, if several regions of cortex can support language acquisition this suggests that the representations involved will emerge given the combination of language input and basic cortical architecture. The second cognitive neuroscience approach I will discuss concerns the attempt to identify neural correlates of language-related processing abilities very early in life. I start by reviewing evidence relevant to the first approach.

6.2 Are some parts of cortex critical for language acquisition?

Language acquisition has become a focal point for studies designed to investigate the extent to which particular cortical areas are prespecified to support specific functions. Two complementary directions have been taken, with one set of studies examining the extent to which language functions can be supported by other regions of the cortex, and another group of studies concerned with whether other functions can "occupy" regions that normally support language. The first of these lines of research has asked whether children suffering from perinatal lesions to "language areas" can still acquire language. The second line of research has involved testing congenitally deaf children to see what functions occupy regions of cortex which are normally (spoken) language areas, and also by studying the consequences of brain damage on the ability to produce sign language.

If particular cortical regions are uniquely prespecified to support language then it is reasonable to assume that early damage to such regions will impair the acquisition of language. This implicit hypothesis has motivated a large body of research, the conclusions of which still remain somewhat controversial. In an influential book, Lenneberg (1967) argued persuasively that if localized left hemisphere damage occurred early in life it had little or no effect on subsequent language acquisition. This contrasted both with the effect of similar lesions in adults or older children, and to several congenital abnormalities in which language is delayed or never emerges (see chapter 4). Lenneberg's view lost adherents in the 1970s, as evidence accumulated from studies of children with hemispherectomies suggesting that left hemisphere removal always leads to selective subtle deficits in language, especially for syntactic and phonological tasks (e.g. Dennis and Whitaker, 1976). Similar results were also reported for children with early focal brain injury due to strokes (Vargha-Khadem et al., 1994). These findings were compatible with studies of normal infants showing a left hemisphere bias at birth in processing speech and other complex sounds (Molfese, 1989), and led some researchers to the conclusion that functional asymmetries for language in the human brain are established at birth, and cannot be reversed. Unfortunately, some of the secondary sources that summarized the work on hemispherectomies and/or early focal injury failed to note that the deficits shown by these children are far more subtle than the frank aphasias displayed by adults with homologous forms of brain damage (see Bishop, 1983, for a critique of the Dennis and Whitaker, 1976 study). Indeed, most of the children with left hemisphere injury that have been studied to date fall within the normal range (Stiles and Thal, 1993), and those that fall outside the normal range often have complications in addition to their focal brain injury.

While most studies to date have involved assessing language competence in children that acquired perinatal lesions many years beforehand, Stiles and her colleagues have recently carried out *prospective* studies of language and spatial cognition in children who have suffered a single unilateral injury to either the right or the left hemisphere, prenatally or before 6 months of life, confirmed by at least one radiological technique (Stiles and Thal, 1993). Children in these studies are identified prior to the onset of measurable language skills and were examined longitudinally. This team has now studied more than 20 cases between 8 and 31 months of age, all with unilateral lesions which occurred prenatally or before 6 months of age (i.e. before language development would normally begin). Regardless of the lesion site, infants with focal brain lesions were delayed suggesting, not surprisingly, that there is a general non-specific cost to early brain injury. However, the prospective study of these infants also produced a number of rather surprising results. Based on the adult aphasia literature, delays in word comprehension would be expected to be most severe in children with damage to left posterior sites. In contrast to this, it appears that comprehension deficits are actually more common in the right hemisphere infant group. This deficit is rarely reported in adults with right hemisphere damage. This and other findings lead these authors to suggest that the regions responsible for language learning are not necessarily the regions responsible for language use and maintenance in the adult (Bates, 1994).

Another complicating factor revealed by prospective studies of focal lesion infants comes from a recent study of language production by Reilly et al. (in press). This study used the same population of pre- or perinatal lesions just discussed. Reilly and colleagues looked at many different aspects of lexical, grammatical, and discourse structure in a storytelling task, in focal lesion children, and normal controls between 3 and 8 years of age. In this study (like many others within this age range), there were no significant differences between the left and right hemisphere groups on any of the language measures. However, the focal lesion sample as a whole performed worse than normal controls on several measures of morphology, syntax, and narrative structure. Each of these disadvantages appears to resolve over time in the focal lesion group, but each time the child moves on to the next level of development (in language acquisition), differences between the focal lesion infants and normals reappear. Thus, functional recovery does not appear to be a one-off event, but rather may re-occur at several critical points during acquisition.

To summarize, the effects of early focal lesions on language acquisition are complex. However, in general the evidence supports the following conclusions:

1   While regions of the left temporal lobe may be best suited to language processing, they are not critical since language can develop in a close to normal way without this region (Bates, 1994).
2   Focal pre- and perinatal lesions often cause delay in language acquisition regardless of the site of the lesion.
3   Different regions of the cortex may be involved in the acquisition of language from those which are important for language in adults.
4   Functional compensation may have to re-occur at several points in language acquisition, and is not a one-off event.

Another approach to studying the extent to which the cortical areas supporting language are prespecified is to see whether other functions can occupy the cortical regions that normally support aspects of language. Such experiments would be analogous in logic to the neurobiological studies mentioned in chapter 2 in which input to a developing region of cortex was "re-wired" such that representations generated from a new sensory modality were produced.

Neville and colleagues (see Neville, 1991, for review) have used ERPs (chapter 2) to examine cortical plasticity related to intersensory competition. Evidence from visual and spatial tasks in deaf subjects suggests that visual processing in the cortex is different among subjects reared in the absence of auditory input. Specifically, the congenitally deaf seem more sensitive to events in the peripheral visual field than are hearing subjects. ERPs recorded over classical auditory regions, such as portions of the temporal lobe, are two or three times larger for deaf than for hearing subjects following peripheral visual field stimulation. Thus, the lack of auditory input has resulted in a normally auditory area becoming at least partially allocated to visual functions.

Thus, the evidence described so far indicates that regions of the cortex are not prespecified for language processing, and that other functions may be able to "capture" areas that normally end up processing language. However, it is still possible that small variations on the basic architecture of the cortex may be sufficient to "attract" language processing to some regions during normal functional brain development. For example, one possibility is that some regions, such as the left temporal lobe, may be most suited for processing the rapid temporal information that is necessary for language.

Some evidence for this view comes from studies of deaf signers with acquired focal brain lesions. After reviewing evidence that sign language has many of the same formal properties as spoken languages, Bellugi et al. (1989) found that deaf signers with adult-acquired left hemisphere lesions are aphasic in sign language, while showing intact performance on several other visuospatial tasks. Adult patients with recently acquired right hemisphere lesions, on the other hand, showed the reciprocal pattern of performance. In this latter group, signing was fluent even to the extent of being able to sign fluently about the contents of their room while showing gross spatial distortion in their description of its contents! This, and other evidence, led Bellugi and colleagues to propose that it is the computations required for linguistic processing, rather than its modality, that determines cortical localization.

6.3 Neural correlates of speech processing

The second general approach to investigating the extent to which language is "biologically special" involves attempting to identify language-relevant processes in the brains of very young infants. A further question then concerns how specific to language these correlates are. The implicit reasoning here is that, if there are specific neural correlates of language observable very early in life, this may indicate language-specific neural processing prior to significant experience.

One example of this approach concerns the ability to discriminate speech-relevant sounds such as phonemes. Behavioral experiments have revealed that young infants show enhanced (categorical) discrimination at phonetic boundaries used in speech such as /ba/ /pa/. These observations initially caused excitement as evidence for a language-specific detection mechanism in humans. That is, a graded phonetic transition from /ba/ to /pa/ is perceived as a sudden categorical shift by infants. However, over the past decade it has become clear that other species, such as chinchillas, show similar acoustical discrimination abilities, indicating that this ability may merely reflect general characteristics of the mammalian auditory processing system, and not an initial spoken language-specific mechanism (see Kuhl, 1993). In human infants, however, Werker and Polka (1993) have reported that, while young infants can discriminate a very wide range of phonetic constructs, including those not found in the native language (e.g. Japanese infants, but not Japanese adults, can discriminate between "r" and "l" sounds), this ability becomes restricted to the phonetic constructs of the native language around 12 months of age.

If brain correlates of this process could be identified, it may be possible to study the mechanisms underlying this language-specific selective loss of sensitivity. As mentioned earlier, ERPs offer an excellent opportunity to study the neural correlates of cognition in normal infants in a relatively non-invasive manner. This excellent temporal resolution of ERPs can be complemented by some spatial resolution through the use of high-density ERPs (HD-ERP). When components of ERP differ in both latency (following the event) and spatial resolution, we may be confident that different neural circuitry is being activated. An example of this approach comes from a recent HD-ERP study of phonetic discrimination in 3-month-old infants.

Dehaene-Lambertz and Dehaene (1994) presented their subjects with trials in which a series of four identical syllables (the standard) was followed by a fifth that was either identical or phonetically different (deviant). They time locked the ERP to the onset of the syllable and observed two peaks with different scalp locations (see figure 6.1). The first peak occurred around 220 ms after stimulus onset and did not habituate to repeated presentations (except after the first presentation) or dishabituate to the novel syllable. Thus the generators of this peak, probably primary and secondary auditory areas in the temporal lobe, did not appear to be sensitive to the subtle acoustical differences that encoded phonetic information.

The second peak reached is maximum around 390 ms after stimulus onset and again did not habituate to repetitions of the same syllable, except after the first presentation. However, when the deviant syllable was introduced the peak recovered to at least its original level. Thus, the neural generators of the second peak, also in the temporal lobe but in a distinct and more posterior location, are sensitive to phonetic information. Further studies need to be done to see if the recovery of the second peak is due to the categorical perception of phonemes, or whether it

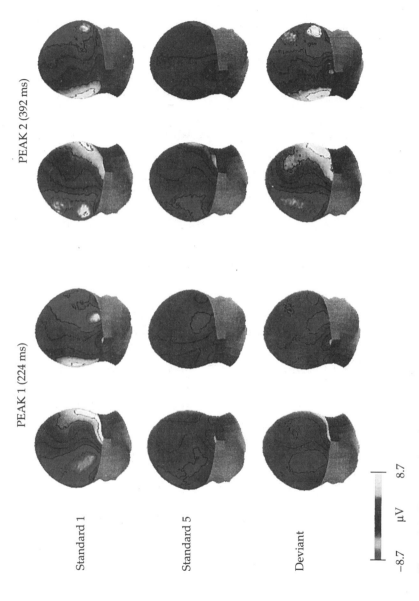

PEAK 1 (224 ms)   PEAK 2 (392 ms)

Standard 1

Standard 5

Deviant

−8.7   µV   8.7

Figure 6.1   Topography of evoked potentials at the maximum of peak 1 and peak 2. Graphics show voltages as measured on the scalp surface.

would be elicited by any acoustical change. A later peak was observed over frontal regions following the deviant stimuli, a finding common to many paradigms with unexpected auditory or visual stimuli. This peak probably represents detection of novelty regardless of the input modality and, as discussed earlier, may reflect the updating of working memory.

While this study must necessarily be regarded as a preliminary analysis of the neural mechanisms underlying speech discrimination and processing by young infants, it has opened up a number of intriguing avenues for further research. As mentioned earlier, infants' discrimination of phonetic constructs becomes restricted to the phonetic constructs of the native language around 12 months of age. Examining which, if any, of the three peaks observed by Dehaene-Lambertz and Dehaene (1994) declined with the loss of discrimination would be informative (see Christophe and Morton, 1994).

As discussed earlier, the left temporal lobe may be particularly adept at the rapid temporal information necessary for phonemic discrimination and normal language acquisition. Tallal and colleagues have argued that children with oral language delay often have deficits in the perception and discrimination of rapidly changing acoustic information (e.g. Tallal, 1980; Tallal et al., 1980). The inability to discriminate some phonemes with rapid temporal transitions, such as "ba" and "da", may have consequences for oral speech recognition. Recently, Tallal, Merzenich and colleagues have produced preliminary evidence that the inability to process rapid temporal transitions in children with specific language delay can be rectified by training with adapted speech in which the temporal transitions are extended (Merzenich et al., 1996; Tallal et al., 1996). Whether such remediation can be successfully extended to a wider range of language and reading disorders remains to be seen. However, some reports have indicated that children with language delay sometimes develop reading problems symptomatic of some types of dyslexia.

Dyslexia was perhaps the first developmental disorder to be associated with a particular underlying neural abnormality. In 1907 Hinshelwood postulated that it was a developmental version of alexia (failure to recognize words) and associated it with abnormality of the left angular gyrus of the cortex (Hinshelwood, 1907). Key symptoms of dyslexia are difficulties in learning to read and spell, with letter and number reversals, and unusual errors. These correlated deficits (such as in naming, and verbal short-term memory) are thought to be due to primary cognitive deficit in the phonological coding of written language. There is both structural and physiological evidence from the brains of dyslexics consistent with Hinshelwood's original proposal that developmental abnormalities in the left hemisphere are important.

The structural evidence comes from the work of Galaburda and colleagues (e.g. Galaburda et al., 1985) who conducted autopsies on the brains of several dyslexic individuals. They observed symmetry (between the right and left side) of a particular part of the temporal lobe of the cortex, the planum temporale. This region is part of the so-called Wernicke's area, which has been implicated in phonological processing. Galaburda and colleagues also observed malformations in the clustering of neurons in this region, and to a lesser extent elsewhere in the cortex of these individuals. These cellular abnormalities are not evident in structural MRI or CT scanning, making the point that developmental abnormalities at the cellular or molecular level will not always be evident in terms of gross brain structure.

Turning to functional studies of the brain of this subject group, Wood et al. (1991) described studies from blood flow, PET, and scalp-recorded evoked responses. Consistent with the postmortem studies, they concluded that dyslexics showed abnormal processing in the left temporal lobe in both phonemic discrimination and orthographic tasks. Recently, a functional PET study on five adults with dyslexia was conducted by Paulesu and colleagues (Paulesu et al., in press). A rhyming task and a short-term memory task for visually presented letters were used to compare brain activity in these subjects to subjects with no difficulties in phonological processing. The results showed that only a subset of the regions normally active during these tasks were activated in the dyslexics. Specifically, Broca's area and

Wernicke's area were never activated in concert as is normal. In addition, the left insula was never activated. The authors suggested that the insula normally provides a link between left anterior and posterior speech areas, which may be absent or impaired in dyslexics.

The above studies are all consistent with involvement of regions of the left hemisphere around the temporal lobe in both phonemic discrimination and dyslexia. However, it is important to stress that there is considerable controversy about the exact nature of the cognitive deficits observed in dyslexia (e.g. Pennington and Welsh, 1995) and that there is also evidence for abnormalities elsewhere in the brain (e.g. Livingstone et al., 1991). Further, the putative involvement of the left temporal lobe in this disorder need not be interpreted in terms of a causal epigenesis pathway. It is tempting to infer that a neural deficit or abnormality in the left temporal lobe gives rise to a failure to process the rapid temporal transitions necessary for phonemic discrimination, and that in some cases this might be related to subtypes of dyslexia. However, the evidence on cortical development and plasticity discussed in chapter 2, and the apparent initial success of the training studies by Tallal, Merzenich, and colleagues, suggests a more probabilistic epigenetic view.

Roughly speaking, this view is that the left temporal lobe is engaged by inputs which require rapid temporal processing due to having a detailed architecture slightly different from the basic structure common to the cortex. This makes this region the most efficient, but not the only possible, "home" for speech processing. If this region is damaged, other parts of cortex can also support these representations, though perhaps not quite so efficiently. Processing speech within this region influences its synaptic and dendritic microstructure through some of the mechanisms discussed in chapter 2. Through interaction with a certain type of input, it thus becomes increasingly specialized and differentiated from other regions. Some degree of plasticity may remain during development, resulting in a reconfiguration of the microcircuitry of the region following specific training. Differences in neural structure between this region in adult dyslexics and "normals" would reflect this deviant developmental pathway, much of which may have occurred postnatally. Thus, a slight initial bias can be compounded through development into greater anatomical and functional specialization and deviation from the norm.

6.4 Neural correlates of normal and abnormal language acquisition

Bates et al. (1992) have reviewed and identified a number of correlations between neuroanatomical developments in the human cerebral cortex and "landmarks" in language acquisition. Such correlations cannot be used to establish firm links between neural events and cognitive ones. However, the approach is useful for identifying specific hypotheses which can then be tested with more direct methodologies.

Consistent with the evidence reviewed in this chapter so far, Bates et al. (1992) suggested that the evidence for some neuro-anatomical differences between the right and left hemispheres at birth (see chapter 8) may set up computational differences that "bias" language toward the left hemisphere. As discussed later, it is likely that these differences between the hemispheres are due to differential timing of development, rather than a genetic encoding of a specific architecture. Bates et al. (1992) identify a peak transition in both behavioral and neural development at around 8–9 months after birth. They discuss the establishment of long-range connections (especially from the frontal cortex) and the onset of an adult distribution of metabolic activity (from the PET study of Chugani, 1994, reviewed in chapter 2) at this age, and suggest these neural developments enable the onset of a number of language-related skills such as word comprehension, and the inhibition of non-native speech contrasts.

Around 16–24 months there is a "burst" in vocabulary and grammar, and Bates and colleagues argue that this correlates with a steep increase in synaptic density in many cortical regions. The increased synaptic density, they speculate, enables a larger capacity for storage and information processing. At around 4 years of age most normal children have acquired the basic morphological and syntactic structures of their native language, and thus have reached the end of the "grammar burst." Bates and colleagues point out that this "stabilization" of language coincides with the decline in overall brain metabolism and synaptic density (although, as mentioned in chapter 2, the peaks of these two measures may not coincide exactly).

Developmental disorders involving language can also be informative about the neurodevelopmental basis of these abilities. Some authors have argued that developmental disorders in which language is relatively intact, despite impairment in other domains, constitute evidence for an "innate language module." For example, in Williams syndrome (WS) (see chapter 4), language can be strikingly intact, despite severe deficits in other domains. Several studies have demonstrated that linguistic and face-processing skills are surprisingly preserved in WS subjects, despite low IQs (typically in the 50s–60s) and serious deficits on visuospatial, number, motor, planning, and problem-solving tasks (see Karmiloff-Smith et al., 1995, for review). The linguistic ability of these subjects is not just superficial (such as repetition of previously heard sentences), but is generative in the sense that they can create new sentences with appropriate grammatical structure. The depth of this linguistic knowledge is currently the subject of continuing research. In certain cases the dissociation between linguistic ability and other abilities can be very marked. For example, the following is the spontaneous speech of a 21-year-old WS subject (studied by Annette Karmiloff-Smith and colleagues) with performance equivalent to a mental age of 5 and a half years as assessed on a standardized spatial cognition task (Ravens Matrices):

> [*discussing a trip to Australia*]
> And I met my two cousins who were twins, so that was great fun being with them. They took us out, meals, boat trips and things and we went to [um] Harbour Bridge and the Opera House. I liked that because it was so massive.

[*talking about her job at the hospital where she helps with the catering staff*]
Well sometimes I do and sometimes I don't. They just tell you how many cups you put on the tray and the saucers and how many [um] spoons and sugars and creams you put on the tray and how many sandwiches they want for how many people.

[*Experimenter*: But do you count them yourself, the cups?]
No, they count them and I just put them on the trays. So, I put them in with cling film on top so they don't get wet.

Thus, in this latter example, while this subject is unable to count relatively small numbers (the number of cups on a tray), she is able to express herself grammatically and has a fairly wide vocabulary. While it seems initially attractive to account for such cases of isolated intact language in terms of innate representations for language, the evidence on cortical development in chapter 2 and that discussed earlier in this chapter should make us wary of jumping to this conclusion. Perhaps a better way to view such cases is that some deviation from the normal trajectory of brain development results in a slightly maladaptive architecture in some structures. This slightly deviant aspect of neural architecture has much more effect on some domains of computation than others. Once early postnatal development deviates from the normal trajectory, then it is likely that this deviation will be amplified by abnormal interactions with the environment.

chapter seven

Frontal Cortex, Object Permanence, and Planning

The frontal cortex shows the most prolonged development of any region of cortex. In this chapter, two approaches to understanding the role of this part of cortex in cognitive development are outlined. The first approach has entailed associating the preservative errors of young infants on object permanence and retrieval tasks with maturation of the dorsolateral prefrontal cortex by means of data from human infants, infant monkeys, and adult monkeys with prefrontal cortex lesions. These data support the view that maturation of this part of the cortex allows integration of information across space and time, and the inhibition of prepotent responses. This account of the functional consequences of frontal cortex development will require some modification in the light of recent evidence from marker tasks with younger infants involving looking, rather than reaching, as the relevant response. A second view of the role of prefrontal cortex in cognitive development comes from studies of EEG coherence. These studies suggest a role for prefrontal regions in the cyclical reorganization of cortical representations during cognitive development. Some of the problems with this approach are outlined. It is concluded that the specificity of prefrontal cortex functioning probably arises from a combination of initial neurochemical and connectivity biases, and the relatively delayed development of the region.

As discussed in chapter 2, the frontal cortex shows the most prolonged period of postnatal development of any region of the human brain, with detectable changes in synaptic density even into the teenage years (Huttenlocher, 1990). For this reason, it has probably been the cortical region most commonly associated with developments in cognitive abilities. Further, several developmental abnormalities present with some "frontal" deficit symptoms. Two major unresolved issues concerning frontal cortex development are:

- Are the specialized computations performed by frontal cortex due to its unique neuroanatomy/neurochemistry, or to other factors?
- How are we to resolve evidence for prefrontal cortex functioning in the first 6 months of life, with the continuing neuroanatomical development of the region until the teenage years?

We will return to these issues at the end of the chapter. Initially, however, we will explore two alternative views that have been taken of the relation between frontal cortex structural development and increases in cognitive ability in childhood. The first of these is that structural developments in the frontal cortex occur at a particular age, allowing certain increases in cognitive ability (a recent refinement of this general view is that the frontal lobes are composed of a number of regions which subserve different functions and show differential rates of maturation; see e.g. Diamond, 1991). The alternative view is that the frontal cortex is consistently involved in the acquisition of new skills and knowledge from very early in life, and that it may also play a role in organizing other parts of cortex (e.g. Thatcher, 1992). By this second view, regions of frontal cortex play a fundamental role in cognitive transitions primarily because of the region's involvement in the acquisition of *any* new skill or knowledge. A corollary of this hypothesis is that frontal involvement in a particular task or situation may decrease with experience of the task. Currently there is some evidence consistent with both positions. I begin by reviewing attempts to relate the maturation of particular regions of prefrontal cortex to aspects of cognitive development.

One of the most comprehensive attempts to relate a cognitive change to underlying brain developments has concerned the emergence of object permanence in infants. In particular, Diamond, Goldman-Rakic, and colleagues (Goldman-Rakic, 1987; Diamond and Goldman-Rakic, 1989; Diamond, 1991) have argued that the maturation of prefrontal cortex during the second half of the human infant's first year of life accounts for both Piaget's (1954) observations about object permanence and a variety of other transitions in related tasks which involve working memory and the inhibition of prepotent responses (e.g. Diamond et al., 1994).

The region of the frontal lobe anterior to the primary motor and premotor cortex, commonly called the prefrontal cortex, accounts for almost one-third of the total cortical surface in humans (Brodmann, 1909, 1912; see figure 2.6) and is considered by most investigators to be the locus of control for many abilities central to higher-level cognition. Extensive clinical (Milner, 1982) and experimental observations of the effects of injury to this region have also supported the notion that prefrontal cortex subserves important aspects of cognition (for reviews, see Goldman-Rakic, 1987; Fuster, 1989). While there are no universally accepted theories of frontal cortex functioning, the particular forms of cognitive processing that have been consistently linked to frontal cortex in adults pertain to the planning or carrying out of sequences of actions, the maintenance of information "on-line" during short temporal delays, and the ability to inhibit a set of responses that are appropriate in one context but not another.

Piaget first observed that infants younger than around 7 months fail to retrieve a hidden object accurately after a short delay period if the object's location is changed from one where it was previously and successfully retrieved. Infants of this age make a particular preservative error. They often reach to the hiding location where the object was found on the immediately preceding trial. This characteristic pattern of error, called "A not B", was cited by Piaget (1954) as evidence for the failure of infants to understand that objects retain their existence or permanence when moved from view. Between $7\frac{1}{2}$ and 9 months, infants begin to succeed in the task at successively longer delays of 1–5 seconds (Diamond, 1985). However, their performance is unreliable; infants continue to make the A not B error up to about 12 months if the delay between hiding and retrieval is incremented according to the infant's age (Diamond, 1985).

Diamond and Goldman-Rakic (1989) tested monkeys in a version of Piaget's object permanence task. In the object permanence task, subjects are shown an object hidden at location A and are permitted to retrieve it. After a predetermined number of successful retrievals at location A (usually three), the object is then hidden at location B. Infant monkeys failed to retrieve the hidden object at location B when the delay between hiding and retrieval was 2 seconds or more. Diamond and Goldman-Rakic (1989) found that adult animals with lesions to the parietal cortex, a brain region closely associated with spatial processing, did not show this performance deficit; nor did lesions to the hippocampal formation, a region thought to be crucial for other memory-related tasks, impair monkey performance on A not B (Diamond et al., 1989). However, lesions to the dorsolateral prefrontal cortex severely impaired the adult monkeys' performance in this task.

Developmental evidence that links maturation in frontal cortical regions to the emergence of working memory abilities comes from studies (Diamond and Goldman-Rakic, 1986, 1989) which showed that infant monkeys failed in both the A not B and an object retrieval task (in which the subject has to retrieve an object from behind a barrier) in ways similar to frontal cortex lesioned monkeys. In contrast older, unlesioned monkeys succeeded in these tasks and showed an ability to withstand longer delays. Evidence linking this change in behavior to brain maturation also comes from studies which show that prefrontal afferents and efferents myelinate later than other cortical areas (Yakovlev and Lecours, 1967). Furthermore, in a series of EEG studies with normal human infants, increases in frontal EEG responses have been shown to correlate with the ability to respond successfully over longer delays in delayed response tasks (Fox and Bell, 1990; Bell, 1992a,b; Bell and Fox, in press).

Further evidence for the importance of frontal cortex maturation comes from studies on children with a neurochemical deficit in the prefrontal cortex resulting from phenylketonuria (PKU) (Welsh et al., 1990). Even when treated, this inborn error of metabolism can have the specific consequence of reducing the levels of a neurotransmitter, dopamine, in the dorsolateral prefrontal cortex (see chapter 2). These reductions in dopamine levels in the dorsolateral prefrontal cortex result in these infants and children being impaired on tasks thought to involve prefrontal cortex such as the object permanence task and object retrieval tasks, and being relatively normal in tasks thought to be dependent on other regions of cortex such as delayed non-matching to sample (Welsh et al., 1990; Diamond et al., submitted).

In Diamond's (1991) view, the emergence of the ability to demonstrate knowledge about an object's permanence results from the maturation of prefrontal cortical regions between the ages of 5 and 12 months. Diamond proposed that this region of the cortex is important when a subject has *both* to retain information over spatial delays and to inhibit prepotent (previously reinforced) responses. To review the evidence for this position briefly: human infants younger than $7\frac{1}{2}$ months fail to retrieve hidden objects when any delay is imposed between hiding and retrieval. In this sense, human infants behave like adult monkeys with prefrontal lesions and infant monkeys, as discussed previously. In addition, human infants of this age make similar retrieval errors to these other groups in both the A not B task, in which the side of hiding is switched after several repeated hidings on one side, and in an object retrieval task when the side of hiding is varied randomly (Diamond and Doar, 1989). This suggests that Piaget's observations about object permanence reflect the state of development of one or more underlying neural mechanisms common to performance on both the object permanence and retrieval tasks. Since successful performance on these tasks requires both memory for the most recently hidden location and the inhibition of an incorrect reach to the last rewarded location, the underlying neural mechanism may subserve both functions. Consequently, Diamond and colleagues have presented a strong case for the importance of dorsolateral prefrontal cortex development.

Two recent lines of evidence suggest that the prefrontal cortex maturation hypothesis is not the whole story, and that some modification or elaboration of the original account will be required. The first of these lines of evidence concerns a different marker task for the dorsolateral prefrontal cortex that was discussed in chapter 3, the oculomotor delayed response task. Gilmore and Johnson (1995) found that infants can succeed on this task at a much younger age than is indicated by the object retrieval tasks, even though it also requires the subject to maintain spatial information over a delay and inhibition of a prepotent response (to make a saccade to the cue when it appears). One explanation of the discrepancy between performance in Piaget's object permanence task and the results of Gilmore and Johnson (1995) is that tasks in which the response is an eye movement (looking) are easier since oculomotor planning develops more rapidly than other forms of motor output such as reaching. This proposal is consistent with several studies showing that infants can perform successfully in analogous object permanence tasks as young as 4 or 5 months of age if looking rather than reaching performance is measured (Lecuyer et al., 1992). Further, studies by Baillargeon (1987, 1993) and others, entailing infants viewing "possible" and "impossible" events involving occluded objects, have found that infants as young as $3\frac{1}{2}$ months look longer at the impossible events indicating that they have an internal representation of the occluded object.

In order to account for the apparent discrepancy between these results, and those with the reaching measures, some have provided "means–ends" explanations, arguing that infants do not know how to coordinate the necessary sequence of motor behaviors to retrieve a hidden object (Diamond, 1991; Baillargeon, 1993). In a recent series of experiments, Munakata et al. (1994) trained 7-month-olds to retrieve objects placed at a distance from them by means of pulling on a towel or pressing a button. Infants retrieved objects when a transparent screen was interposed between them and the toy, but not if the screen was sufficiently opaque to make the object invisible. Since the same means–ends planning is required whether the screen is transparent or opaque, it was concluded that this cannot account for the discrepancy between the looking and the reaching tasks. Munakata et al. (1994) proposed an alternative "graded" view of the discrepancy implemented as a connectionist model. In chapter 9, I will discuss this model which illustrates how weak internal representations of a stimulus can be sufficient to drive a simple output, such as an eye movement, but may be insufficient to initiate a more complex output, such as reaching.

An alternative approach to understanding the role of the prefrontal cortex in cognitive development has been advanced by several authors who have suggested that the region plays a critical role in the *acquisition* of new information and tasks. Three concomitants of this general view are that (a) the cortical regions crucial for a particular task will change with the stage of acquisition; (b) the prefrontal cortex plays a role in organizing or allocating information to other regions of cortex; and (c) that development involves the establishment of hierarchical control structures, with frontal cortex maintaining the currently highest level of control. One example of this theoretical approach to functional prefrontal cortex development has recently been advanced by Thatcher (1992) and Case (1992) (for another related approach, see Stuss, 1992).

Thatcher (1992) and colleagues have collected EEG data from a large number of subjects at various ages between 2 months and 18 years. While recording, the subjects sit quietly and, as far as can be ascertained, are not responding to any stimuli. From 16 leads placed evenly across the scalp, the spontaneous EEG rhythms of the brain are recorded before being subjected to a complex analysis which ascertains the extent to which the recordings from each lead "cohere" (roughly speaking, correlate in their activity) with other leads. From the large amount of raw data that such an analysis generates, the major factors (which leads cohere) can be adduced for each age group, and the age "peaks" of rate of increase in coherence for these leads computed.

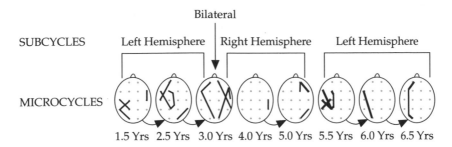

Figure 7.1 Summary of the sequence and anatomical distribution of the co-herence patterns reported by Thatcher (1992). Lines connecting electrode locations indicate a measure of strong coherence. "Microcycles" are a developmental sequence that involves a lateral-medial rotation that cycles from the left hemisphere to bilateral to right hemisphere in approximately 4 years. Note the hypothesized involvement of the frontal cortex in the "bilateral" subcycle.

Thatcher then adds two working assumptions to these data, namely that scalp electrode locations provide reasonable indications of underlying cortical activity, and that the extent of correlation between the activity of regions (leads) reflects the strength of neural connections between them. The result is a hypothesis about recurring cycles of cortical reorganization orchestrated by the frontal cortex.

Figure 7.1 illustrates the hypothesis put forward by Thatcher on the basis of a complex analysis of a subset of his data. The lines in between points indicate the leads that show the greatest rate of increase in cohesion at that age. Thatcher's claim is that there are cycles of cortical reorganization which begin with microcycles involving reorganization of short-range connections in the left hemisphere. Following this, longer-range frontal connections become important, at first only on the left side, but then bilaterally. The cycle is then completed by reorganization of short-range connections on the right-hand side. According to Thatcher, a complete cycle of this kind takes approximately 4 years, though subcycles and microcycles provide the basis for shorter-term periods of stability and transition. By virtue of the longer-range connections related to the frontal cortex, Thatcher suggests that this part of cortex plays an integral role in the reorganization of the cortex as a whole.

Case (1992) attempted to use these EEG findings to relate brain reorganizations to cognitive change by arguing that (a) cognitive change has a similarly "recursive" character, and (b) that many limitations on cognitive performance are due to functions such as working memory commonly associated with the frontal cortex. One example used to illustrate that neural and cognitive changes may be both manifestations of a common underlying process is the rate of change in EEG coherence between a particular pair of leads (frontal and parietal) and the rate of growth in working memory span during the same ages (see figure 7.2). While the change in the rate of growth in the two variables may seem compelling at first glance, there are several reasons why it cannot be regarded as more than suggestive at present. One of these is that there is no clear rationale for choosing the particular pair of electrodes presented: there are, after all, 56 possible pairs to select from and there are always likely to be a few that show peaks in growth at similar ages to some developing cognitive function.

Even assuming that watertight correlations between the peaks in rates of increase in cognitive abilities and EEG coherence could be obtained, this association between brain and cognition would still be based only on temporal correlation, a form of evidence which, when take in isolation, is not very compelling. Further research also needs to be done on the neural generators of EEG signals and coherence, which at present remains controversial and poorly understood. It is to be hoped that, in the future, this approach will attempt to consider the fact the EEG coherence shows phases of significant decreases of coherence as well as increases, which may be associated with "dips" in performance at the behavioral level, and more recursive, as opposed to stage-based, accounts of cognitive change.

Two different viewpoints on the development of prefrontal cortex have been reviewed in this chapter. The view that the maturation of regions of the prefrontal cortex enable particular

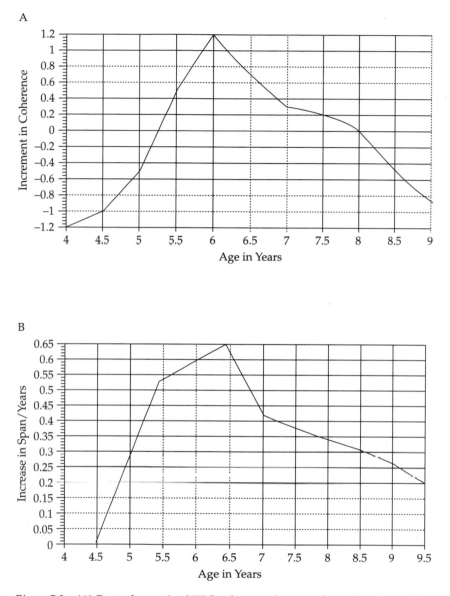

Figure 7.2 (A) Rate of growth of EEG coherence between frontal and posterior lobes during middle childhood (F 7–P 3). (Thatcher, 1992). (B) Rate of growth of working memory (counting span and spatial span) during the same age range.

cognitive functions is, of course, a *causal epigenesis* type of account (chapter 1), and such accounts will always be vulnerable to demonstrations of partial functioning of the region in question at earlier ages. On the other hand, the second approach discussed, in which the frontal lobes are a critical part of the cyclical self-organization of cortex, is relatively unspecified with only preliminary evidence to support it at the moment. Nevertheless, bearing the evidence for these two approaches in mind, we can return to the unresolved issues raised at the start of the chapter.

The first of these issues concerned whether the specialized computations performed by frontal cortex are due to a unique neuroanatomy and/or neurochemistry, or to other factors. The view put forward in chapter 2 was that, while the cerebral cortex provides architectural constraints on the representations that emerge during ontogeny, there are no innate representations. However, it seems likely that graded differences in neurotransmitter densities, and differences in patterns of interconnectivity to other regions of cortex (see Goldman-Rakic, 1988), will provide initial biases that may subsequently lead to some regional differences in microcircuitry. In addition, however, the relatively delayed development of the frontal cortex means that it is likely to develop representations which capture invariances in the structure of the external world, and interactions with the external environment, at greater spatial and temporal distances than other regions of cortex. In other words, it will tend to integrate information over larger time and space intervals than other regions of cortex. Thus, a combination of small intrinsic biases and relatively delayed development may give rise to the unique information-processing properties of this region of cortex.

The second unresolved issue concerned how to reconcile evidence for continuing neuroanatomical development in the frontal cortex until the teenage years, on the one hand, and evidence for some functioning in the region as early as 6 months of age, on the other. One possible resolution to this issue is that representations that emerge with this region of cortex are initially weak, and sufficient only to control some types of output, such as saccades, but not others, such as reaching (Munakata et al., 1994). This view is explored further in chapter 9. Other plausible resolutions of this issue come from Diamond's (1991) proposal that different regions of frontal cortex are differentially delayed in their development, and Thatcher's (1992) suggestion that prefrontal regions may have a continuing role in the cyclical reorganization of the rest of cortex.

chapter eight

Cerebral Lateralization

Three models of laterality are presented: the biased gene model, biased brain model, and the biased head model. Some of these models also address the relation between manual lateralization and hemispheric specialization for cognitive functions. A variety of genetic models of handedness and hemispheric specialization have been put forward. While these models are increasing in their complexity, none of them has yet achieved universal acceptance, and there are remaining doubts about the heretability of handedness. Biased brain models are designed to account for neuroanatomical evidence of hemispheric specialization in newborns. This evidence mainly relates to gross aspects of brain anatomy such as gyral development, and not to the cytoarchitectonics of the hemispheres. Consequently, no firm conclusions can be drawn about prespecified computational properties of the two hemispheres. Biased head models argue that motor biases in the newborn, such as the tendency to turn the head to the right when lying on their backs, result in some visual inputs being biased to one visual field. Thus motor lateralization may indirectly initiate hemispheric specialization. Within the first year of life, hemispheric specialization for cognitive functions such as language and face processing emerges. Several authors have proposed that these specializations are not due to prespecified computations (innate representations), but rather due to an initial difference in the timing between the two hemispheres. Such an initial difference in developmental state could result in certain types of inputs being more readily processed by one hemisphere. Subsequent dynamic inhibition between the hemispheres could increase this functional lateralization to such an extent that the other hemisphere can no longer take over processing the inputs in question following damage to the opposite side. Thus, slight differences in timing between the hemispheres may mean that the detailed architecture of one side is engaged more readily by certain inputs. Processing these inputs increases the specialization of these circuits to the extent that the other hemisphere eventually cannot replace them.

A number of domains of adult cognition appear to be differentially processed in the two hemispheres, such as face recognition, language, and spatial cognition. In developmental neuropsychology, debate has ensued about the extent to which such hemispheric specialization is prespecified (generally equated with being present from birth), as opposed to being an emergent product of differential timing of development. This debate has been further complicated by the fact that empirical studies of hemispheric functional and structural specialization have sometimes produced apparently contradictory results during postnatal development, with the left hemisphere appearing to be more mature at some points of development and the right at others (e.g. Spreen et al., 1995). A further source of difficulty has concerned the extent of the interrelationship (if any) between the hemispheric specialization of cognitive functions and the lateralization of motor functions (such as handedness).

It is now generally agreed that there is some degree of neuroanatomical hemispheric lateralization present from shortly after birth in the human infant. However, there is still considerable disagreement about how this laterality arises and its relation to subsequent adult hemispheric specialization. Hopkins (1993) has discussed a number of hypotheses about the developmental origins of handedness and hemispheric laterality. He divided the range of theories into a number of types including "biased gene models," "biased brain models," and "biased head/uterus models."

Biased gene models provide genetic accounts of laterality. Among the most prominent of these is the "right shift theory" of Annett (1985) and the model of McManus and Bryden (1993). Briefly, the right shift theory states that the majority of individuals inherit a gene which predisposes them to left hemisphere control of speech as a by-product of right-handedness. The minority of individuals that do not have this "right shift gene" have their laterality determined by environmental factors. Specifically, this model accounts for the high percentage of right-handedness observed in the children of two left-handed parents. McManus and Bryden (1993) have pointed out a number of problems with the right shift theory, and proposed a more complicated alternative which incorporates the influence of a second, sex-linked, modifier gene. This modifier gene allows them to account for some of the sex differences observed (left-handedness being more common in males and left-handed mothers giving rise to more left-handed offspring than left-handed fathers). The increasingly complex genetic models of laterality reflect the fact that the heritability of handedness remains controversial, and the effects that have been reported are subtle and interact with other factors such as sex and early experience. A further problem is that the relation between handedness and cognitive lateralization remains unclear (see below). Finally, until the ontogenetic function of the putative genes in question are known, the behavior genetic approach is necessarily limited in its explanatory value. We need not assume that these putative gene(s) have their effect in the central nervous system. Instead, they may bias some other factor that indirectly influences brain development.

The *biased brain model* refers to neuroanatomical observations of hemispheric differences around the time of birth. A number of neuroanatomical studies have shown differences between parts of left and right cerebral cortex in adults. For example, Geschwind and Levitsky (1968) reported that the left planum temporale, an area thought to be involved in language, was larger than the right in 65 percent of adult brains studied. A number of groups have looked for similar differences in infant brains. Chi et al. (1977) investigated the timing of gyral and sulcal development in the fetus. In certain cases these developed earlier on the right than on the left. In particular, a region of the temporal lobe thought to be important for language decoding and comprehension, Heschl's gyrus, was found to develop a little earlier on the right than on the left. In apparent contradiction to this finding of earlier development of the right hemisphere are several studies that report that as early as the 29th week of gestation the left planum temporale is usually larger than the right (Teszner et al., 1972; Witelson and Pallie, 1973; Wada et al., 1975). It is important to remember, however, that these measures refer simply to the extent of folding in the cortex. As reviewed in chapter 2, the cerebral cortex is a thin flat sheet that becomes convoluted as it grows within the skull. Gyral and sulcal measures can therefore only tell us about the quantity of cortical tissue within a region (roughly speaking, the more tissue, the more folding) and cannot be used to argue for architectural prespecification. The latter can only be established by examining the detailed cytoarchitecture of the regions concerned. Until such studies are conducted with postmortem tissue from newborn infants, no definite conclusions can be reached about different computational properties of the left and right cerebral hemispheres at birth.

Even if empirical evidence for the "biased brain" hypothesis were obtained, the question of the factors responsible for this bias remains. The model of Geschwind, Behan, and Galburda (GBG) (Geschwind and Behan, 1982; Geschwind and Galaburda, 1987) provides a causal account of how some of these neuroanatomical differences may arise and their consequences for later life. Briefly, these authors argued for a causal relationship between hormone levels in the uterus and the development of cerebral dominance, and a further relationship between the former and the immune system. More specifically, they argued that higher or lower levels of the hormone testosterone *in utero* can slow down or accelerate the embryological migration of neurons from the neural crest into the cortex. Raised testosterone levels, more commonly found in males, are said to delay migration specifically in the left hemisphere resulting in "anomalous dominance" in which a reduced degree of hemispheric specialization is observed. A characterization of the GBG hypothesis is illustrated in figure 8.1.

Various theoretical and empirical problems with this theory

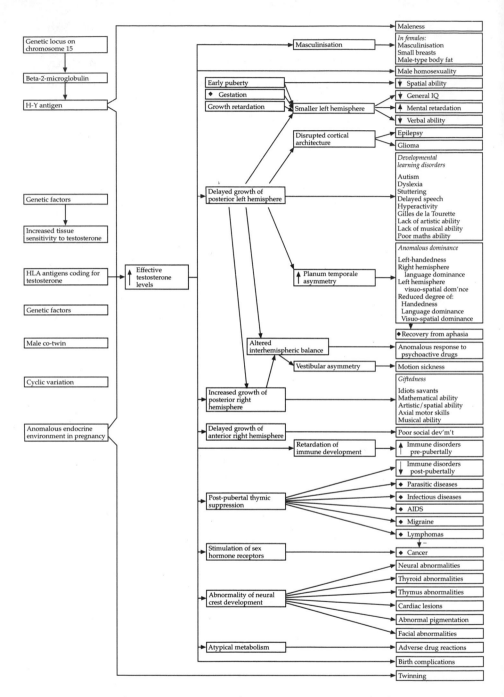

Figure 8.1 A summary diagram of the model proposed by Geschwind, Behan, and Galaburda. Arrows between boxes indicate direct causal links (McManus and Bryden, 1991).

have been reviewed by McManus and Bryden (1993) (see also *Brain and Cognition,* Special Issue (1992), 20, devoted to the theory). Among the more serious problems with the theory are that it posits that those who are not right-handed are part of the "abnormal dominance" population, and such an over-inclusive category does not seem likely to be clinically useful. Another problem is that the theory does not differentiate between a number of possible outcomes: for example, why does elevated testosterone sometimes lead to autism and sometimes to dyslexia?

The third class of model Hopkins (1993) refers to as the *biased head or uterus model.* This model shares the assumption that laterality, and possibly also hemispheric specialization, result from a strong tendency for young infants to angle their head to one side. A number of researchers have noted that when lying on their back newborn infants commonly orient their head toward the right side (though a minority orient strongly to the left). This can be demonstrated both in spontaneous behavior and after a period in which the head is held at the midline (e.g. Turkewitz and Kenny, 1982). This head bias may be caused by the most common position in the uterus restricting the extent of possible head and hand movement to one side (Michel, 1981). These restrictions, in turn, are imposed by asymmetries in the shape of the uterus. A consequence of a bias to turn the head to one side when supine are that one hand (most commonly the right) falls into view more frequently generating a preference for use of that hand for subsequent visually guided reaching. On the other hand, head-turning preference and manual handedness may share a common neural basis. However, since neonates under 12 hours of age do not show this head-turn bias, and some studies have not reported a forced head position in the uterus (van Gelder et al., 1989), the biased head model remains controversial. It also remains unclear whether an early manual bias could influence subsequent hemispheric specialization for cognitive functions.

Whichever of the above models of laterality turns out be most correct, it is clear that by 4 or 5 months of age infants start to show some hemispheric specialization for cognitive functions.

For example, in adults the right hemisphere shows an advantage in certain kinds of face-processing tasks. De Schonen and Mathivet (1989) reviewed a number of studies indicating that the right hemisphere (left visual field) has an advantage for the recognition of faces in the human infant by 4 or 5 months of age. One way to interpret these findings is that the right hemisphere has innate representations for face processing. However, de Schonen and colleagues (de Schonen and Mathivet, 1989; de Schonen and Mancini, 1995) believe that this emergent right hemisphere specialization for face processing is a product of small biases in the detailed architecture of this hemisphere relative to the left, since other (abstract) patterns also differentially engage processing in the two hemispheres. The architectural differences are argued by these authors to arise from slightly different timing of development in the two hemispheres, with the right temporal lobe being a little ahead of its counterpart on the left. This differential timing means that the right temporal lobe processes the lower spatial frequency input which carries most of the information about facial identity. Thus, on this view, differential timing of development between the two hemispheres in early infancy may be sufficient to bias each of them to process particular types of inputs.

Similar views have been expressed with regard to hemispheric specialization for language (see chapter 6). For example, Bullock et al. (1987) argued against Witelson's (1987) view that the left hemisphere is innately prespecified to process language, and that the ability of the right hemisphere to support language following early damage to the left is due to specialized trauma-induced plasticity mechanisms. Bullock et al. (1987) argued instead that developmental timing differences cause an initial small bias for language to be processed on the left. This initial bias, when combined with dynamic inhibition between the hemispheres, leads to increasing lateralization of cognitive function with development. By this view, the end of the "sensitive period" within which the right hemisphere can compensate for damage to the left is a function of the extent of hemispheric specialization for language that has occurred prior to the damage.

Thus, a dynamic probabilistic epigenesis view of hemispheric specialization of function, which supposes an initial difference in the timing of development between the two hemispheres, may account for some of the evidence on recovery of function following early unilateral damage. It may also be consistent with neuroanatomical observations of gyral differences between the hemispheres in newborns. Lateralization of cognitive functions may be further enhanced by newborn motoric asymmetries that bias the visual field within which certain inputs are observed.

chapter nine

Representational Change in Development

In this chapter various mechanisms for the emergence and transformation of representations during development are outlined. The first of these concerns localization: what factors determine the location within the cortex that a representation emerges? Some sources of constraint on this are mentioned, but I focus on chronotopic factors, and suggest that there is a graded differential timing of cortical development both between the hemispheres and running approximately posterior–anterior in the cortex. When combined with other constraints, such as thalamic projection patterns, differentiation of the cortex into functional regions with (sometimes) domain-specific representations occurs. Next, I turn to the emergence of new representations, with the assumption that understanding the principles of re-mapping in the cerebral cortex will illuminate our understanding of processes of perceptual and cognitive change. I put forward a speculative proposal regarding the basis for re-mapping information within cerebral cortex, which involves using cortical space to map out higher-order stimulus dimensions once the lower-order invariances have been extracted by "earlier" cortical areas. The next mechanism for transforming representations during development is selectionism. Different types of selectionist theories are outlined, but all have the common belief that the loss of synapses and circuits during postnatal development increase the specificity of neural and cognitive functioning. The loss of synaptic contacts and circuits is also invoked in a developmental process called "parcellation." Parcellation is the increasing encapsulation (informational isolation) of neural circuits. This process is argued to have a number of computational consequences, such as a reduction in interference, and a reduction in informational exchange, between neural systems. Finally, I turn to the graded strengthening of representations during ontogeny. It is suggested that this process can account for a number of transitions in cognitive development in which different task outputs give different estimates of success in infants.

9.1 Localization

Various themes have emerged from our review of several domains of cognitive development. I argued in chapter 2 that evidence from other mammals indicated that the cerebral cortex does not contain innate representations, and that most of the areal divisions of cortex arise from a combination of intrinsic spatial and timing factors, and extrinsic input. However, the six-layered structure of the neocortex imposes certain architectural constraints on the representations that can emerge within these regions. One example of this from a more primitive forebrain was the spatially invariant object representations that emerged within O'Reilly and Johnson's (1994) model of the chick forebrain (chapter 4). In several of the preceding chapters evidence from human infants and children was consistent with this general viewpoint. In most of the cases examined there was evidence that cortical representations for cognitive functions emerged postnatally, and partially under the influence of the informational structure of the input in question. In those cases where there was evidence of specific information about the world in the newborn, such as the preferential responses to face patterns (chapter 4), subcortical circuits appeared to play an important contributory role in controlling the behavior.

One question that has been raised in most of the domains covered in previous chapters concerns the emergence of localization of function. It was argued that the type of representations that emerge within cortical tissue is constrained by the informational structure of the input in collaboration with the intrinsic structure of the basic neocortical network. This may be able to account for the relative consistency of cognitive abilities across individuals of the same species that follow the normal developmental trajectory. However, it does not offer a satisfactory explanation of why these representations tend to be located in approximately the same regions of cortex between different individuals of a species.

I propose that a partial answer to this localization question comes from differential timing of development within the neocortex (see also Shrager and Johnson, 1995). Elman et al. (1996) introduced the notion of *chronotopic nativism*. That is, the idea that the timing of events in brain development is critical, and can be a powerful source of constraint on the type and location of representations that emerge. But can this somewhat ephemeral notion help us with concrete examples, like those we have discussed in earlier chapters? Two aspects of cortical localization that were discussed were hemispheric lateralization and frontal cortex functioning. In both of these cases, differential developmental timing was argued to be important. In the case of the frontal, and especially prefrontal, cortex it seems to be the last region of the cortex to show identifiable neuroanatomical changes (chapter 7). Thus, it may be delayed relative to the rest of the cortex. In the case of hemispheric specialization, several authors have argued for differences in development between the right and left hemispheres (chapter 8). These differences may differentially engage certain types of inputs. Thus, there may be both right–left and anterior–posterior differential development within the human cortex. One speculation is that these two directions of graded differential development are related to the cyclical rotation during development of cortical EEG cohesion described by Thatcher (chapter 7).

This graded differential timing hypothesis raises two immediate questions. The first of these concerns why these putative gradients of developmental timing have not been observed in neuroanatomical measures in non-human primates. In chapter 2, I alluded to the analysis of Finlay and Darlington (1995) which argues that differences in the relative and overall size of mammalian brain structures arises from changes in the length of time taken for brain development. This analysis accounted for the relatively large cortex seen in primates, and especially in man, and confirms the belief that brain development in our own species is stretched out in time relative to other primates. I argued that this stretched out development means that differential growth in both dimensions of the cortex would become more evident than in a more compressed timescale. Perhaps this is why spatial gradients of development are more evident in our species.

The second question concerns how a graded pattern of differential development can contribute to the relatively sharp borders between cortical regions observed in adults. While these sharply differentiated borders may be the product of patterns of afferents from the thalamus, they may also be the product of self-organizing clustering, such as the ocular dominance columns studied in the model of Miller and colleagues (chapter 3).

In the following sections of this chapter, I will describe in more detail some of the neurally inspired mechanisms of representational change that have been alluded to earlier. These approaches have a common assumption that an understanding of functional brain development will both inform and transform our thinking about cognitive transitions.

9.2 The emergence of new representations

One of the central problems of cognitive development has concerned the emergence of new representations (e.g. Karmiloff-Smith, 1992; Mandler, 1992). With few attempts to specify clearly the neurocognitive mechanisms by which new representations emerge, some authors have argued that there are no new representations in postnatal development, just refinement or selection of prespecified ones (for example, Fodor, 1983, Piatelli-Palmarini, 1989). As noted in chapter 2, this has also been a central issue in the development of the cortex, with some authors arguing for prespecified (innate) representations, and others preferring to focus on the factors that influence the emergence of representations. While the review of evidence in this book clearly inclines us to the latter view, the hard work of specifying in detail the neurocognitive mechanisms that constrain the emergence of representations remains. In what follows I sketch out one avenue for further research on this topic.

There are at least three subsidiary questions that must be asked when attempting to specify mechanisms underlying the emergence of new representations. The first concerns the substrate on which the representation is established, the second concerns the factors that constrain the type of representation that emerges, and the third concerns the trigger or generator that initiates the formation of new representations.

In chapter 2, evidence about structural and representational plasticity in the cerebral cortex was discussed. The evidence reviewed supported the argument that, while there are no innate representations in the cerebral cortex, the basic architecture of the cortex enables it to be an effective substrate for maintaining and manipulating representations. Representations in the cortex are assumed to be implemented in a similar way to those in connectionist nets, namely as patterns of link strengths (weight changes or synaptic efficacy). The formation of a new representation can involve either the growth and strengthening of synaptic contacts, the selective loss of existing synaptic contacts, or, most likely, combinations of both.

Given that the cerebral cortex provides a suitable substrate for maintaining a variety of types of representations, the next question concerns the factors that constrain the type of representations that develop. For several of the domains of cognitive development reviewed in chapters 3–8 we were able to identify some of the multiple sources of constraint on the emergence of cortical representations. The main sources of constraint identified were:

- The statistical regularities present in the input to the region.
- The basic architecture (circuitry) of cortex.
- The influence of subcortical structures in structuring the organism's interaction with the external environment.
- Patterns of innervation of thalamic inputs.
- Chronotopic factors ensuring differential timing of development.

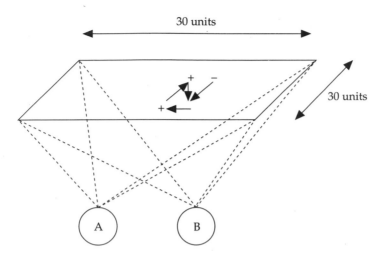

Figure 9.1 Schematic diagram of the structure of the "cortical matrix" model.

In order to investigate the importance of, and interaction between, these factors, various investigators have run simulations with simple cortical matrix network models (Kerszberg et al., 1992; Shrager and Johnson, 1995; Oliver et al., 1996). For example, Kerszberg, Dehaene, and Changeux described several experiments in which they investigated the effects of the correlational structure of input on the development of representation in the cortical matrix. Their model consisted of a single cortical sheet and two sensory node inputs (see figure 9.1). This allowed them to investigate the effect of different patterns of correlation between the input nodes. For example, the input nodes might be in the following states (progressing with time): Node A (1,1,1,0,1,0,0,1,0 . . .) and Node B (0,0,0,1,0,1,1,0,1 . . .). This is a correlation of −1 between the sheets, thus representing an environment in which the two sources of environmental information are completely anticorrelated. With these input nodes it is possible to present a range of input correlations and characterize the units in the cortical sheet according to complexity of the information they encode (specifically, what Boolean function). For example, with certain inputs some nodes in the cortical sheet were only active in response to one or other of the inputs, i.e. they responded to either A or B but not to the other. Other nodes responded to combinations of the two inputs, such as being active when A and B were "1" simultaneously. A few nodes responded in ways thought to be even more complex, such as being active only when A and B are on and also when they are both off (the so-called "XOR function") (see also Elman et al., 1996).

The correlational structure of "sensory" input can be examined by considering different degrees of correlation between the inputs. While the results of such simulations are not as straightforward as might be initially assumed, the correlational structure of the inputs has a marked effect on the proportion of nodes that show different levels of function derived from the inputs. Inputs that are highly, but not completely, correlated result in the greatest number of cortical nodes coding for more complex relations between inputs. Inputs that are either completely uncorrelated, or completely correlated, result in most functional nodes showing first-order functions (responding to input node A or B, but not combinations). In the case of complete correlation between the two inputs, the information is redundant between the two channels, and so there is no pressure for nodes to code for combinations of information. These simulations illustrate that the correlations latent in the "sensory" input have an effect on the level of abstraction of the functions coded for by nodes in the matrix. Sometimes the correlational structure of the environment ensures that most nodes respond to a single source of input, while sometimes units in the cortical sheet integrate information between the two input nodes.

In these simulations, while nodes with similar functions sometimes tend to cluster together (see also Oliver et al., 1996), there is no clear division between areas with different maps as there is in the real cortex. As described in chapter 2, the cerebral cortex is composed of a series of areas with different representations. For example, the primary visual cortex feeds into a number of areas that are involved with extracting more abstract correlations from the input such as motion, objects, etc. Part of the reason why the simulations just described do not form cortical "areas"

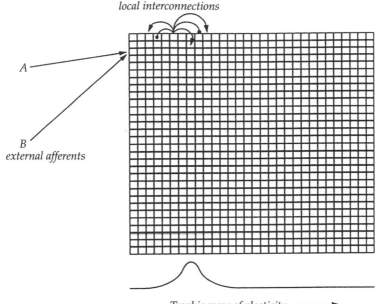

Figure 9.2 Schematic diagram of the dynamic "wave of trophic factor" as implemented in the cortical matrix model.

may be that the information being coded does not have a graded topographical structure to it, and therefore does not induce map representations. However, another reason may be related to the question of what factors initiate the emergence of new representations. My colleagues and I have proposed that to answer this question we need to consider timing (chronotopic) factors (Shrager and Johnson, 1995; Elman et al., 1996).

Indirect evidence reviewed earlier suggests that there may be "waves" of plasticity that pass through the cortex during postnatal development (see Thatcher, 1992; Shrager and Johnson, 1995). In the simple cortical matrix model, this wave can be implemented as a moving peak of "trophic factor." When the peak passes a point on the cortical matrix it has the effect of increasing the link loss (synaptic pruning) in that location (see figure 9.2). More specifically, if the wave of trophic factor moves from left to right across a cortical array, then at the start of the simulation, nodes in column 1 of the cortical sheet have a relative amount of trophic factor equal to 1, those in column 2, 0.86, those in column 3, 0.77 etc. As the simulation proceeds, the peak of the "wave" moves to the right with the effect that the leftmost columns of nodes of the cortical sheet have more trophic factor and are more plastic early on in the simulation, while the rightmost columns of nodes are more plastic later. This has the consequence that the leftmost nodes become fixed in their functionality early on, while nodes to their right remain relatively plastic. In this way the nodes to the left of any given node come to act as an extra source of input for the node. Under certain conditions this leads to the development of a hierarchical structure of representations in which the nodes in the left of the cortical sheet tend to respond to first-order features of the input, while those to the right respond to combinations of inputs. (For those readers with some knowledge of connectionist models the units to the left can be thought of as a "hidden layer" for those on the right, with the exception that these "hidden units" have their representations established and fixed before the final layer) (see also Elman et al., 1996, for discussion of this point).

Simulations such as that described above may begin to help us understand the factors responsible for re-mappings of sensory dimensions in the cortex. As discussed earlier, the cortex contains topographical maps of sensory surfaces and motor outputs. Other cortical regions may also be organized in a similar fashion, though this is hard to ascertain since we do not know what the relevant dimensions of the mapping are. A simple way of stating this is that the basic architectural constraints in the cortex ensure that like things along some dimension are represented together, and more different things further apart. Taking the cortical visual system as an exemplar, it is apparent that multiple maps of visual space are formed. In fact, there are at least 20 visual areas in the primate cortex. Each of these areas re-maps sensory space within some new dimension. In other words, as cortical processing gets further from the sensory input, the representations map higher dimensions of the statistical regularities present in the input. This may be because the input to the "downstream" areas already has lower-order invariances extracted (filtered) from it by other cortical regions. Thus, later developing areas develop representations that map higher-order invariances in the input. Turning to postnatal development, it is possible that as cortical representations of, for example, the visual field get re-mapped, this makes new levels of representation for guiding action available. Consequently, an understanding of the principles that govern representation in the cortex may provide a mechanism for cognitive re-representation.

Edelman and colleagues (e.g. Reeke et al., 1990) have been exploring some related hypotheses in the context of a self-organizing computational system, Darwin III. The behavior of this automaton emerges from representations developed during its interactions with a simple "environment" of simple two-dimensional shapes. The automaton's interactions with the environment at any given "age" is determined by the systems which are functional earliest (sometimes corresponding to subcortical pathways). Through structured interactions with the environment, and by a process of selective loss of synapses, Darwin III comes to develop a number of sensorimotor functions such as tracking and touching objects.

9.3   Selectionism

In chapter 2 the marked postnatal loss of synaptic contacts within the cerebral cortex was reviewed. This ubiquitous observation has led some authors to speculate on the functional consequence of this selective loss process (Changeux et al., 1973; Ebbesson, 1980; Gazzaniga, 1983; Changeux, 1985; Edelman, 1987). One of the broadest and most clearly explicated selectionist accounts has been provided by Changeux and his collaborators. They argue that connections between classes of cells are prespecified, but are initially labile. Synapses in their labile state may either become stabilized or regress, depending on the total activity of the postsynaptic cell. The activity of the postsynaptic cell is, in turn, dependent upon its input. Initially, this input may be the result of spontaneous activity in the network, but rapidly it is evoked by input to the circuit. The critical concept here is that of *selective stabilization*. Changeux proposes that "to learn is to eliminate," as opposed to learning taking place by instruction, or new growth.

Changeux and Dehaene (1989) extended and generalized the earlier neurocomputational account of selective loss. Specifically, they argued that there are definable biological levels in the brain (molecular, circuit level, and cognitive), and that a formalized selectionist theory can be used to bridge these levels. They then introduced a "Darwinian" version of selectionism. In their view, a "Darwinian" change has two stages. The first of these is a constructive process that generates a range of possible options, while the second is a mechanism for selecting among these options. At the neural level, these two stages are implemented as an exuberance of connections specified within a particular genetic envelope, followed by the selection of particular synapses, or groups of synapses, selected as a result of either patterns of spontaneous activity within neural circuitry, and/or as a result of the information structure of sensory input. Changeux and Dehaene (1989) then outlined how an analogous mechanism might operate at the cognitive level. The initial step, the generation of options, they suggest is achieved by the presence of "pre-representations." Pre-representations are described as transient, dynamic, "privileged" spontaneous activity states in neural circuits. The selection process is achieved by particular pre-representations from the set available "resonating" with particular sensory inputs. This process probably takes place in seconds or less, whereas a more prolonged time course may be necessary for the process of attrition at the neural level.

Selectionist-type theories of neurocognitive development vary along a number of dimensions. One of these dimensions is the scale of the unit selected. For example, Edelman (1987) has proposed a similar selectionist account to that outlined above except that particular "neuronal groups" are the unit of selection rather than single synapses. (Crick, 1989, suggests that such neuronal groups will be composed of around 200–1,000 neurons or a "mini-column.") Possibly the cognitive level of selection posited by Changeux and Dehaene (1989) could be implemented as the dynamic selection of large-scale neural circuits or pathways according to particular task demands. Most likely, selection occurs at multiple scales and time courses.

Another dimension along which selectionist theories can vary is the extent to which the selective loss is responsive to sensory input, as opposed to being determined by intrinsic factors. In the model of Changeux and colleagues, sensory input or spontaneous activity determines both the pattern and the timing of the loss. Ebbesson (1988) discusses some examples in which both the pattern and timing of neural connection loss is insensitive to experience, such as when it occurs prenatally. That is, not only is the initial "overwiring" closely genetically specified, but so are the particular patterns and the extent of loss of connectivity. This difference between the Changeux and Ebbesson selection mechanisms is not trivial. It has distinct implications for how plasticity in a developing neural system is terminated. For Changeux, the process is self-terminating, with only connections which are actively employed remaining. For Ebbesson, the end of plasticity is more rigidly determined, i.e. by a given developmental stage a certain proportion of connections *must* be lost, regardless of experience.

A "hybrid" selectionist account of postnatal neural development which draws on aspects of both the Changeux and Ebbesson accounts has also been advanced (see Johnson and Karmiloff-Smith, 1992). The emphasis in this account is on a distinction between *timing* and *patterning* of loss. The hypothesis put forward is that, while the timing and extent of loss of connections or neurons may be a product of interactions intrinsic to the organism (innate by the definition in chapter 1), the specificity or particular pattern of that loss is partly determined by interactions with the extrinsic environment. On this view, there can be an intrinsically determined termination of the phase of selective loss, while the pattern of loss within the "sensitive period" may be determined by experience-driven neural activity. These different possibilities will require systematic investigation in real developing nervous systems, and their different effects at the computational level need to be assessed through neural network modeling.

As discussed in the previous section, a number of modelers have begun to investigate the functional consequences of different variations of link loss (Barto et al., 1983; Kerszberg et al., 1992), including the interaction between activity-dependent link loss and overall network decreases in "trophic" factors (Shrager and Johnson, 1995). However, it is important to note that selective loss is only one of several aspects of postnatal neural development (see Purves, 1994), and so a selectionist account alone can never provide a complete account of neurocognitive development.

Quartz and Sejnowski (in press) have criticized selectionist theories and attempted to provide a "neural constructivist" approach. The essence of this approach is that specificity of neural connections can arise from directed dendritic growth, instead of by selective synaptic growth. These authors suggest that by utilizing a constructive process of growth, as opposed to synaptic loss, development has more flexibility. Their mechanism for directed dendritic growth involves a variation of Hebbian association in which a small volume of neural tissue attracts dendritic growth by passive diffusion (possibly of nitric oxide) and without synaptic contacts. While this is a plausible computational mechanism for directed dendritic growth, there is, as yet, no compelling neurobiological evidence to support it. In addition, directed dendritic growth should be seen as an additional, rather than an alternative, mechanism for increasing the specificity of neural connections.

9.4   Parcellation

Selectionist accounts commonly assume that particular representations are selected from a pre-existing set of representations. However, this set of possible representations could be as wide as all possible representations that can be supported by the basic architecture of the cortex. Given such a broad range of possible representations, the selective loss of synapses could equally well be viewed as the emergence of representations *de novo*. That is, the selection of particular links or synapses to be strengthened or lost need not be taken to imply that the resultant representation is also selected from a pre-existing set of representations. The resulting representation may be no more "pre-existing" than possible future species that could occupy a certain ecological niche.

A complementary approach to understanding the functional consequences of selective synapse loss was proposed by Ebbesson (1984) who maintained that a process called *parcellation* is important in both ontogenetic and phylogenetic development. On the basis of evidence from a variety of species and neural systems, Ebbesson (1984) has argued that the increasing differentiation of the brain into separate processing streams and structures during both phylogeny and ontogeny occurs as a result of the selective loss of synapses and dendrites. The result of this parcellation process is the creation of informationally encapsulated processing streams and structures. At the cognitive level, such systems may correspond to "modules" in the adult mind/ brain (Fodor, 1983). While some authors have viewed parcellation as comparatively insensitive to the effects of experience (Ebbesson, 1984), others have viewed the process as being at least partially experience dependent (O'Leary, 1989; Killackey, 1990). Johnson and Vecera (1996) argued for three possibilities with regard to the extent to which parcellation is experientially driven:

(1)   Processes of neuronal parcellation are due to interactions intrinsic to the brain. Clearly, parcellation processes that occur prenatally and in subcortical structures are of this kind. Further, many of the phylogenetic differences attributable to degrees of parcellation are of this type (see Ebbesson, 1984).

(2)   Processes of selective loss in which the *timing* of the loss is due to intrinsic factors while the *patterning* of the loss is experientially determined: a possible example of this occurs in the

projection from the LGN to layer 4 of the primary visual cortex in the monkey. Lund and Holbach (1991) studied the effects of rearing infant monkeys in various ways on the characteristic increase and subsequent decrease of density of synapses (measured by dendritic spines) on the cells in layer 4 that receive input from the LGN, the spiny stellate cells. As in other systems, the normal overproduction and loss of dendritic spines (there is one spine per synapse) in the developing visual cortex occurs at the time it is most sensitive to interruption of visual input. When comparing monkeys that had been dark reared from the first few days of life with normal monkeys, however, Lund and Holbach observed that there was the normal extent of attrition of synapses from 8–12 days of age to 5 years of age (adult). Although it is unclear as yet whether the time course of the loss is exactly the same for dark-reared monkeys, it is clear that visual experience is not essential for either the initial overproduction of synapses, or for the subsequent loss. Synapses thought to be intrinsic to the layer (type 2: inhibitory) show a later occurring peak and decline than do the spine synapses just mentioned. However, their pattern of development is also comparatively unaffected by visual deprivation (Lund and Holbach, 1991). For this example of selective loss, therefore, the timing of the loss of synapses may be influenced by intrinsic factors.

(3)   Parcellation that is influenced by interactions with the external environment: as reviewed in chapter 2, there is a good deal of evidence that the patterning of selective loss in the mammalian cerebral cortex is activity dependent.

Thus, parcellation is a developmental process that could be influenced by input-driven neural activity, intrinsic factors, or a combination both. Indeed, all three types of parcellation mentioned above probably occur in the course of primate cortical development. Johnson and Vecera (1996) hypothesized that certain behavioral and cognitive changes may be directly related to the increasing segregation of streams of information (i.e. parcellation) at the neuronal level. Clearly, neural parcellation occurs at a number of different levels, and both within and between cortical regions. However, they argued that in all these cases differentiation by selective loss at the neuronal level gives rise to increasingly modular information processing. ("Modular" was used in its most general sense to refer to information-processing systems that are isolated from others.) Specifically, they argued that evidence is consistent with the following consequences of a developmental increase in the extent of cortical modularization:

- less informational exchange between certain brain systems with development
- less interference between certain brain systems with development
- increased specificity in sensory detection

One of the examples of parcellation is the emergence of ocular dominance columns discussed in chapter 3. Recall that ocular dominance columns that received inputs exclusively from one eye emerged from a situation in which most layer 4 cells (in the primary visual cortex) received afferents from both eyes. The parcellation process would lead us to expect that the selective loss of afferents will result in components of the network becoming increasingly encapsulated and inaccessible to other parts. Held and his colleagues (see Held, 1993) tested this idea with the experiment described earlier in which they demonstrated that infants under 4 months had a form of integration between the two eyes not observed in older infants. The older infants did not show this integration between the eyes because by this age neurons in cortical layer 4 of primary visual cortex only receive inputs from one eye.

The example of ocular dominance column formation also demonstrates that parcellation (or segregation) at one level of processing can allow for more adaptive or accurate recombination at another level of processing. Thus, while parcellation may result in a loss of a certain level of integration between systems (e.g. binocular summation in the case of ocular dominance columns), it may be followed by the acquisition of a new level of integration (e.g. binocular vision, as in the current example).

Another domain in which parcellation processes were described by Johnson and Vecera (1996) was cross-modal integration (see also Maurer, 1993). While the example of ocular dominance columns concerned increasing differentiation *within* a sensory projection, it is possible that a similar process may occur *between* sensory modalities. Many mammals appear to have transient connections between different sensory cortices early in life. For example, Dehay et al. (1984, 1988) have reported transient connections between visual, auditory, somatosensory, and motor cortices in the kitten and monkey. The loss of the connections through parcellation would presumably result in less cross-talk between sensory modalities at the level of primary sensory representations. Two consequences of increasing parcellation between sensory modalities were discussed by Johnson and Vecera: (a) sensory input should provide a broader pattern of activation across the cortex prior to parcellation; and (b) there will be more "cross-talk" between sensory modalities prior to parcellation.

With regard to the first of these predictions, Wolff et al. (1974) investigated the cortical-evoked response of 3 and 4-day-old infants to somatosensory and auditory stimulation. Their evidence suggested that auditory input (white noise) had a modulating effect on the somatosensory-evoked responses in these very young infants. However, when a similar experiment was run with adults, no effects of auditory input on somatosensory responses was found. One interpretation of these results is that there is less intersensory integration at this level in adults as a result of parcellation between the auditory and somatosensory modalities.

With regard to the second prediction, it should be noted that there are likely to be multiple levels of information exchange between sensory modalities. This fact means that an infant is likely to go through a sequence of developmental stages in which she integrates increasingly specific forms of information across the sensory modalities. Considering this, the prediction from parcellation is that infants will go through developmental periods in which they show an apparent loss of intersensory integration within a particular cross-modal task. This may then be followed by subsequent reintegration between modalities of a more specific kind, resulting in some cases in an apparent U-shaped pattern of developmental change.

Lewkowicz (1991), when reviewing the development of intersensory functions in human infants, argues that there is strong evidence for nonspecific cross-modal influences early in life. For example, Lewkowicz and Turkewitz (1981) established that the looking preferences of newborn infants for bright or dim stimuli was effected by prior exposure to auditory stimuli. Infants tested in silence looked longer at intermediate intensity lights, whereas infants exposed to an auditory tone looked longest at the dimmest light.

Other cross-modal experiments with infants have been concerned with apparently more complex types of stimuli, such as the matching of numerical quantity (Starkey and Cooper, 1980; Starkey et al., 1983, 1990). When infants succeed in these tasks at a young age, the results can be interpreted in one of two ways. One explanation is that infants have "intelligently" matched input in one sensory modality to input in another. The other explanation is that infants are unable to discriminate the sensory modality of the input and merely respond to some nonspecific aspect of the stimulus such as intensity or quantity. In the first case, the infant is viewed as having separate representations of the visual and auditory input, and then actively extracting the similarity between them. In the second case, the representations from the two sensory modalities are blended within the cortex such that infants cannot discriminate between them. Rather, they just perceive a certain stimulus intensity. The parcellation conjecture predicts an initial state in which there are nonspecific connections between primary sensory representations. These connections will then be pruned resulting in the apparent loss of cross-modal influence. Subsequently, more specific cross-modal matching may emerge. This account of the development of cross-modal effects makes the counterintuitive prediction that early cross-modal influences should decline with development, a surprising prediction for which there is in fact some evidence.

Stetri (1987) and Stetri and Pecheux (1986) investigated whether there is intermodal transfer of shape from touch to vision (and vice versa) in infants from 2 to 5 months old. Infants were familiarized with an object visually or tactually (hand) until they habituated to it. Subsequently, the infant was presented with the same shape in the other modality and the duration of look or grasp recorded. If the infants were capable of cross-modal habituation then they should remain habituated to that shape and show little interest in it. Stetri found no evidence for cross-modal transfer from touch to vision in 5-month-old infants, but strong evidence for such transfer in 2 and 3-month-olds. Older infants have yet to be tested in this experiment.

Meltzoff and Borton (1979) conducted a cross-modal "matching" experiment with 1-month-old infants. These authors reported cross-modal matching between the infant mouthing nubby or smooth pacifiers for 90 seconds and whether they subsequently look more toward a picture of a nubby or smooth pacifier when presented side by side. Maurer and Stager (reported in Maurer, 1993) also found an effect with 1-month-old infants, but failed to find any effects in a group of 3-month-olds in the same experiment. This pattern of loss is consistent with the increasing parcellation of cortical sensory inputs.

Johnson and Vecera (1996) also speculated that since developmental abnormalities may have failed or deviant patterns of parcellation in the cortex, they may also have symptoms of inappropriate cross-modal integration. They then note reports of synesthesia, or multi-channel sensory experiences, in adults with autism (Cesaroni and Garber, 1991). Another area in which parcellation processes may be speculatively applied is in particular aspects of language acquisition. Johnson and Karmiloff-Smith (1992) discuss some examples of language acquisition from Karmiloff-Smith's earlier work in which some components of the language system appear to become modularized as a result of development, in the sense that other information-processing streams no longer have access to its contents. One example of this occurs in a study of awareness of linguistic repairs within a narrative. Younger subjects (11 year olds) were able to detect one type of linguistic repair, "discourse cohesion" repairs, more frequently than adults. Discourse cohesion repairs involved either a change from noun-phrase to pronoun (e.g. then the girl/then she), or a change from pronoun to noun-phrase (e.g. he's got/ the man's got), depending on whether the expression referred to the main or to the subsidiary character in the story, according to the "thematic subject constraint" (Karmiloff-Smith, 1985). The results showed that, while subjects of all ages were successful in detecting all categories of repair and could easily furnish explanations of lexical and referential repairs, they were remarkably poor at providing metalinguistic explanations of discourse cohesion repairs. Although there was some increase in correct responses between 7 and 11 years, this was followed by a decline by adulthood. Karmiloff-Smith and colleagues suggest that discourse cohesion rules can be accessed at some points in development, whereas in adulthood that access is lost. The discourse cohesion system becomes progressively more modular and cognitively impenetrable and begins to operate automatically (thereby allowing for focus on propositional content) (Karmiloff-Smith et al., 1993).

While I believe the association between neural parcellation and increasing cognitive encapsulation may be a fruitful one for further research, there are several limitations and complicating factors which should be acknowledged. The first of these is that refinement of neural connections also occurs at subcortical levels in structures such as the superior colliculus (Stein, 1984) and the hippocampus (Duffy and Rakic, 1983). While parcellation at the subcortical level could also have behavioral consequences, much of the parcellation in these structures appears to occur prenatally. The second caveat is that some aspects of behavioral development that Johnson and Vecera (1996) attributed to cortical-level parcellation could also be attributed to a shift from subcortical to cortical processing. For example, in the cross-modal integration studies, it is known that the superior colliculus contains many multisensory neurons and plays an important role in attending and orienting toward such stimuli (e.g. Stein, 1984). Whether the superior colliculus could support the cross-modal abilities observed in human infants is not known, but this is certainly a possibility that cannot be excluded. Third, the most compelling evidence for cognitive encapsulation comes from apparent decrements in performance during development. Clearly, however, development would not involve these processes unless they led to some eventual computational benefit to the organism. Presumably, a partially modular brain is more efficient in generating behavior in some respects. Finally, the increasing encapsulation of neural systems within a brain could also involve the strengthening of connections within a system, possibly by dendritic growth mechanisms similar to that outlined by Quartz and Sejnowski (in press).

9.5   Strengthening representations

In several of the earlier chapters I suggested that apparently conflicting bodies of evidence could be resolved by invoking the graded development of underlying representations. Indeed, it seems likely that most developmental transitions at both the neural and cognitive levels will be gradual and occur over months or years. Brain-inspired connectionist models, as well as other forms of non-linear dynamic system, offer the opportunity to model gradual transitions in which representations gradually increase in specificity or "strength" as a result of experience (McClelland and Rumelhart, 1986; Munakata et al., 1994; Elman et al., 1996). One example of the use of connectionist modeling to investigate the graded development of partial representations concerns object permanence.

In chapter 7 we discussed an apparent conflict between studies of object permanence (such as the A not B error) that involved reaching as the output, and those which merely required looking. This dissociation between looking and reaching responses was also observed in marker tasks for dorsolateral prefrontal cortex, with infants succeeding in the marker task involving looking (the oculomotor delayed response task) at a younger age than with reaching (object retrieval or permanence tasks). There are several ways to account for these reaching–looking dissociations. One of the most parsimonious is to assume that reaching is a more complex form of response in that it requires more information for its accurate execution. For example, there are more degrees of freedom involved in reaching than in looking, since it requires the coordination of many more muscle groups. It is conceivable that the greater specification required for reaching requires a more detailed, or stronger, representation than looking. The strength of a representation could be important if the pattern of activation it produces has to engage several subsystems. By this general view, cognitive development entails the elaboration and strengthening of representations, and infants will succeed in tasks that are less demanding of the representation in question first. In addition to task difficulty, defined in terms of the output required, other factors such as the length of time that the representation is active following presentation of the triggering stimulus, and the familiarity of the stimulus in question, are likely to influence success through the strength of the representation. This would be consistent with Diamond's (1991) report that the length of time that can be tolerated by infants between training and test in the A not B task increases with age.

To explore this idea in a more computational way, some groups have run simulations in which connectionist networks are trained to develop representations of occluded objects (Munakata et al., 1994; Mareschal et al., 1995). For example, Munakata and colleagues trained a simple "predictive" network on a series of views of an object moving behind an occluder. After some training, the internal representation of the object (defined as a pattern of activations across a particular set of nodes) tends to persist for some time after occlusion of the object (see figure 9.3). Thus, in a sense, the network can be said to show some degree of permanence of object representations. With further training, the representation maintained in the absence of the stimulus gets stronger and lasts for longer after occlusion. The hypothesis explored by Munakata and colleagues is that, with a small amount of training, the weak representation of an occluded object

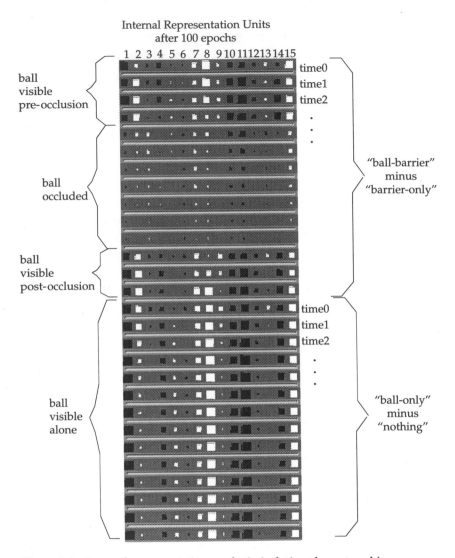

Internal Representation Units
after 100 epochs

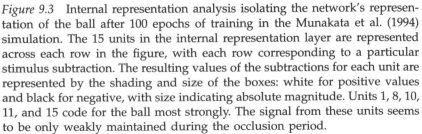

Figure 9.3 Internal representation analysis isolating the network's representation of the ball after 100 epochs of training in the Munakata et al. (1994) simulation. The 15 units in the internal representation layer are represented across each row in the figure, with each row corresponding to a particular stimulus subtraction. The resulting values of the subtractions for each unit are represented by the shading and size of the boxes: white for positive values and black for negative, with size indicating absolute magnitude. Units 1, 8, 10, 11, and 15 code for the ball most strongly. The signal from these units seems to be only weakly maintained during the occlusion period.

may be sufficient to drive a low-threshold output such as looking, but not a complex output such as reaching. With further training, the representation of an occluded object gets stronger, allowing it to guide more complex forms of output such as reaching.

This model, and a related model of Mareschal et al. (1995), makes some empirically testable predictions about infants' behavior in a variety of object permanence related tasks. For example, familiar objects should elicit a stronger representation which is capable of (a) being retained for a longer period; and (b) initiating a more complex response. These and related predictions are currently the focus of empirical research. While the graded representations approach seems promising, there is still a lot of computational work and empirical research that needs to be done. One challenge is that it is likely that there are multiple representations of, for example, an object within the brain, suggesting that future models will have to incorporate competition between different neural pathways. A related challenge will be to increase the neural plausibility of these models, possibly by incorporating some of the recent findings from multicellular recordings in monkeys.

chapter ten

Toward an Integrated Developmental Cognitive Neuroscience

This final chapter attempts to tie together some themes of the book, and points out some future directions. The first issue discussed is the value of the molecular genetic analysis of cognitive development. While this approach is likely to prove powerful over the next decade, some reasons for caution about the interpretation of findings are outlined. It is suggested that the role of genes in functional development can only be interpreted from within a developmental cognitive neuroscience approach. Next, the value of a level of neural network modeling that can make contact with both neural and cognitive data is expounded. I suggest that this approach can also be extended to developmental disorders, and to assessing the effects of developmental changes in levels of neuromodulators. Finally, I stress the need for applying multiple methods to cognitive transitions, and for training a future generation of developmental cognitive neuroscientists.

The earlier chapters of this book have introduced the reader to the newly emerging field of developmental cognitive neuroscience (or at least my perspective on it). No doubt it is evident that there is a long way to go before it becomes a cohesive and well-integrated field of inquiry. However, the extent to which previously disparate fragments of information are coming together encourages optimism for the future. In this final chapter some conclusions and recommendations are presented which may facilitate further progress in the field.

The first issue concerns the relation between genes and cognition. Molecular biological techniques are unquestionably going to have a major impact on our understanding of genetic contributions to cognitive change. However, it is important to bear in mind that genes do not "code for" functional components of cognition in any direct sense. We are never likely to discover a "gene for language" for the same reason as there is not a gene for the big toe. Both language and big toes are the result of complex interactions between many genes, their products, and multiple levels of environments. Similarly, with regard to brain structure, it is likely that most relevant genes have widespread effects throughout several or all brain regions, and commonly other organs, such as the heart, too. As attractive as the notion may seem at first sight, there is little evidence for gene expression being localized to, for example, a particular area of cerebral cortex. Since brain structure is not directly "coded for" in genes, but rather is the product of complex self-organizing interactive processes, then providing causal accounts of cognitive change purely in terms of gene action are certain to be inadequate. Rather, expression of particular genes will have to be located within a developmental cognitive neuroscience framework that includes some account of the interactions at molecular, cellular, and organism–environment levels. Ultimately, development is the path from genotype to phenotype, and no cognitive "function" for a gene can be attributed without some account of this mapping.

Ironically, it is the genes that play a role in synaptic plasticity and transmission that perhaps offer the best hope for our understanding of their computational consequences. In these cases, we can study changes due to gene expression that take place sometimes even in the adult animal. Regulation of synaptic density and activity through neuromodulators may be a way in which the action of specific genes on the formation of representations could be studied. Another area is the expression of genes involved in synaptic plasticity, so-called "immediate early" genes. This special class of genes is involved in rapid plastic changes in cortex and other regions, and is probably also involved in developmental plasticity. It may be, therefore, that there are a limited number of genes which are critical for maintaining or terminating plasticity in neural circuits. In addition to molecular biological studies of these types of genes, one approach to understanding the contribution of the expression of the genes may be in detailed cellular neural network modeling in which the effects of gene expression can be simulated, and then compared to real neurobiological systems.

A related side issue is that it is not sufficient for understanding the role of a gene(s) in a developmental sequence to demonstrate that knocking out the gene in question eliminates a particular behavior in later life. In these experimental cases, and in human developmental disorders with an identifiable genetic abnormality, we may say that the gene defect *causes* the deficit. However, this does not allow the inference that the gene codes for the aspect of behavior which is disrupted, or that this aspect of behavior is the "function" of the gene, for the reasons discussed above.

Another issue that surfaced in several of the preceding chapters was the apparent discrepancy between structural and functional development. For example, with regard to the frontal cortex, there is evidence of neuroanatomical changes occurring until the teenage years, yet infants as young as 6 months old appear to pass some marker tasks of prefrontal cortex functioning such as the oculomotor delayed response task (chapter 3). These findings are, however, only a problem for a causal epigenesis view (chapter 1) in which cause operates in a single direction from brain development to cognitive change. The data can be resolved by taking a probabilistic epigenesis view, in which there are two-way interactions between brain and cognitive development. More specifically, there are at least two ways that they can be reconciled. One way is to invoke the graded development of representations in which input helps to tune the fine structure of a network over time (chapter 9). The other is the view advanced by Thatcher (1992) and others that there are dynamic changes in the connectivity between cortical regions which lead to a reorganization of representations at several points in development.

Throughout this book I have made use of comparisons with connectionist-style neural network models (see also Elman et al., 1996). The use of these models does not necessarily commit one to an empiricist (behaviorist) viewpoint on development as some critics have suggested. Rather, as we have seen in this book, these models are excellent research tools for exploring interactions between intrinsic and extrinsic information during the emergence of representations, and interpreting the functional consequence of partial or weak representations. When information about brain structure is added to the network architecture, neural network models can potentially provide a theoretical bridge between neurobiology and cognitive psychology.

Putting these two applications of connectionist modeling together, we can devise models in which aspects of postnatal developmental neuroanatomy can be simulated, such as the selective loss of synapses, and the interacting effects of different variables studied. In my opinion, for such models to be useful they need to be pitched at an appropriately abstract level to make contact with both neural and cognitive data. To date, most connectionist models of cognitive development make little or no attempt to relate to brain development data (see also Elman et al., 1996). Similarly, some network models of neural development are pitched at a detailed cellular level that does not allow any inferences about cognitive representations. In order to study the possible functional consequence of developments in neural structure, we need models that make contact with both sets of data. Other types of non-linear models, such as those derived from dynamical systems theory (Thelen and Smith, 1994), may be useful in certain contexts, such as motor development. However, although such analyses tend to give good descriptions of the shape of developmental change in a given task or behavior, they do not address the fundamental (in my view) issue of representational transformation (see Karmiloff-Smith and Johnson, 1994). Consequently, they may be of limited utility for studying some types of cognitive transitions during development.

One of the general assumptions that pervades this book is that an understanding of cognitive change during ontogeny will be best achieved at a neurocomputational level. Looking for mechanisms of cognitive change at this level does not imply a maturationist, empiricist, or reductionist viewpoint. It does, however, require a belief that a level of explanation closer to neural mechanisms will bring benefits. While this belief remains largely untested, it is no less plausible than the widely held assumption that cognitive models can provide the best explanation of behavioral change.

Another way in which the developmental cognitive neuroscience approach differs from more traditional unidisciplinary approaches to behavioral and cognitive development is that the organism's interaction with its current external environment is taken into account. Taking this more "ethological" view of cognitive development changes the types of representations we consider in our models of cognitive development in two ways. First, it inclines the researcher to consider the entire neurocognitive path from input to output. This is done because the nature of the input representations, and the nature of the representations necessary for certain outputs, severely restrict the possible intermediate representations. In other words, there is a need for models that, while less detailed, attempt to capture the functioning of several brain systems within a given domain. The second, and related, difference in an ethological approach is that taking the structure of the external environment in which the organism develops into account means that the information contained in representations can be relatively impoverished but still be adaptive. In other words, the representation need only be as detailed as that which is sufficient for adaptive behavior in a given context. For example, in chapter 4 I reviewed the hypothesis that the face representation possessed by newborn infants is merely a primitive "sketch" of the face (something like three blobs corresponding to the eyes and mouth) (Johnson and Morton, 1991). This somewhat impoverished representation is sufficient for adaptive behavior, however, given that faces engage this representation, and that the early environment of the infant is guaranteed to have faces present. Few stimuli (other than those generated by developmental psychologists for experiments!) are likely to engage the same representation.

The developmental cognitive neuroscience perspective advanced in this book also has implications for developmental disorders. The developmental disorders discussed – autism, Williams syndrome, PKU, and dyslexia – are those in which the most research has been done that attempts to link cognitive and neural deficits. However, even in these cases, the mapping from neural to cognitive remains far from clear. In some cases, multiple brain regions have been implicated despite apparently focal cognitive deficits. In my opinion, a number of factors contribute to the complexity of this mapping:

- If a region that develops relatively early in the course of brain development is abnormal, then this is likely to have knock-on consequences for later developing regions. For example, if the projections from the thalamus to the cortex are abnormal, then the subsequent parcellation of the cortex into areas will be disturbed. Further, it is likely that cognitive deficits result from a combination of primary and secondary neural abnormalities. It is possible that the primary cognitive deficits arise from secondary neural effects.
- It is likely that the most devastating forms of brain injury in development are those that affect a major brain system, rather than, for example, a particular cortical area. In most cases of genetic abnormality, or insult early in gestation, the neural consequences are likely to be widespread. Thus they are more likely to disturb whole brain systems than are focal lesions acquired in later life. Focal lesions commonly result in compensation at neural and cognitive levels in primate infants.
- It is possible that a number of different types of developmental brain damage can result in the same cognitive profiles. This could be because the same brain system is ultimately affected and/or because the self-organizing and adaptive nature of brain development channels deviant developmental trajectories to one of a small number of adaptive outcomes. This consideration highlights the importance of taking a probabilistic epigenesis, as opposed to a causal epigenesis, approach to developmental disorders (see chapter 1). Developmental disorders are unlikely to yield to the same types of

neuropsychological analysis as applied to adults with acquired brain damage.

Given that current "static" neuropsychological analysis can only provide, at best, a preliminary analysis of the neural basis of developmental disorders, what could the constructivist approach provide? At present there are very few attempts at computational modeling of developmental trajectories. However, there are some examples of neuroconnectionist models being applied to dyslexia (Plaut and Shallice, 1993), and a preliminary analysis of aspects of autism (Gustafsson, 1995).

As a preliminary attempt to study the ways in which the "normal" formation of structured representations in the cortex can go wrong, my colleagues and I have developed simulations with the simple cortical matrix model discussed earlier (chapter 9) in which we deliberately change one or other of the critical parameters (Johnson and Oliver, unpublished manuscript; Oliver et al., 1996). The results of one such simulation is illustrated in figure 10.1. In this case, when we manipulated an aspect of the intrinsic structure of the network, the relative length of excitatory and inhibitory links, we totally disrupted the formation of structured representations. In other simulations, representations can emerge, but distorted in different ways relative to the "normal" case. By developing a taxonomy of the ways that structured representations can go awry, we hope to be able to generate hypothetical developmental disorders, some of which may correspond to problems that occur in the real brain.

Within the same general constructivist viewpoint, we can also consider developmental disorders in terms of Waddington's intuitive conceptualization of developmental trajectories in the form of an epigenetic landscape (see chapter 1; figure 1.3). In the epigenetic landscape, a perturbance to the trajectory early in development (possibly corresponding to prenatal) will lead to an entirely different pathway (valley) being taken. However, a variety of different sources of perturbance could lead to the same alternative path being taken, and therefore the same behavioral phenotype could result. This corresponds to the fact

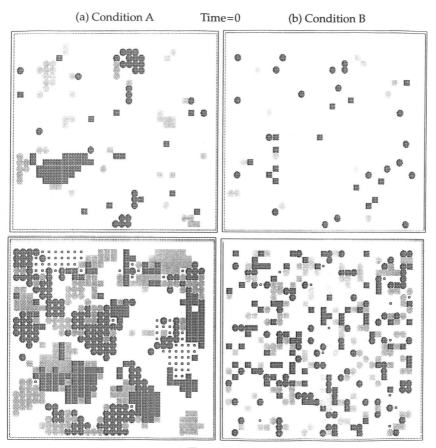

Figure 10.1 The formation of representations in the cortical matrix model under two different architectural conditions. The left upper panel shows the starting state and the left lower the final state. In the final state, "structured" representations emerge in which stimuli that have features in common tend to be clustered together (spatially aligned). With just a minor change in the architecture of the network (changing the relative average lengths of intrinsic excitatory and inhibitory links: the right-hand side) nodes in the network fail to form structured clustered representations.

that there are probably several sources of perturbation that can result in autistic symptoms, for example. Waddington's analysis would, however, predict that these perturbations occur around the same developmental stage. Perturbations to development that occur later in development when the organism is in a chreod (possibly corresponding to perinatal or early postnatal) are compensated for by self-regulatory (adaptive) processes which ensure that the same behavioral phenotype results. I suggest that this latter type of perturbation corresponds to the effects of perinatal and early postnatal acquired cortical damage. As we have seen, if perinatal damage is limited to regions of the cortex, there is often a degree of functional compensation not seen in adults and older children. For example, lesions to the left temporal lobe early in life do not have a devastating effect on language acquisition (chapter 6). The effects are subtle and influence other domains of cognition also. Thus, in these cases, the injured brain adapts to preserve the patterns of specialization which result from normal development. Obviously, major perturbations, such as the loss of most of the cortex, or prolonged rearing in darkness or social isolation, are likely to push the child into a different phenotype.

Two other lines of research in developmental cognitive neuroscience that might be fruitful to pursue in the near future are the effects of changing neuromodulators and dynamic oscillatory firing patterns in neural circuits. In chapter 2, a number of changes in neurotransmitters during postnatal development were described. In the case of some neurotransmitters, such as norepinephrine (also known as noradrenalin), there are specific hypotheses about function at the neurobiological level, which some authors have related to information processing at the cognitive level in adults (e.g. Cohen and Servan-Schreiber, 1992). Such models could fairly readily be applied to developmental issues and related to data on neurotransmitter levels, such as the effects of reduced dopamine in PKU children discussed in chapter 7.

Thelen and Smith (1994) and Thatcher (1992), among others, have argued that information about oscillatory activity in the brain could inform our thinking about the development of brain functions. As discussed in chapter 7, attempts to relate neural oscillations to cognitive function have been somewhat indirect. However, as Thatcher has demonstrated, the pattern of correlation between regions in their resting oscillations changes with age. While the cognitive significance of natural brain EEG rhythms (such as the "alpha" rhythm) are poorly understood, Abeles and Prut (1995), and others concerned with multiple cellular recording in monkeys, have evidence for organized "synfire" chains of spatiotemporal firing patterns in cerebral cortex. Theoretical EEG (or ERP) activation could potentially be computed from models of these oscillatory firing chains. Developmental studies of these organized spatiotemporal patterns of firing in monkeys may shed light on aspects of the different patterns of EEG coherence observed during human infancy.

Another theme of this book concerns the need to apply multiple different methods to study the same cognitive transitions. One reason that this is necessary is so that we can better relate brain and behavioral observations. Another reason is that in both cognitive and brain development studies it is clear that hypotheses based on a single methodology are hazardous to interpret. For example, in chapters 7 and 9 dissociations between looking and reaching measures of object permanence in infants were discussed. If converging evidence from a number of methods and output measures is obtained, conclusions could perhaps be drawn with more confidence. When using multiple measures and methods, we will likely find task-dependent differences as well as similarities. The task-dependent differences may turn out to be as instructive as the converging evidence (see Munakata, in press).

Finally, the short-term future of developmental cognitive neuroscience is dependent on successful collaboration between developmental neurobiologists, cognitive developmentalists, and computational modelers. In the longer term, we will depend on the next generation who will need some familiarity with all of these fields. My hope is that this book will help to nurture some of them.

Further Reading

The following selection of books provides more detailed coverage of some of the topics covered. There are, of course, many other useful references cited throughout the text.

Chapter 1

Gottlieb (1992) and Oyama (1985) provide useful introductions to historical viewpoints on biological development. Gottlieb (1992) focuses in particular on the relation between evolutionary mechanisms and behavioral ontogeny. Elman et al. (1996) present a more detailed analysis of ways in which aspects of neural structure may be innate.

Chapter 2

Purves and Lichtman (1985) and Hopkins and Brown (1984) provide general introductions to neural development. Purves (1994) is a brief and easy to read constructivist view of neural development. A detailed structural MRI atlas of human postnatal brain development is provided by Salamon et al. (1990). Aspects of human brain development are also covered in the edited volumes listed for chapters 3–8 below.

Chapters 3–8

Several edited volumes provide coverage of the neural basis of these domains of cognition, including Dawson and Fischer (1994), de Boysson-Bardies et al. (1993), and Diamond (1991). A companion reader to this book is Johnson (1993a). Developmental neuropsychological deficits are excellently reviewed in Spreen et al. (1995) and Cicchetti and Cohen (1995).

Chapters 9 and 10

The integration between cognitive development, brain development, and connectionist modeling is explored in more detail by Elman et al. (1996).

References

Abeles, M. and Prut, Y. (1995) Spatio-temporal firing patterns in the frontal cortex. In M. Burrows, T. Matheson, Philip L. Newland and Hansjurgen Schuppe (eds), *Nervous Systems and Behaviour: Proceedings of the 4th International Congress of Neuroethology*, p. 109. Georg Thieme Verlag: Stuttgart, Germany.

Akhtar, N. and Enns, J. T. (1989) Relations between covert orienting and filtering in the development of visual attention. *Journal of Experimental Child Psychology*, 48: 315–34.

Akshoomoff, N. A. and Courchesne, E. (1994) ERP evidence for a shifting attention deficit in patients with damage to the cerebellum. *Journal of Cognitive Neuroscience*, 6: 388–99.

Alexander, G. E., DeLong, M. R. and Strick, P. L. (1986) Parallel organization of functionally segregated circuits linking basal ganglia and cortex. *Annual Review of Neuroscience*, 9: 357–82.

Anderson, D. A. and Zipser, D. (1988) The role of the posterior parietal cortex in coordinate transformations for visual-motor integration. *Canadian Journal of Physiology and Pharmacology*, 66: 488–501.

Andrew, R. J. (1991) *Neural and Behavioural Plasticity: the Use of the Domestic Chick as a Model*. Oxford: Oxford University Press.

Annett, M. (1985) *Left, Right, Hand and Brain: the Right Shift Theory*. Hillsdale, NJ: Lawrence Erlbaum.

Aslin, R. N. (1981) Development of smooth pursuit in human infants. In D. F. Fisher, R. A. Monty and J. W. Senders (eds), *Eye Movements: Cognition and Visual Perception*, pp. 31–51. Hillsdale, NJ: Lawrence Erlbaum.

Atkinson, J. (1984) Human visual development over the first six months of life: a review and a hypothesis. *Human Neurobiology*, 3: 61–74.

Bachevalier, J. and Mishkin, M. (1984) An early and a late developing system for learning and retention in infant monkeys. *Behavioural Neuroscience*, 98: 770–8.

Bachevalier, J., Brickson, M. and Hagger, C. (1993) Limbic-dependent recognition memory in monkeys develops early in infancy. *Neuroreport*, 4: 77–80.

Baillargeon, R. (1987) Object permanence in very young infants. *Cognition*, 20: 191–208.

Baillargeon, R. (1993) The object concept revisited: new directions in the investigation of infants' physical knowledge. In C. Granrud (ed.), *Visual Perception and Cognition in Infancy*, pp. 265–315. Hillsdale NJ: Lawrence Erlbaum.

Banks, M. S. and Shannon, E. (1993) Spatial and chromatic visual efficiency in human neonates. In C. E. Granrud (ed.), *Visual Perception and Cognition in Infancy*, pp. 1–46. Hillsdale, NJ: Lawrence Erlbaum.

Baron-Cohen, S. (1995) Theory of mind and face-processing: how do they interact in development and psychopathology? In D. Cicchetti and D. J. Cohen (eds), *Developmental Psychopathology, Vol. 1: Theory and Methods*, pp. 343–56. New York: John Wiley.

Baron-Cohen, S., Leslie, A. M. and Frith, U. (1985) Does the autistic child have a "theory of mind"? *Cognition*, 21: 37–46.

Baron-Cohen, S., Leslie, A. M. and Frith, U. (1986) Mechanical, behavioural and intentional understanding of picture stories in autistic children. *British Journal of Developmental Psychology*, 4: 113–25.

Baron-Cohen, S., Cox, A., Baird, G., Swettenham, J., Nightingale, N., Morgan, K., Drew, A. and Charman, T. (in press) Psychological markers in the detection of autism in infancy in a large population. *British Journal of Psychiatry*.

Barto, A. G., Sutton, R. S. and Anderson, C. W. (1983) Neuronlike adaptive elements that can solve difficult learning control problems. *IEEE Transactions on System, Man and Cybernetics*, 15: 835–46.

Bates, E. (1994) Language development in children after early focal injury. Paper Presented at the 9th International Conference on Infant Studies, Paris, France.

Bates, E., Thal, D. and Janowsky, J. S. (1992) Early language development and its neural correlates. In I. Rapin and S. Segalowitz (eds), *Handbook of Neuropsychology*, vol. 7, pp. 69–110. Amsterdam: Elsevier.

Bateson, P. and Horn, G. (1994) Imprinting and recognition memory: a neural net model. *Animal Behaviour*, 48: 695–715.

Bear, M. F. and Singer, W. (1986) Modulation of visual cortical plasticity by acetylcholine and noradrenaline. *Nature*, 320: 172–6.

Becker, L. E., Armstrong, D. L., Chan, F. and Wood, M. M. (1984) Dendritic development on human occipital cortex neurones. *Brain Research*, 315: 117–24.

Bell, M. A. (1992a) Electrophysiological correlates of object search performance during infancy. *International Conference on Infant Studies*, Miami Beach.

Bell, M. A. (1992b) A not B task performance is related to frontal EEG asymmetry regardless of locomotor experience. *International Conference on Infant Studies*, Miami Beach.

Bell, M. A. and Fox, N. A. (in press) The relations between frontal brain electrical activity and cognitive development during infancy. *Child Development*.

Bellugi, U. and Morris, C. A. (eds) (in press) Williams syndrome: from cognition to gene. Abstracts from the Williams Syndrome Association Sixth International Professional Conference, *Genetic Counselling*, 2.

Bellugi, U., Poizner, H. and Klima, E. S. (1989) Language, modality and the brain. *Trends in the Neurosciences*, 12: 380–8.

Bellugi, U., Bihrle, A., Neville, H., Jernigan, T. and Doherty, S. (1992) Language, cognition and brain organization in a neurodevelopmental disorder. In M. Gunnar and C. Nelson (eds), *Developmental Behavioural Neuroscience*, pp. 201–32. Hillsdale, NJ: Lawrence Erlbaum.

Benes, F. M. (1994) Development of the corticolimbic system. In G. Dawson and K. W. Fischer (eds) *Human Behaviour and the Developing Brain*, pp. 176–206. New York: Guilford Press.

Berman, S. and Friedman, D. (1995) The development of selective attention as reflected by event-related brain potentials. *Journal of Experimental Child Psychology*, 59: 1–31.

Bishop, D. V. M. (1983) Linguistic impairment after left hemidecortication for infantile hemiplegia. A reappraisal. *Quarterly Journal of Experimental Psychology*, 35A: 199–207.

Blass, E. (1992) Linking developmental and psychobiological research. *Society for Research in Child Development Newsletter*, pp. 3–10.

Bolhuis, J. J. (1991) Mechanisms of avian imprinting: a review. *Biological Reviews*, 66: 303–45.

Bolhuis, J. J. and Bateson, P. P. G. (1990) The importance of being first: a primacy effect in filial imprinting. *Animal Behaviour*, 40: 472–83.

Bolhuis, J. J. and Johnson, M. H. (1990) Sensory templates: mechanism or metaphor? *Behavioral and Brain Sciences*, 14: 349–50.

Bolhuis, J. J., McCabe, B. J. and Horn, G. (1986) Androgens and imprinting: differential effects of testosterone on filial preferences in the domestic chick. *Behavioral Neuroscience*, 100: 51–6.

Bolhuis, J. J., Johnson, M. H., Horn, G. and Bateson, P. (1989) Long-lasting effects of IMHV lesions on the social preferences of domestic fowl. *Behavioral Neuroscience*, 103: 438–41.

de Boysson-Bardies, B., de Schonen, S., Jusczyk, P., McNeilage, P. and Morton, J. (eds) (1993) *Developmental Neurocognition: Speech and Face Processing in the First Year of Life*. Dordrecht, Netherlands: Kluwer.

Braddick, O. J., Atkinson, J., Hood, B., Harkness, W., Jackson, G. and Vargha-Khadem, F. (1992) Possible blindsight in infants lacking one cerebral hemisphere. *Nature*, 360: 461–3.

Braitenberg, V. (1984) *Vehicles: Experiments in Synthetic Psychology*. Cambridge, Mass.: MIT Press.

Bremner, J. G. (1988) *Infancy*. Oxford: Blackwell.

Brodal, A. (1981) *Neurological Anatomy in Relation to Clinical Medicine*. Oxford: Oxford University Press.

Brodmann, K. (1909) *Vergleichende Lokalisationslehre der Grosshirnrinde in ihren Prinzipien Dargestellt auf Grund des Zellenbaues.* Leipzig: Barth.

Brodmann, K. (1912) Neue ergebnisse über die vergleichende histologische lokalisation der grosshirnrinde mit besonderer berücksichtigung des stirnhirns. *Anatomischer Anzeiger* (Suppl.), 41: 157–216.

Bronson, G. W. (1974) The postnatal growth of visual capacity. *Child Development*, 45: 873–90.

Bronson, G. W. (1982) *The Scanning Patterns of Human Infants: Implications for Visual Learning.* Norwood, NJ: Ablex.

Brooksbank, B. W. L., Atkinson, D. J. and Balasz, R. (1981) Biochemical development of the human brain. II: Some parameters of the GABAergic system. *Developmental Neuroscience*, 1: 267–84.

Brothers, L. and Ring, B. (1992) A neuroethological framework for the representation of minds. *Journal of Cognitive Neuroscience*, 4: 107–18.

Bruinink, A., Lichtensteinger, W. and Schlumpf, M. (1983) Pre- and postnatal ontogeny and characterization of dopaminergic D2, serotonergic S2, and spirodecan on binding sites in rat forebrain. *Journal of Neurochemistry*, 40: 1227–37.

Bruyer, R., Laterre, C., Serron, X., Feyereisn, P., Strypstein, E., Pierrand, E. and Rectem, D. (1983) A case of prosopagnosia with some preserved covert remembrance of familiar faces. *Brain and Cognition*, 2: 157–281.

Bullock, D., Liederman, J. and Todorovic, D. (1987) Reconciling stable asymmetry with recovery of function: an adaptive systems perspective on functional plasticity. *Child Development*, 58: 689–97.

Canfield, R. L. and Haith, M. M. (1991) Young infants' visual expectations for symmetric and asymmetric stimulus sequences. *Developmental Psychology*, 27: 198–208.

Case, R. (1992) The role of the frontal lobes in the regulation of cognitive development. *Brain and Cognition*, 20: 51–73.

Cesaroni, L. and Garber, M. (1991) Exploring the experience of autism through firsthand accounts. *Journal of Autism and Developmental Disorders*, 21. 303–13.

Changeux, J-P. (1985) *Neuronal Man: the Biology of Mind.* New York: Pantheon.

Changeux, J-P. and Dehaene, S. (1989) Neuronal models of cognitive functions. *Cognition*, 33: 63–109.

Changeux, J-P., Courrege, P. and Danchin, A. (1973) A theory of the epigenesis of neuronal networks by selective stabilization of synapses. *Proceedings of the National Academy of Sciences of the USA*, 70: 2974–8.

Chapman, M. (1981) Dimensional separability or flexibility of attention? Age trends in perceiving configural stimuli. *Journal of Experimental Child Psychology*, 31: 332–49.

Chi, J. G., Dooling, E. and Gilles, F. H. (1977) Gyral development of the human brain. *Annals of Neurology*, 1: 86.

Christophe, A. and Morton, J. (1994) Comprehending baby-think. *Nature*, 370: 250–1.

Chugani, H. T. (1994) Development of regional brain glucose metabolism in relation to behavior and plasticity. In G. Dawson and K. W. Fischer (eds), *Human Behaviour and the Developing Brain*, pp. 153–75. New York: Guilford Press.

Chugani, H. T. and Phelps, M. E. (1986) Maturational changes in cerebral function determined by 18FDG positron emission tomography. *Science*, 231: 840–3.

Chugani, H. T., Phelps, M. E. and Mazziotta, J. C. (1987) Positron emission tomography study of human brain functional development. *Annals of Neurology*, 22: 487–97.

Chugani, H. T., Hovda, D. A., Villablanca, J. R., Phelps, M. E. and Xu, W-F. (1991) Metabolic maturation of the brain: a study of local cerebral glucose utilization in the developing cat. *Journal of Cerebral Blood Flow and Metabolism*, 11: 35–47.

Cicchetti, D. and Cohen, D. J. (eds) (1995) *Developmental Psychopathology, Vol. 1: Theory and Methods*. New York: John Wiley.

Clarke, P. G. H. (1985) Neuronal death in the development of the vertebrate nervous system. *Trends in the Neurosciences*, 8: 345–9.

Clohessy, A. B., Posner, M. I., Rothbart, M. K. and Vecera, S. P. (1991) The development of inhibition of return in early infancy. *Journal of Cognitive Neuroscience*, 3(4): 345–50.

Cohen, J. D. and Servan-Schreiber, D. (1992) Context, cortex and dopamine: a connectionist approach to behavior and biology in schizophrenia. *Psychological Review*, 99: 45–77.

Conel, J. L. (1939–67) *The Postnatal Development of the Human Cerebral Cortex*. Cambridge, Mass.: Harvard University Press.

Cooper, N. G. F. and Steindler, D. A. (1986) Lectins demarcate the barrel subfield in the somatosensory cortex of the early postnatal mouse. *Journal of Comparative Neurology*, 249: 157–69.

Courchesne, E. (1991) The theory of mind deficit in autism: possible biological bases. Paper presented to the Society for Research in Child Development, Seattle, WA, April.

Courchesne, E., Hesselink, J. R., Jernigan, T. L. and Yeung-Courchesne, R. (1987) Abnormal neuroanatomy in a nonretarded person with autism: unusual findings with magnetic resonance imaging. *Archives of Neurology*, 44: 335–41.

Courchesne, E., Yeung-Courchesne, R., Press, G. A., Hesselink, J. R. and Jernigan, T. L. (1988) Hypoplasia of cerebellar vermal lobules VI and VII in autism. *New England Journal of Medicine*, 318: 1349–54.

Cowan, W. M., Fawcett, J. W., O'Leary, D. D. M. and Stanfield, B. B. (1984) Regressive events in neurogenesis. *Science*, 225: 1258–65.

Coyle, J. T. and Molliver, M. (1977) Major innervation of newborn rat cortex by monoaminergic neurons. *Science*, 196: 444–7.

Crick, F. (1989) Neural Edelmanism. *Trends in the Neurosciences*, 12: 240–8.

Cromer, R. E. (1992) A case study of dissociation between language and cognition. In H. Tager-Flusberg (ed.), *Constraints on Language Acquisition: Studies of Atypical Children*, pp. 141–53. Lawrence Erlbaum: Hillsdale, NJ.

Culler, F., Jones, K. and Deftos, L. (1985) Impaired calcitonin secretion in patients with Williams syndrome. *Journal of Pediatrics*, 107: 720–3.

Damasio, A. R. and Maurer, R. G. (1978) A neurological model for childhood autism. *Archives of Neurology*, 35: 777–86.

Davies, D. C., Horn, G. and McCabe, B. J. (1985) Noradrenaline and learning: the effects of noradrenergic neurotoxin DSP4 on imprinting in the domestic chick. *Behavioral Neuroscience*, 99: 652–60.

Dawson, G. and Fischer, K. W. (eds) (1994) *Human Behavior and the Developing Brain*. New York: Guildford Press.

Dehaene-Lambertz, G. and Dehaene, S. (1994) Speed and cerebral correlates of syllable discrimination in infants. *Nature*, 370: 292–5.

Dehay, C., Bullier, J. and Kennedy, H. (1984) Transient projections from the frontoparietal and temporal cortex to areas 17, 18, and 19 in the kitten. *Experimental Brain Research*, 57: 208–12.

Dehay, C., Kennedy, H., Bullier, J. and Berland, M. (1988) Absence of inter-hemispheric connections of area 17 during development in the monkey. *Nature*, 331: 348 50.

Dehay, C., Horsburgh, G., Berland, M., Killackey, H. and Kennedy, H. (1989) Maturation and connectivity of the visual cortex in monkey is altered by prenatal removal of retinal input. *Nature*, 337: 265–7.

Dennis, M. and Whitaker, H. (1976) Language acquisition following hemi-decortication: linguistic superiority of the left over the right hemisphere. *Brain and Language*, 3: 404–33.

Desimone, R. (1991) Face-selective cells in the temporal cortex of monkeys. *Journal of Cognitive Neuroscience*, 3: 1–8.

Diamond, A. (1985) Development of the ability to use recall to guide action, as indicated by infants' performance on AB. *Child Development*, 56: 868–83.

Diamond, A. (1991) Neuropsychological insights into the meaning of object concept development. In S. Carey and R. Gelman (eds), *The Epigenesis of Mind: Essays on Biology and Cognition*, pp. 67–110. Hillsdale, NJ: Lawrence Erlbaum.

Diamond, A. and Doar, B. (1989) The performance of human infants on a measure of frontal cortex function: the delayed response task. *Developmental Psychobiology*, 22: 271–94.

Diamond, A. and Goldman-Rakic, P. S. (1986) Comparative development in human infants and infant rhesus monkeys of cognitive functions that de-pend on prefrontal cortex. *Society for Neuroscience Abstracts*, 12: 742.

Diamond, A. and Goldman-Rakic, P. S. (1989) Comparison of human infants and infant rhesus monkeys on Piaget's AB task: evidence for dependence on dorsolateral prefrontal cortex. *Experimental Brain Research*, 74: 24–40.

Diamond, A., Zola-Morgan, S. and Squire, L. R. (1989) Successful performance by monkeys with lesions of the hippocampal formation on AB and object retrieval, two tasks that mark developmental changes in human infants. *Behavioral Neuroscience*, 103: 526–37.

Diamond, A., Werker, J. F. and Lalonde, C. (1994) Toward understanding commonalities in the development of object search, detour navigation, categorization and speech perception. In G. Dawson and K. W. Fischer (eds), *Human Behavior and the Developing Brain*, pp. 380–426. New York: Guilford Press.

Diamond, A., Hurwitz, W., Lee, E. Y., Bockes, T., Grover, W. and Minarcik, C. (submitted) Cognitive deficits on frontal cortex tasks in children with early treated PKU: results of two years of longitudinal study.

Diebler, M. F., Farkas-Bargeton, E. and Wehrle, R. (1979) Developmental changes of enzymes associated with energy metabolism and synthesis of some neurotransmitters in discrete areas of human neocortex. *Journal of Neurochemistry*, 32: 429–35.

Duffy, C. J. and Rakic, P. (1983) Differentiation of granule cell dendrites in the dentate gyrus of the rhesus monkey: a quantitative Golgi study. *Journal of Comparative Neurology*, 214: 224–37.

Ebbesson, S. O. E. (1980) The parcellation theory and its relation to interspecific variability in brain organization, evolutionary and ontogenetic development, and neuronal plasticity. *Cell and Tissue Research*, 213: 179–212.

Ebbesson, S. O. E. (1984) Evolution and ontogeny of neural circuits. *Behavioral and Brain Sciences*, 7: 321–66.

Ebbesson, S. O. E. (1988) Ontogenetic parcellation: dual processes. *Behavioral and Brain Sciences*, 11: 548–9.

Eckenhoff, M. F. and Rakic, P. (1988) Nature and fate of proliferative cells in the hippocampal dentate gyrus during the life span of the rhesus monkey. *Journal of Neuroscience*, 8: 2729–47.

Edelman, G. M. (1987) *Neural Darwinism: the Theory of Neuronal Group Selection*. New York: Basic Books.

Elman, J., Bates, E., Johnson, M. H., Karmiloff-Smith, A., Parisi, D. and Plunkett, K. (1996) *Rethinking Innateness: a Connectionist Perspective on Development*. Cambridge, Mass.: MIT Press.

Enns, J. T. and Brodeur, D. A. (1989) A developmental study of covert orienting to peripheral visual cues. *Journal of Experimental Child Psychology*, 48: 171–89.

Enns, J. T. and Girgus, J. S. (1985) Developmental changes in selective and integrative visual attention. *Journal of Experimental Child Psychology*, 40: 319–37.

Ewart, A. K., Morris, C. A., Atkinson, D., Jin, W., Sternes, K., Spallone, P., Dean Stock, A., Leppert, M. and Keating, M. T. (1993) Hemizygosity at the elastin locus in a developmental disorder, Williams syndrome. *Nature Genetics*, 5: 11–16.

Ewert, J-P. (1987) Neuroethology of releasing mechanisms: prey-catching in toads. *Behavioral and Brain Sciences*, 10: 337–405.

Fantz, R. L. (1964) Visual experience in infants: decreased attention to familiar patterns relative to novel ones. *Science*, 46: 668–70.

Farah, M. J. (1990) *Visual Agnosia*. Cambridge, Mass.: MIT Press.

Finlay, B. L. and Darlington, R. B. (1995) Linked regularities in the development and evolution of mammalian brains. *Science*, 268: 1578–84.

Fischer, B. and Breitmeyer, B. (1987) Mechanisms of visual attention revealed by saccadic eye movements. *Neuropsychologia*, 25: 73–83.

Fodor, J. (1983) *The Modularity of the Mind*. Cambridge, Mass.: MIT Press.

Fosse, V. M., Heggelund, P. and Fonnum, F. (1989) Postnatal development of glutamatergic, GABAergic and cholinergic neurotransmitter phenotypes in the visual cortex, lateral geniculate nucleus, pulvinar and superior colliculus in cats. *Journal of Neuroscience*, 9: 426–35.

Fox, N. A. and Bell, M. A. (1990) Electrophysiological indices of frontal lobe development. In A. Diamond (ed.), *The Development and Neural Bases of Higher Cognitive Functions*, pp. 677–98. New York: New York Academy of Sciences.

Frith, U. (1989) *Autism: Explaining the Enigma*. Oxford: Basil Blackwell.

Frost, D. O. (1990) Sensory processing by novel, experimentally induced cross-modal circuits. *Annals of the New York Academy of Sciences*, 608: 92–109.

Funahashi, S., Bruce, C. J. and Goldman-Rakic, P. S. (1989) Mnemonic coding of visual space in the monkey's dorsolateral prefrontal cortex. *Journal of Neurophysiology*, 61: 331–49.

Funahashi, S., Bruce, C. J. and Goldman Rakic, P. S. (1990) Visuospatial coding in primate prefrontal neurons revealed by oculomotor paradigms. *Journal of Neurophysiology*, 63: 814–31.

Fuster, J. M. (1989) *The Prefrontal Cortex*, 2nd edn. New York: Raven Press.

Galaburda, A. M. and Pandya, D. N. (1983) The intrinsic architectonic and connectional organization of the superior temporal region of the rhesus monkey. *Journal of Computational Neurology*, 221: 169–84.

Galaburda, A. M., Sherman, G. F., Rosen, G. D., Aboitiz, F. and Geschwind, N. (1985) Developmental dyslexia: four consecutive patients with cortical anomalies. *Annals of Neurology*, 18: 222–32.

Galaburda, A. M., Wang, P. P., Bellugi, U. and Rosen, M. (1994) Cytoarchitectonic anomalies in a genetically based disorder: Williams syndrome. *Neuroreport*, 5: 753–7.

Gazzaniga, M. (1983) Right-hemisphere damage following brain bisection. *American Psychologist*, 25: 549.

van Gelder, R. S., Dijkman, M. M. T. T., Hopkins, B., van Geijn, G. P. and Homeau-Long, D. C. (1989) Fetal head orientation preference at the gestational ages of 16 and 24 weeks. *Journal of Clinical and Experimental Neuropsychology*, 11: 364.

Geschwind, N. and Behan, P. (1982) Left-handednesss: association with immune disease, migraine and developmental learning disorder. *Proceedings of the National Academy of Sciences of the USA*, 79: 5097–100.

Geschwind, N. and Galaburda, A. (1987) *Cerebral Lateralization: Biological Mechanisms, Associations, and Pathology*. Cambridge, Mass.: MIT Press.

Geschwind, N. and Levitsky, W. (1968) Left-right asymmetries in the temporal speech region. *Science*, 161: 166.

Gibson, J. J. (1979) *The Ecological Approach to Visual Perception*. Boston: Houghton Mifflin.

Gilles, F. H., Shankle, W. and Dooling, E. C. (1983) Myelinated tracts: growth patterns. In F. H. Gilles, A. Leviton and E. C. Dooling (eds), *The Developing Human Brain: Growth and Epidemiological Neuropathology*, pp. 117–83. Boston: John Wright-PSG.

Gilmore, R. O. and Johnson, M. H. (1995a) Egocentric action in early infancy: spatial frames of reference. Developmental Cognitive Neuroscience Technical Report, No. 95.4.

Gilmore, R. O. and Johnson, M. H. (1995b) Working memory in six-month-old infants revealed by versions of the oculomotor delayed response task. *Journal of Experimental Child Psychology*, 59: 397–418.

Goldman-Rakic, P. S. (1971) Functional development of the prefrontal cortex in early life and the problem of neuronal plasticity. *Experimental Neurology*, 32: 366–87.

Goldman-Rakic, P. S. (1987) Development of cortical circuitry and cognitive function. *Child Development*, 58: 601–22.

Goldman-Rakic, P. S. (1988) Topography of cognition: parallel distributed networks in primate association cortex. *Annual Review of Neuroscience*, 11: 137–56.

Goldman-Rakic, P. S. (1994) Introduction. In G. Dawson and K. W. Fischer (eds), *Human Behavior and the Developing Brain*. New York: Guilford Press.

Goldman-Rakic, P. S. and Brown, R. M. (1982) Postnatal development of monoamine content and synthesis in the cerebral cortex of rhesus monkeys. *Brain Research*, 256: 339–49.

Goren, C. C., Sarty, M. and Wu, P. Y. K. (1975) Visual following and pattern discrimination of face-like stimuli by newborn infants. *Pediatrics*, 56: 544–9.

Gottlieb, G. (1992) *Individual Development and Evolution*. New York: Oxford University Press.

Greenberg, F. (1990) Introduction to special issue on Williams syndrome. *American Journal of Medical Genetics Supplement*, 6: 85–8.

Greenough, W. T., Black, J. E. and Wallace, C. S. (1987) Experience and brain development. *Child Development*, 58: 539–59.

Guitton, H. A., Buchtel, H. A. and Douglas, R. M. (1985) Frontal lobe lesions in man cause difficulties in suppressing reflexive glances and in generating goal-directed saccades. *Experimental Brain Research*, 58: 455–72.

Gustafsson, L. (1995) Effects of inadequate features maps on memory and higher cognitive functions in autism. Lulea University of Technology, Division of Industrial Electronics Technical Report, No. 1995: 44.

Haith, M. M., Hazan, C. and Goodman, G. S. (1988) Expectation and anticipation of dynamic visual events by 3.5-month-old babies. *Child Development*, 59: 467–79.

Hallett, P. E. (1978) Primary and secondary saccades to goals defined by instructions. *Vision Research*, 18: 1270–96.

Happe, F. (1994 *Autism: an Introduction to Psychological Theory*. London: UCL Press.

Happe, F. and Frith, U. (in press) The neuropsychology of autism. *Brain*.

Held, R. (1985) Binocular vision: behavioral and neuronal development. In

J. Mehler and R. Fox (eds), *Neonate Cognition: Beyond the Blooming, Buzzing Confusion*, pp. 37–44. Hillsdale, NJ: Lawrence Erlbaum.

Held, R. (1993) Development of binocular vision revisited. In M. H. Johnson (ed.), *Brain Development and Cognition: a Reader*, pp. 159–66. Oxford: Blackwell.

Hellige, J. B. (1993) *Hemispheric Asymmetry: What's Right and What's Left*. Cambridge, Mass.: Harvard University Press.

Hinde, R. A. (1961) The establishment of parent–offspring relations in birds, with some mammalian analogies. In W. H. Thorpe and O. L. Zangwill (eds), *Current Problems in Animal Behaviour*, pp. 175–93. Cambridge: Cambridge University Press.

Hinde, R. A. (1974) *Biological Bases of Human Social Behaviour*. New York: McGraw-Hill.

Hinshelwood, J. (1907) Four cases of cogenital word-blindness occurring in the same family. *British Medical Journal*, 2: 1229–32.

Hobson, R. P. (1993) Understanding persons: the role of affect. In S. Baron-Cohen, H. Tager-Flusberg and D. J. Cohen (eds), *Understanding Other Minds*, pp. 201 27. Oxford: Oxford University Press.

von Hofsten, C. (1984) Developmental changes in the organisation of prereaching movements. *Developmental Psychology*, 20: 378–88.

Hood, B. (1993) Inhibition of return produced by covert shifts of visual attention in 6-month-old infants. *Infant Behavior and Development*, 16: 245–54.

Hood, B. (1995) Shifts of visual attention in the human infant: a neuroscientific approach. In C. Rovee-Collier and L. Lipsitt (eds), *Advances in Infancy Research*, vol. 9. Norwood, NJ: Ablex.

Hood, B. and Atkinson, J. (1991) Shifting covert attention in infants. Poster presented at the Society for Research in Child Development, 8, Seattle, WA.

Hopkins, B. (1993) On the developmental origins of human handedness. In Annual Report 1992–1993, no. 16, Research and Clinical Center for Child Development, Hokkaido University, Sapporo, Japan.

Hopkins, W. G. and Brown, M. C. (1984) *Development of Nerve Cells and their Connections*. Cambridge: Cambridge University Press.

Horn, G. (1985) *Memory, Imprinting, and the Brain: an Inquiry into Mechanisms*. Oxford: Clarendon Press.

Horn, G. and Johnson, M. H. (1989) Memory systems in the chick: dissociations and neuronal analysis. *Neuropsychologia*, 27 (special issue: Memory): 1–22.

Horn, G. and McCabe, B. J. (1984) Predispositions and preferences: effects on imprinting of lesions to the chick brain. *Brain Research*, 168: 361–73.

Huttenlocher, P. R. (1990) Morphometric study of human cerebral cortex development. *Neuropsychologia*, 28: 517–27.

Huttenlocher, P. R. (1994) Synaptogenesis, synapse elimination, and neural plasticity in human cerebral cortex. In C. A. Nelson (ed.), *Threats to Optimal Development: the Minnesota Symposia on Child Psychology*, vol. 27, pp. 35–54. Hillsdale, NJ: Lawrence Erlbaum.

Huttenlocher, P. R., de Courten, C., Garey, L. G. and van der Loos, H. (1982)

Synaptogenesis in human visual cortex – evidence for synapse elimination during normal development. *Neuroscience Letter*, 33: 247–52.

Janowsky, J. S. (1993) The development and neural basis of memory systems. In M. H. Johnson (ed.), *Brain Development and Cognition: a Reader*, pp. 665–78. Oxford: Blackwell.

Janowsky, J. S. and Findlay, B. L. (1986) The outcome of perinatal brain damage: the role of normal neuron loss and axon retraction. *Developmental Medicine and Child Neurology*, 28: 375–89.

Jernigan, T. L. and Bellugi, U. (1994) Neuroanatomical distinctions between Williams and Down syndromes. In S. Broman and J. Grafman (eds), *Atypical Cognitive Deficits in Developmental Disorders: Implications for Brain Function*, pp. 57–66. Hillsdale, NJ: Lawrence Erlbaum.

Jernigan, T. L., Press, G. A. and Hesselink, J. R. (1990) Methods for measuring brain morphological features on magnetic resonance images: validation and normal aging. *Archives of Neurology*, 47: 27–32.

Johnson, M. H. (1990) Cortical maturation and the development of visual attention in early infancy. *Journal of Cognitive Neuroscience*, 2: 81–95.

Johnson, M. H. (1991) Information processing and storage during filial imprinting. In P. G. Hepper (ed.), *Kin Recognition*, pp. 335–57. Cambridge: Cambridge University Press.

Johnson, M. H. (1993a) *Brain Development and Cognition: a Reader*. Oxford Blackwell.

Johnson, M. H. (1993b) Constraints on cortical plasticity. In M. H. Johnson (ed.), *Brain Development and Cognition: a Reader*, pp. 703–21. Oxford: Blackwell.

Johnson, M. H. (1994) Visual attention and the control of eye movements in early infancy. In C. Umilta and M. Moscovitch (eds), *Attention and Performance XV: Conscious and Nonconscious Processing*, pp. 291–310. Cambridge, Mass.: MIT Press.

Johnson, M. H. (1995) The inhibition of automatic saccades in early infancy. *Developmental Psychobiology*, 28: 281–91.

Johnson, M. H. and Bolhuis, J. J. (1991) Imprinting, predispositions and filial preference in the chick. In R. J. Andrew (ed.), *Neural and Behavioral Plasticity*, pp. 133–56. Oxford: Oxford University Press.

Johnson, M. H. and Gilmore, R. O. (1996) Developmental cognitive neuroscience: A biological perspective on cognitive change. In R. Gelman and T. Au (eds), *Handbook of Perception and Cognition: Perceptual and Cognitive Development*, pp. 333–70. Orlando, Fla.: Academic Press.

Johnson, M. H. and Horn, G. (1986) Dissociation of recognition memory and associative learning by a restricted lesion of the chick forebrain. *Neuropsychologia*, 24: 329–40.

Johnson, M. H. and Horn, G. (1987) The role of a restricted region of the chick forebrain in the recognition of individual conspecifics. *Behavioural Brain Research*, 23: 269–75.

Johnson, M. H. and Horn, G. (1988) The development of filial preferences in the dark-reared chick. *Animal Behaviour*, 36: 675–83.

Johnson, M. H. and Karmiloff-Smith, A. (1992) Can neural selectionism be applied to cognitive development and its disorders? *New Ideas in Psychology*, 10: 35–46.

Johnson, M. H. and Morton, J. (1991) *Biology and Cognitive Development: the Case of Face Recognition*. Oxford: Blackwell.

Johnson, M. H. and Oliver, A. (unpublished manuscript) Deviations in the formation of cortical representations: a new theoretical framework for interpreting developmental disorders.

Johnson, M. H. and Tucker, L. A. (1993) The ontogeny of covert visual attention: facilitatory and inhibitory effects. *Abstracts of the Society for Research in Child Development*, 9: 424.

Johnson, M. H. and Tucker, L. A. (in press) The development and temporal dynamics of spatial orienting in infants. *Journal of Experimental Child Psychology*.

Johnson, M. H. and Vecera, S. P. (1996) Cortical differentiation and neurocognitive development: the parcellation conjecture. *Behavioural Processes*, 36: 195–212.

Johnson, M. H., Bolhuis, J. J. and Horn, G. (1985) Interaction between acquired preferences and developing predispositions during imprinting. *Animal Behaviour*, 33: 1000–6.

Johnson, M. H., Dziurawiec, S., Ellis, H. D. and Morton, J. (1991a) Newborns' preferential tracking of face-like stimuli and its subsequent decline. *Cognition*, 40: 1–19.

Johnson, M. H., Posner, M. I. and Rothbart, M. (1991b) The development of visual attention in infancy: contingency learning, anticipations and disengaging. *Journal of Cognitive Neuroscience*, 3: 335–44.

Johnson, M. H., Dziurawiec, S., Bartrip, J. and Morton, J. (1992a) The effects of movement of internal features on infants' preferences for face-like stimuli. *Infant Behavior and Development*, 15: 129–36.

Johnson, M. H., Siddons, F., Frith, U. and Morton, J. (1992b) Can autism be predicted on the basis of infant screening tests? *Developmental Medicine and Child Neurology*, 34: 316–20.

Johnson, M. H., Posner, M. I. and Rothbart, M. K. (1994) Facilitation of saccades toward a covertly attended location in early infancy. *Psychological Science*, 5: 90–3.

Johnson, M. H., Gilmore, R. O., Tucker, L. A. and Minister, S. L. (1995) Cortical development and saccadic control: vector summation in young infants. *Developmental Cognitive Neuroscience Technical Report*, No. 95.3.

Johnston, T. D. (1988) Developmental explanation and the ontogeny of birdsong: nature/nurture redux. *Behavioural and Brain Sciences*, 11: 617–63.

Johnston, M. V., McKinney, M. and Coyle, J. T. (1979) Evidence for a cholinergic projection to neocortex from neurons in basal forebrain. *Proceedings of the National Academy of Sciences of the USA*, 76: 5392–6.

Jonides, J., Smith, E. E., Koeppe, R. A., Awh, E., Minoshima, S. and Mintun, M. A. (1993) Spatial working memory in humans as revealed by PET. *Nature*, 363: 623–5.

Kalsbeek, A., Voorn, P., Buijs, R. M., Pool, C. W. and Uylings, H. B. (1988) Development of the dopaminergic innervation in the prefrontal cortex of rat. *Journal of Comparative Neurology*, 269: 58–72.

Karmiloff-Smith, A. (1985) Language and cognitive processes from a developmental perspective. *Language and Cognitive Processes*, 1: 61–85.

Karmiloff-Smith, A. (1992) *Beyond modularity: a Developmental Perspective on Cognitive Science*. Cambridge, Mass.: MIT Press/Bradford Books.

Karmiloff-Smith, A. and Johnson, M. H. (1994) Thinking on one's feet (review of *A Dynamic Systems Approach to the Development of Cognition and Action*, by Esther Thelan and Linda Smith). *Nature*, 372: 53–4.

Karmiloff-Smith, A., Johnson, M. H., Grant, J., Jones, M-C., Karmiloff, Y-N., Bartrip, J. and Cuckle, P. (1993) From sentential to discourse functions: detection and explanation of speech repairs by children and adults. *Discourse Processes*, 16: 565–89.

Karmiloff-Smith, A., Klima, E., Bellugi, U., Grant, J. and Baron-Cohen, S. (1995) Is there a social module? Language, face processing, and theory of mind in individuals with Williams syndrome. *Journal of Cognitive Neuroscience*, 7: 196–208.

Karten, H. J. and Shimizu, T. (1989) The origins of neocortex: connections and lamination as distinct events in evolution. *Journal of Cognitive Neuroscience*, 1: 291–301.

Kasamatsu, T. and Pettigrew, J. W. (1976) Depletion of brain catecholamines: failure of monocular dominance shift after monocular conclusion in kittens. *Science*, 194: 206–9.

Kennedy, H. and Dehay, C. (1993) The importance of developmental timing in cortical specification. *Perspectives on Developmental Neurobiology*, 1: 93–9.

Kerszberg, M., Dehaene, S. and Changeux, J-P. (1992) Stabilization of complex input-output functions in neural clusters formed by synapse selection. *Neural Networks*, 5: 403–13.

Killackey, H. P. (1990) Neocortical expansion: an attempt toward relating phylogeny and ontogeny. *Journal of Cognitive Neuroscience*, 2: 1–17.

Kinsbourne, M. and Hiscock, M. (1983) The normal and deviant development of functional lateralization of the brain. In M. Haith and J. Campos (eds), *Handbook of Child Psychology*, pp. 157–280. New York: John Wiley.

Klein, R. M., Kingstone, A. and Pontefract, A. (1992) Orienting of visual attention. In K. Rayner (eds), *Eye Movements and Visual Cogniton: Scene Perception and Reading*. New York: Springer-Verlag.

Kostovic, I., Pentanjek, Z. and Judas, M. (1990) The earliest areal differentiation of the human cerebral cortex: entorhinal area. *Society for Neuroscience Abstracts*, 16: 846.

Kuhl, P. K. (1993) Innate predispositions and the effects of experience in speech perception: the native language magnet theory. In B. de Boysson-Bardies, S. de Schonen, P. Jusczyk, P. McNeilage and J. Morton (eds), *Developmental Neurocognition: Speech and Face Processing in the First Year of Life*, pp. 259–74. Dordrecht, Netherlands: Kluwer.

Kwong, K. E., Belliveau, J. W., Chesler, D. A., Goldberg, I. E., Weisskoff, R. M., Poncelet, B. P., Kennedy, D. N., Hoppel, B. E., Cohen, M. S., Turner, R., Cheng, H. M., Brady, T. J. and Rosen, B. R. (1992) Dynamic magnetic resonance imaging of human brain activity during primary sensory stimulation. *Proceedings of the National Academy of Sciences of the USA*, 89: 5675–9.

Lecuyer, R., Abgueguen, I. and Lemarie, C. (1992) 9- and 5-month-olds do not make the AB error if not required to manipulate objects. In C. Rovee-Collier (ed.), *Proceedings of the VIII th International Conference on Infant Studies*, p. 514. Miami, Florida.

Lenneberg, E. (1967) *Biological Foundations of Language*. New York: John Wiley.

Leslie, A. (1987) Pretence and representation: the origins of "theory of mind". *Psychological Review*, 94: 412–26.

Lewis, T. L., Maurer, D. and Milewski, A. (1979) The development of nasal detection in young infants. *Investigative Ophthalmology and Visual Science*, 271 (suppl.).

Lewkowicz, D. J. (1991) Development of intersensory functions in human infancy: auditory/visual interactions. In M. J. S. Weiss and P. Zelazo (eds), *Newborn Attention: Biological Constraints and the Influence of Experience*, pp. 308–38. Norwood, NJ: Ablex.

Lewkowicz, D. J. and Turkewitz, G. (1981) Intersensory interaction in newborns: modification of visual preferences following exposure to sound. *Child Development*, 52: 827–32.

Lipsitt, L. P. (1990) Learning processes in the human newborn: sensitization, habituation, and classical conditioning. *Annals of the New York Academy of Sciences*, 608: 113–27.

Livingstone, M. S., Rosen, G. D., Drislane, F. W. and Galaburda, A. M. (1991) Physiological and anatomical evidence for a magnocellular defect in developmental dyslexia. *Proceedings of the National Academy of Sciences of the USA*, 88: 7943–7.

Lorenz, K. S. (1965) *Evolution and Modification of Behaviour*. Chicago: Chicago University Press.

Lu, S. T., Hamalainen, M. S., Hari, R., Ilmoniemi, R. J., Lounasamaa, O. V., Sams, M. and Vilkman, V. (1991) Seeing faces activates three separate areas outside the occipital visual cortex in man. *Neuroscience*, 43: 287–90.

Lund, J. S. and Holbach, S. M. (1991) Postnatal development of thalmic recipient neurons in the monkey striate cortex. I: Comparison of spine acquisition and dendritic growth of layer 4C alpha and beta spiny stellate neurons. *Journal of Comparative Neurology*, 309: 115–28.

McCabe, B. J., Cipolla-Neto, J., Horn, G. and Bateson, P. P. G. (1982) Amnesic effects of bilateral lesions placed in the hyperstriatum ventrale of the chick after imprinting. *Experimental Brain Research*, 48: 13–21.

McClelland, J. L. and Rumelhart, D. E. (eds) (1986) *Parallel Distributed Processing: Explorations in the Microstructure of Cognition*. Cambridge, Mass.: MIT Press.

McManus, I. C. and Bryden, M. P. (1991) Geschwind's theory of cerebral lateralization: developing a formal, causal model. *Psychological Bulletin*, 110: 237–53.

McManus, I. C. and Bryden, M. P. (1993) The neurobiology of handedness, language and cerebral dominance: a model for the molecular genetics of behavior. In M. H. Johnson (ed.), *Brain Development and Cognition: a Reader*, pp. 679–702. Oxford: Blackwell.

MacPhail, E. M. (1982) *Brain and Intelligence in Vertebrates*. Oxford: Clarendon Press.

Maier, V. and Scheich, H. (1983) Acoustic imprinting leads to differential 2-deoxy-D-glucose uptake in the chick forebrain. *Proceedings of the National Academy of Sciences of the USA*, 80: 3860–4.

Mandler, J. M. (1992) How to build a baby. II: Conceptual primitives. *Psychological Review*, 99: 587–604.

Marcusson, J. O., Morgan, D. G., Winblad, B. and Finch, C. E. (1984) Serotonin-2 binding sites in human frontal cortex and hippocampus: selective loss of S-2 A sites with age. *Brain Research*, 311: 51–6.

Mareschal, D., Plunkett, K. and Harris, P. (1995) Developing object permanence: a connectionist model. In J. D. Moore and J. F. Lehman (eds), *Proceedings of the Seventeenth Annual Conference of the Cognitive Science Society*, pp. 170–5. Hillsdale, NJ.: Lawrence Erlbaum.

Marin-Padilla, M. (1990) The pyramidal cell and its local-circuit interneurons: a hypothetical unit of the mammalian cerebral cortex. *Journal of Cognitive Neuroscience*, 2: 180–94.

Marler, P. (1991) The instinct to learn. In S. Carey and R. Gelman (eds), *The Epigenesis of Mind: Essays on Biology and Cognition*, pp. 37–66. Hillsdale, NJ: Lawrence Erlbaum.

Maurer, D. (1985) Infants' perception of faceness. In T. N. Field and N. Fox (eds), *Social Perception in Infants*, pp. 73–100. Norwood, NJ: Ablex.

Maurer, D. (1993) Neonatal synesthesia: implications for the processing of speech and faces. In B. de Boysson-Bardies, S. de Schonen, P. Jusczyk, P. McNeilage and J. Morton (eds), *Developmental Neurocognition: Speech and Face Processing in the First Year of Life*, pp. 109–24. Dordrecht, Netherlands: Kluwer.

Maurer, D. and Barrera, M. (1981) Infants' perception of natural and distorted arrangements of a schematic face. *Child Development*, 47: 523–7.

Maylor, E. A. (1985) Facilitory and inhibitory components of orienting in visual space. In M. I. Posner and O. M. Marin (eds), *Attention and Performance XI*, pp. 189–204. Hillsdale, NJ: Lawrence Erlbaum.

Meltzoff, A. N. and Borton, R. W. (1979) Intermodal matching by human neonates. *Nature*, 282: 403–4.

Merzenich, M. M., Jenkins, W. M., Johnston, P., Schreiner, C., Miller, S. L. and Tallal, P. (1996) Temporal processing deficits of language-learning impaired children ameliorated by training. *Science*, 271: 77–81.

Michel, G. F. (1981) Right-handedness: a consequence of infant supine heard-orientation? *Science*, 212: 685–7.

Miller, K. D. (1990) Correlation-based models of neural development. In M. A. Gluck and D. E. Rumelhart (eds), *Neuroscience and Connectionist Theory*, pp. 267–353. Hillsdale, NJ: Lawrence Erlbaum.

Miller, K. D., Keller, J. B. and Stryker, M. P. (1989) Ocular dominance column development: analysis and simulation. *Science*, 245: 605–15.

Milner, B. (1982) Some cognitive effects of frontal-lobe lesions in man. *Philosophical Transactions of the Royal Society of London*, 298: 211–26.

Molfese, D. (1989) Electrophysiological correlates of word meanings in 14-month-old human infants. *Developmental Neuropsychology*, 5: 70–103.

Molnar, Z. and Blakemore, C. (1991) Lack of regional specificity for connections formed between thalamus and cortex in co-culture. *Nature*, 351: 475–7.

Morton, J. and Johnson, M. H. (1991) CONSPEC and CONLERN: a two-process theory of infant face recognition. *Psychological Review*, 98: 164–81.

Morton, J., Mehler, J. and Jusczyk, P. W. (1984) On reducing language to biology. *Cognitive Neuropsychology*, 1: 83–116.

Muir, D. W., Clifton, R. K. and Clarkson, M. G. (1989) The development of a human auditory localization response: a U-shaped function. *Canadian Journal of Psychology*, 43: 199–216.

Munakata, Y. (in press) Task-dependency in infant behavior: toward an understanding of the processes underlying cognitive development. In Lacerda, von Hofsten, and Heimann (eds), *Transitions in Perception, Cognition, and Action in Early Infancy*.

Munakata, Y., McClelland, J. L., Johnson, M. H. and Siegler, R. S. (1994) Now you see it, now you don't: a gradualistic framework for understanding infants' successes and failures in object permanence tasks. *Technical Report PDP.CNS. 94.2.* Carnegie Mellon University.

Nelson, C. A. (1994) Neural correlates of recognition memory in the first potential year of life. In G. Dawson and K. Fischer (eds), *Human Behaviour and the Developing Brain*, pp. 269–313. New York: Guilford Press.

Nelson, C. A. (1995) The ontogeny of human memory: a cognitive neuroscience perspective. *Developmental Psychology*, 31: 723–38.

Nelson, C. A. and Collins, P. F. (1992) Neural and behavioural correlates of recognition memory in 4- and 8-month-old infants. *Brain and Cognition*, 19: 105–21.

Nelson, C. A. and de Haan, M. (in press) Neural correlates of infants' visual responsiveness to facial expressions of emotion. *Developmental Psychobiology*.

Nelson, C. A. and Ludemann, P. M. (1989) Past, current and future trends in infant face perception research. *Canadian Journal of Psychology*, 43: 183–98.

Neville, H. J. (1991) Neurobiology of cognitive and language processing: effects of early experience. In K. R. Gibson and A. C. Petersen (eds), *Brain Maturation and Cognitive Development: Comparative and Cross-cultural Perspectives*, pp. 355–80. New York: Aldine de Gruyter.

Nowakowski, R. S. (1987) Basic concepts of CNS development. *Child Development*, 58: 568–95.

O'Leary, D. D. M. (1989) Do cortical areas emerge from a protocortex? *Trends in the Neurosciences*, 12: 400–6.

O'Leary, D. D. M. and Stanfield, B. B. (1985) Occipital cortical neurons with transient pyramidal tract axons extend and maintain collaterals to subcortical but not intracortical targets. *Brain Research*, 336: 326–33.

O'Leary, D. D. M. and Stanfield, B. B. (1989) Selective elimination of axons extended by developing cortical neurons is dependent on regional locale: experiments utilizing fetal cortical transplants. *Journal of Neuroscience*, 9: 2230–46.

Oliver, A., Johnson, M. H. and Shrager, J. (1996) The emergence of hierarchical clustered representations in a Hebbian neural network model that simulates aspects of development in the neocortex. *Network*, 7: 291–9.

O'Reilly, R. and Johnson, M. H. (1994) Object recognition and sensitive periods: a computational analysis of visual imprinting. *Neural Computation*, 6: 357–90.

Overman, W., Bachevalier, J., Turner, M. and Peuster, A. (1992) Object recognition versus object discrimination: comparison between human infants and infant monkeys. *Behavioral Neuroscience*, 106: 15–29.

Oyama, S. (1985) *The Ontogeny of Information*. Cambridge: Cambridge University Press.

Ozonoff, S., Pennington, B. F. and Rogers, S. J. (1991) Executive function deficits in high-functioning autistic individuals: relationship to theory of mind. *Journal of Child Psychology and Psychiatry*, 32: 1081–105.

Pandya, D. N. and Yeterian, E. H. (1985) Architecture and connections of cortical assocation areas. In A. Peters and E. G. Jones (eds), *Cerebral Cortex, Vol. 4: Association and Auditory Cortices*. New York: Plenum Press.

Pandya, D. N. and Yeterian, E. H. (1990) Architecture and connections of cerebral cortex: implications for brain evolution and function. In A. B. Scheibel and A. F. Weschsler (eds), *Neurobiology of Higher Cognitive Function*, pp. 53–84. New York: Guilford Press.

Parmelee, A. H. and Sigman, M. D. (1983) Perinatal brain development and behavior. In M. M. Haith and J. Campos (eds), *Infancy and the Biology of Development, Vol. 2: Handbook of Child Psychology*. New York: Oxford University Press.

Pascalis, O., de Schonen, S., Morton, J., Deruelle, C. and Fabre-Grenet, M. (1995) Mother's face recognition by neonates: a replication and an extension. *Infant Behavior and Development*, 18: 79–86.

Paulesu, E., Frith, U., Snowling, M., Gallagher, A., Morton, J., Frackowiak, R. S. J. and Frith, C. D. (1996) Is developmental dyslexia a disconnection syndrome? Evidence from PET scanning. *Brain*, 119: 143–57.

Pearson, D. A. and Lane, D. M. (1990) Visual attention movements: a developmental study. *Child Development*, 61: 1779–95.

Pennington, B. F. and Welsh, M. (1995) Neuropsychology and developmental psychopathology. In D. Cicchetti and D. J. Cohen (eds), *Developmental Psychopathology, Vol. 1: Theory and Methods*, pp. 254–90. New York: John Wiley.

Petersen, S. E., Fox, P., Posner, M., Mintun, M. and Raichle, M. (1988) Positron emission tomographic studies of the cortical anatomy of single-word processing. *Nature*, 331: 585–9.

Piaget, J. (1954) *The Construction of Reality in the Child.* New York: Basic Books.

Piatelli-Palmarini, M. (1989) Evolution, selection and cognition: from "learning" to parameter setting in biology and in the study of language. *Cognition*, 31: 1–44.

Piven, J., Berthier, M. L., Starkstein, S. E., Nehme, E., Pearlson, G. and Folstein, S. (1990) Magnetic resonance imaging evidence for a deficit of cerebral cortical development in autism. In S. Chase and M. E. Hertzig (eds), *Annual Progress in Child Psychiatry and Child Development*, pp. 455–65. New York: Brunner/Mazel.

Plaut, D. C. and Shallice, T. (1993) Deep dyslexia: a case study of connectionist neuropsychology. *Cognitive Neuropsychology*, 10: 377–500.

Posner, M. I. (1988) Structures and functions of selective attention. In T. Boll and B. Bryant (eds), *Clinical Neuropsychology and Brain Function: Research, Measurement, and Practice*, pp. 171–202. Washington, DC: American Psychological Association.

Posner, M. I. and Cohen, Y. (1980) Attention and the control of movements. In G. E. Stelmach and J. Roguiro (eds), *Tutorials in Motor Behavior*, pp. 243–58. Amsterdam: North Holland.

Posner, M. I. and Cohen, Y. (1984) Components of visual orienting. In H. Bouma and D. G. Bouwhis (eds), *Attention and Performance*, pp. 531–56. Hillsdale, NJ: Lawrence Erlbaum.

Posner, M. I. and Peterson, S. E. (1990) The attention system of the human brain. *Annual Review of Neuroscience*, 13: 25–42.

Posner, M. I. and Rothbart, M. K. (1980) The development of attentional mechanisms. In J. H. Flower (ed.), *Nebraska Symposium on Motivation*. Lincoln, Nebr.: University of Nebraska Press.

Posner, M. I., Rafal, R. D., Choate, L. S. and Vaughan, J. (1985) Inhibition of return: neural basis and function. *Cognitive Neuropsychology*, 2: 211–28.

Purpura, D. P. (1975) Normal and aberrant neuronal development in the cerebral cortex of human fetus and young infant. In N. A. Buchwald and M. A. B. Brazier (eds), *Brain Mechanisms of Mental Retardation*, pp. 141–69. New York: Academic Press.

Purves, D. (1994) *Neural Activity and the Growth of the Brain.* Accademia Nazionale Dei Lincei/Cambridge: Cambridge University Press.

Purves, D. and Lichtman, J. W. (1985) *Principles of Neural Development.* Sunderland, Mass.: Sinauer Associates.

Quartz, S. R. and Sejnowski, T. J. (in press) A neural basis of cognitive development: a constructivist manifesto.

Rabinowicz, T. (1979) The differential maturation of the human cerebral cortex. In F. Falkner and J. M. Tanner (eds), *Human Growth, Vol. 3: Neurobiology and Nutrition*, pp. 141–69. New York: Plenum Press.

Rafal, R., Smith, J., Krantz, J., Cohen, A. and Brennan, C. (1990) Extrageniculate vision in hemianopic humans: saccade inhibition by signals in the blind field. *Science*, 250: 1507–18.

Raichle, M. E. and Malinkrodt, M. E. (1987) Circulatory and metabolic correlates of brain function in normal humans. In V. B. Mountcastle, F. Plum and S. R. Geiger (eds), *Handbook of Physiology: The Nervous System*, pp. 643–74. Bethesda, Md.: American Physiological Association.

Rakic, P. (1987) Intrinsic and extrinsic determinants of neocortical parcellation: a radial unit model. In P. Rakic and W. Singer (eds), *Neurobiology of Neocortex*. New York: John Wiley.

Rakic, P. (1988) Specification of cerebral cortical areas. *Science*, 241: 170–6.

Rakic, P. (1995) Corticogenesis in human and nonhuman primates. In M. S. Gazzaniga (ed.), *The Cognitive Neurosciences*, pp. 127–45. Cambridge, Mass.: MIT Press.

Rakic, P., Bourgeois, J-P., Eckenhoff, M. F., Zecevic, N. and Goldman-Rakic, P. S. (1986) Concurrent overproduction of synapses in diverse regions of primate cerebral cortex. *Science*, 232: 153–7.

Rauschecker, J. P. and Singer, W. (1981) The effects of early visual experience on the cat's visual cortex and their possible explanation by Hebb synapses. *Journal of Physiology (London)*, 310: 215–39.

Ravikumar, B. V. and Sastary, P. I. (1985) Muscarinic cholinergic receptors in human foetal brain: characterization and ontogeny of [3H]quinuclidinyl benzilate bind sites in frontal cortex. *Journal of Neurochemistry*, 44: 240–6.

Reeke, G. N., Jr, Sporns, O. and Edelman, G. M. (1990) Synthetic neural modeling: the "Darwin" series of recognition automata. *Proceedings of the Institute of Electrical and Electronics Engineers*, 78 (9): 1498–530.

Reilly, J., Bates, E. and Marchman, V. (in press) Narrative discourse in children with early focal brain injury. In M. Dennis (ed.), *Special Issue: Discourse in Children with Anomalous Brain Development or Acquired Brain Injury. Brain and Language*.

Richards, J. E. (1989a) Sustained visual attention in 8-week old infants. *Infant Behavior and Development*, 12: 425–36.

Richards, J. E. (1989b) Development and stability of HR-defined, visual sustained attention in 14, 20, and 26 week old infants. *Psychophysiology*, 26: 422–30.

Richards, J. E. (1991) Infant eye movements during peripheral visual stimulus localization as a function of central stimulus attention status. *Psychophysiology*, 28.

Rizzolatti, G., Riggio, L., Dascola, I. and Umilta, C. (1987) Reorienting attention across the horizontal and vertical meridians: evidence in favor of a premotor theory of attention. *Neuropsychologia*, 25: 31–40.

Rizzolatti, G., Riggio, L. and Sheliga, B. M. (1994) Space and selective attention. In C. Umilta and M. Moscovitch (eds), *Attention and Performance XV: Conscious and Nonconscious Information Processing*, pp. 231–65. Cambridge, Mass.: MIT Press.

Rodman, H. R., Gross, C. G. and Scalaidhe, S. P. (1993) Development of brain substrates for pattern recognition in primates: physiological and connectional studies of inferior temporal cortex in infant monkeys. In B. de Boysson-Bardies, S. de Schonen, P. Jusczyk, P. McNeilage and J. Morton (eds),

Developmental Neurocognition: Speech and Face Processing in the First Year of Life, pp. 63–76. Dordrecht, Netherlands: Kluwer.

Roe, A. W., Pallas, S. L., Hahm, J. O. and Sur, M. (1990) A map of visual space induced in primary auditory cortex. *Science*, 250: 818–20.

Rogers, S. J. and Pennington, B. F. (1991) A theoretical approach to deficits in infantile autism. *Development and Psychopathology*, 3: 137–62.

Rolls, E. (1989) Functions of neuronal networks in the hippocampus and neocortex in memory. In J. Berne and W. Berry (eds), *Neural Models of Plasticity*, pp. 240–65. New York: Academic Press.

Rovee-Collier, C. K. (1993) The capacity for long-term memory in infancy. *Current Directions in Psychological Science*, 2 (4): 130–5.

Salamon, G., Raynand, C., Regis, J. and Rumeau, C. (1990) *Magnetic Resonance Imaging of the Pediatric Brain: an Anatomical Atlas*. New York: Raven Press.

Sargent, P. L., Nelson, C. A. and Carver, L. J. (1992) *Cross-species Recognition in Infants and Adult Humans: ERP and Behavioral Measures*. Miami: ICIS.

Schacter, D. and Moscovitch, M. (1984) Infants, amnesia and dissociable memory systems. In M. Moscovitch (ed.), *Infant Memory*, pp. 173–216. New York: Plenum Press.

Schiller, P. H. (1985) A model for the generation of visually guided saccadic eye movements. In D. Rose and V. G. Dobson (eds), *Models of the Visual Cortex*, pp. 62–70. Chicester: John Wiley.

Schlagger, B. L. and O'Leary, D. D. M. (1991) Potential of visual cortex to develop an array of functional units unique to somatosensory cortex. *Science*, 252: 1556–60.

Schlagger, B. L. and O'Leary, D. D. M. (1993) Patterning of the barrel field in somatosensory cortex with implications for the specification of neocortical areas. *Perspectives on Developmental Neurobiology*, 1: 81–91.

Schliebs, R., Kullman, E. and Bigl, V. (1986) Development of glutamate binding sites in the visual structures of the rat brain: effect of visual pattern deprivation. *Biomedica Biochemica Acta*, 45: 495–506.

Schneider, W., Noll D. C. and Cohen, J. D. (1993) Functional topographic mapping of the cortical ribbon in human vision with coventional MRI scanners. *Nature*, 365: 150–3.

de Schonen, S. and Mancini, J. (1995) About functional brain specialization: the development of face recognition. *Developmental Cognitive Neuroscience Technical Report no. 95.1.*

de Schonen, S. and Mathivet, H. (1989) First come, first served: a scenario about the development of hemispheric specialization in face recognition during infancy. *European Bulletin of Cognitive Psychology*, 9: 3–44.

Scoville, W. B. and Milner, B. (1957) Loss of recent memory after bilateral hippocampal lesions. *Journal of Neurology, Neurosurgery and Psychiatry*, 20: 11–21.

Shatz, K. (1992) Dividing up the neocortex. *Science*, 258: 237–8.

Shepherd, G. M. (1972) The neuron doctrine: a revision of functional concepts. *Yale Journal of Biology and Medicine*, 45: 584–99.

Shimojo, S., Birch, E. and Held, R. (1983) Development of vernier acuity assessed by preferential looking. *Investigative Ophthalmology and Visual Science* (Suppl.), 24: 93.

Shrager, J. and Johnson, M. H. (1995) Waves of growth in the development of cortical function: a computational model. In B. Julesz and I. Kovacs (eds), *Maturational Windows and Adult Cortical Plasticity*, pp. 31–44. Reading, Mass.: Addison-Wesley.

Siegler, R. S. (1991) *Children's Thinking*, 2nd edn. Englewood Cliffs, NJ: Prentice-Hall.

Silva, A. J., Paylor, R., Wehner, J. M. and Tonegawa, S. (1992a) Impaired spatial learning in α-calcium-calmodulin kinase II mutant mice. *Science*, 257: 206–11.

Silva, A. J., Stevens, C. F., Tonegawa, S. and Wang, Y. N. (1992b) Deficient hippocampal long-term potentiation in α-calcium-calmodulin kinase II mutant mice. *Science*, 257: 201–6.

Simion, F., Valenza, E., Umilta, C. and Dalla Barba, B. (1995) In newborns preferential orienting to faces is subcorticaly mediated. Unpublished manuscript.

Spreen, O., Risser, A. T. and Edgell, D. (1995) *Developmental Neuropsychology*. New York: Oxford University Press.

Squire, L. R. (1986) Mechanisms of memory. *Science*, 232: 1612–19.

Starkey, P. and Cooper, R. G. (1980) Perception of number by human infants. *Science*, 200: 1033–5.

Starkey, P., Spelke, E. S. and Gelman, R. (1983) Detection of intermodal numerical correspondences by human infants. *Science*, 222: 179–81.

Starkey, P., Spelke, E. S. and Gelman, R. (1990) Numerical abstraction by human infants. *Cognition*, 36: 97–127.

Stechler, G. and Latz, E. (1966) Some observations on attention and arousal in the human infant. *Journal of the American Academy of Child and Adolescent Psychiatry*, 5: 517–25.

Stein, B. E. (1984) Multimodal representation in the superior colliculus and optic tectum. In H. Vanegas (ed.), *Comparative Neurology of the Optic Tectum*, pp. 819–41. New York: Plenum Press.

Stetri, A. (1987) Tactile discrimination of shape and intermodal transfer in 2 to 3 month old infants. *British Journal of Developmental Psychology*, 5: 213–20.

Stetri, A. and Pecheux, M-G. (1986) Vision-to-touch and touch-to-vision transfer of form in 5 month old infants. *British Journal of Developmental Psychology*, 4: 161–7.

Stiles, J. and Thal, D. (1993) Linguistic and spatial cognitive development following early focal brain injury: patterns of deficit and recovery. In M. H. Johnson (ed.), *Brain Development and Cognition: a Reader*, pp. 643–64. Oxford: Blackwell.

Streit, P. (1984) Glutamate and aspartate as transmitter candidates for systems of the cerebral cortex. In E. G. Jones and A. Peters (eds), *Cerebral Cortex, Vol. 2: Functional Properties of Cortical Cells*. New York: Plenum Press.

Stryker, M. P. and Harris, W. (1986) Binocular impulse blockade prevents the formation of ocular dominance columns in cat visual cortex. *Journal of Neuroscience*, 6: 2117–33.

Stuss, D. T. (1992) Biological and psychological development of executive functions. *Brain and Cognition*, 20: 8–23.

Sur, M. (1993) Cortical specification: microcircuits, perceptual identity, and overall perspective. *Perspectives on Developmental Neurobiology*, 1: 109–13.

Sur, M., Garraghty, P. E. and Roe, A. W. (1988) Experimentally induced visual projections into auditory thalamus and cortex. *Science*, 242: 1437–41.

Sur, M., Pallas, S. L. and Roe, A. W. (1990) Cross-modal plasticity in cortical development: differentiation and specification of sensory neocortex. *Trends in Neuroscience*, 13: 227–33.

Tallal, P. (1980) Speech perception of language delayed children. In G. H. Yeni-Komshian, J. F. Kavanagh and C. A. Ferguson (eds), *Child Phonology: Perception*. New York: Academic Press.

Tallal, P., Stark, R. E., Clayton, K. and Mellits, D. (1980) Developmental dysphasia: relation between acoustic processing deficits and verbal processing. Neuropsychologia, 18: 273–84.

Tallal, P., Miller, S. L., Bedi, G., Byma, G., Wang, X., Nagarajan, S. J., Srikantan, S., Schreiner, C., Jenkins, W. M. and Merzenich, M. M. (1996) Language comprehension in language-learning impaired children improved with acoustically modified speech. *Science*, 271: 81–4.

Teszner, D., Tzavaras, A., Gruner, J. and Hecaen, H. (1972) L'asymmetrie droite-gauche du planum temporale: a propos de l'étude anatomique de 100 cerveaux. *Revue Neurologique*, 126: 444.

Thatcher, R. W. (1992) Cyclic cortical reorganization during early childhood. *Brain and Cognition*, 20: 24–50.

Thelen, E. and Smith, L. B. (1994) *A Dynamic Systems Approach to the Development of Cognition and Action*. Cambridge, Mass.: MIT Press.

Thompson, D. W. (1917) *On Growth and Form*. Cambridge: Cambridge University Press.

Tinbergen, N. (1951) *The Study of Instinct*. Oxford: Clarendon Press.

Tipper, S. P., Bourque, T. A., Anderson, S. H. and Brehaut, J. C. (1989) Mechanisms of attention: a developmental study. *Journal of Experimental Child Psychology*, 48: 353–78.

Tombol, T., Csillag, A. and Stewart, M. G. (1988) Cell types of the hyperstriatum ventrale of the domestic chicken, *Gallus domesticus*: a Golgi study. *Journal für Hinforschung*, 29: 319–34.

Townsend, J. and Courchesne, E. (1994) Parietal damage and narrow "spotlight" spatial attention. *Journal of Cognitive Neuroscience*, 6: 220–32.

Tramo, M. J., Loftus, W. C., Thomas, C. E., Green, R. L., Mott, L. A. and Gazzaniga, M. S. (1994) The surface area of human cerebral cortex and its gross morphological subdivisions. Unpublished manuscript, University of California, Davis.

Tranel, D. and Damasio, A. R. (1985) Knowledge without awareness: an autonomic index of facial recognition by prosopagnosics. *Science*, 228: 1453–4.

Turkewitz, G. and Kenny, P. A. (1982) Limitation on input as a basis for neural organization and perceptual development: a preliminary theoretical statement. *Developmental Psychobiology*, 15: 357.

Udwin, O. and Yule, W. (1991) A cognitive and behavioural phenotype in Williams syndrome. *Journal of Clinical and Experimental Neuropsychology*, 13: 232–44.

Valenza, E., Simion, F., Cassia, V. M. and Umilta, C. (in press) Face preference at birth. *Journal of Experimental Psychology: Human Perception and Performance*.

Vargha-Khadem, F., Isaacs, E. and Muter, V. (1994) A review of cognitive outcome after unilateral lesions sustained during childhood. *Journal of Child Neurology*, 9: 2S67–73.

Vecera, S. P. and Johnson, M. H. (1995) Eye gaze detection and the cortical processing of faces: evidence from infants and adults. *Visual Cognition*, 2: 101–29.

Volpe, J. J. (1987) *Neurology of the Newborn*, 2nd edn. Philadelphia: Saunders.

Wada, J. A., Clark, R. and Hamm, A. (1975) Cerebral hemispheric asymmetry in humans. *Archives of Neurology*, 32: 239.

Waddington, C. H. (1975) *The Evolution of an Evolutionist*. Edinburgh: Edinburgh University Press.

Wallace, R. B., Kaplan, R. and Werboff, J. (1977) Hippocampus and behavioral maturation. *International Journal of Neuroscience*, 7: 185.

Wattam-Bell, J. (1990) The development of maximum velocity limits for direction discrimination in infancy. *Perception*, 19: 369.

Wattam-Bell, J. (1991) Development of motion-specific cortical responses in infants. *Vision Research*, 31: 287–97.

Webster, M. J., Bachevalier, J. and Ungerleider, L. G. (1995) Development and plasticity of visual memory circuits. In B. Julesz and I. Kovacs (eds), *Maturational Windows and Adult Cortical Plasticity*. New York: Addison-Wesley.

Welsh, M. C., Pennington, B. F., Ozonoff, S., Rouse, B. and McCabe, E. R. B. (1990) Neuropsychology of early-treated phenylketonuria: specific executive function deficits. *Child Development*, 61: 1697–713.

Werker, J. F. and Polka, L. (1993) The ontogeny and developmental significance of language-specific phonetic perception. In B. de Boysson-Bardies, S. de Schonen, P. Jusczyk, P. McNeilage and J. Morton (eds), *Developmental Neurocognition: Speech and Face Processing in the First Year of Life*, pp. 275–88. Dordrecht, Netherlands: Kluwer.

Wiesel, T. N. and Hubel, D. H. (1965) Comparison of the effects of unilateral and bilateral eye closure on cortical unit responses in kittens. *Journal of Neurophysiology*, 28: 1029–40.

Wimmer, H. and Perner, J. (1983) Beliefs about beliefs: representation and constraining function of wrong beliefs in young children's understanding of deception. *Cognition*, 13: 103–28.

Witelson, S. F. (1987) Neurobiological aspects of language in children. *Child Development*, 58: 653–88.

Witelson, S. F. and Pallie, W. (1973) Left hemisphere specialization for language in the newborn: neuroanatomical evidence of asymmetry. *Brain*, 96: 641.

Wolff, P. H., Matsumiya, Y., Abroms, I. F., van Velzar, C. and Lombroso, C. T. (1974) The effect of white noise on the somatosensory evoked response in sleeping newborn infants. *Electroencephalography and Clinical Neurophysiology,* 37: 269–74.

Wood, F., Flowers, L., Buchsbaum, M. and Tallal, P. (1991) Investigation of abnormal left temporal functioning in dyslexia through rCBF, auditory evoked potentials, and positron emission tomography. In B. F. Pennington (eds), *Reading Disabilities: Genetic and Neurological Influences,* pp. 379–93. Dordrecht, Netherlands: Kluwer.

Yakovlev, P. I. and Lecours, A. (1967) The myelogenetic cycles of regional maturation of the brain. In A. Minokowski (ed.), *Regional Development of the Brain in Early Life.* Philadelphia: Davis.

Zipser, D. and Anderson, R. A. (1988) A back-propagation programmed network that simulates response properties of a subset of posterior parietal neurons. *Nature,* 331: 679–84.

Index